Raymond Mertens

About the Author

BECKY A. BAILEY, PH.D., holds a doctorate in psychology, with a concentration in early childhood education and development. Through her dynamic and inspiring lectures and seminars, she reaches more than fifty thousand people annually. She is the author of numerous research articles and five books, including *I Love You Rituals,* winner of a Parent's Guide Children's Media Award. Four of her parenting audiotapes have won the prestigious Parents' Choice Award. She has made many radio and television appearances, including United Nations Radio, CNN's *Daybreak,* and *Dr. Robert Schuller's Hour of Power.* She is being featured in her own public television special. She lives in Oviedo, Florida.

*This book is dedicated with boundless love and gratitude
to my mom and dad.*

*It is also dedicated to the love between all parents and children.
This love is a gift from the universal power
that unites us all.*

A hardcover edition of this book was published in 2000
by William Morrow.

EASY TO LOVE, DIFFICULT TO DISCIPLINE. Copyright © 2000 by
Becky A. Bailey, Ph.D. All rights reserved. Printed in the United
States of America. No part of this book may be used or reproduced
in any manner whatsoever without written permission except in the
case of brief quotations embodied in critical articles and reviews. For
information address HarperCollins Publishers Inc.,
10 East 53rd Street, New York, NY 10022.

HarperCollins books may be purchased for educational, business,
or sales promotional use. For information please write:
Special Markets Department, HarperCollins Publishers Inc.,
10 East 53rd Street, New York, NY 10022.

First Quill edition published 2002.

Designed by Meryl Sussman Levavi / DIGITEXT, INC.

The Library of Congress has catalogued
the hardcover edition as follows:

Bailey, Rebecca Anne.
    Easy to love, difficult to discipline : the seven basic skills
for turning conflict into cooperation / Becky A. Bailey.
        p.   cm.
    Includes bibliographical references and index.
    ISBN 0-688-16116-2
    1. Discipline of children.   2. Child rearing.   3. Parenting.
4. Parent and child.   5. Self-control.   I. Title.
HQ770.4.B3   2000
649'.64—dc21   99-44313
                                                              CIP

ISBN 0-06-000775-3 (pbk.)

04 05 06 FG/RRD 10 9

Easy to Love, Difficult to Discipline

The Seven Basic Skills for Turning Conflict into Cooperation

Becky A. Bailey, Ph.D.

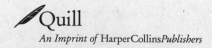

Quill

An Imprint of HarperCollins*Publishers*

Acknowledgments

I have been fortunate to be bathed in love and support for my work. The following people have taught me the power of giving and contributed to the writing of this book. Indeed, they have helped me learn the material it contains.

I am grateful to:

My mother and father, Frances and Talmadge Bailey, for the discipline they showed me and the constant encouragement they offer. To Dr. Mary Thelma Brainard for encouraging me to write and guiding me to discipline myself. To Linda Harris Dragnich, who willingly shared her parenting journey with me. To Mildred Leinweber Dawson, who took my words and with clarity and style reworked them and fed them back to me. Her editing, writing ability, and wisdom as a parent were gifts to me and I am honored to have worked with her on this book. To Lorrie Cabral, who ran between Milly and myself, ensuring that the changes were made and the book was done. To Kate O'Neil, who ran my business, grounded my anxiety, and offered her love and insights. To Casey Doran, who inspired me by making changes in her own life. To Charlene Bell, who wrote the original book proposal that sparked the project's beginning. To Gareth Esersky, my literary agent, who believed in the material. To William Morrow and Toni Sciarra for helping me manifest a dream. To the University of Central Florida for allowing me leave to complete the project. To Sarah Sprinkle, who gave of her precious time to offer suggestions on the original manuscript. To all the children and families who have taught me to deepen my understanding of myself; through that process I have been able to help others. To the creative force of the universe that links us all as one and models love and acceptance. I am honored to relay the message of love and peace.

Contents

Easy to Love, Difficult to Discipline

From Willful
to Willing

A wonderful woman who lived in a shoe
Had so many children,
And she knew exactly what to do.
She held them,
She rocked them,
She tucked them in bed,
"I love you, I love you"
Is what she said.

Have you ever thought, I have tried everything possible to get my child to get dressed (or do his homework, or clean his room) and then sadly said to yourself, "I give up"? Have you ever punished your child and later felt guilty for having behaved in a way that you swore you never would? Have you ever promised yourself to exercise regularly, eat better, or spend more time with loved ones, but found that the promises you made to yourself are difficult to keep? Have you then given up, or felt guilty?

I wrote this book to help you permanently change your own behavior, because only by learning to discipline yourself will you be able to successfully guide your children's behavior. I will show why achieving self-control and self-discipline allows you to know exactly what to do in order to discipline your children.[1]

If I asked you to teach a class in nuclear physics, could you do it? Probably not. Could you teach your child how to pole-vault? Again, probably not. You cannot teach what you do not know.

Yet we often demand that children acquire skills that we ourselves lack. We ask children to do as we say, not as we do. Parents *yell*, "Go to your room until you are in control of yourself." A mother *grabs* a toy that two preschoolers are tussling over and says, "You know better than to grab toys from your friends. It's mine now!" Husbands and wives battle with each other, using attack skills such as name-calling and withdrawal. Then they demand that their children resolve conflicts calmly, by discussing them. Our own emotional intelligence is primitive at best, and whether we admit it or not, we pass our emotional clumsiness on to our children.

For most of us, being consistently in control of ourselves represents a major change. So this book is about change: It's about learning to change your own behavior, and your children's behavior, so that you can grow closer, embrace and resolve conflict, and enjoy life. Once you model self-control for your children, they will show better self-control than you have ever imagined they could achieve. Delightful surprises await you.

Once you model self-control for your children, they will show better self-control than you have ever imagined they could achieve.

Imagine telling your child *one* time to take a shower—and him actually marching off to do it! Imagine promising yourself to either conquer your clutter, or to relax about it—and then keeping your

---

[1] A note on my use of pronouns: I did not want to refer to your child as "he" throughout this book, but using "he or she" and "him or her" felt awkward. Instead, I alternate the use of masculine and feminine pronouns chapter by chapter. In chapter 1 I use "he" and "him," in chapter 2, "she" and "her," and so on.

promise. This book will help you realize these possibilities and many, many others.

Easy to Love, Difficult to Discipline can help you become the person you want your child to emulate. It will take your self-discipline and child-rearing skills to new levels. You will learn how to move beyond policing your children with rules and consequences, and discover how to create a home in which healthy relationships flourish and your children voluntarily choose to cooperate.

Sounds impossible? The revised Mother Goose nursery rhyme at the start of this chapter contains all the needed ingredients. If you want your children to change, you must begin by becoming a wonderfully loving adult. You must focus on what you *want* to have happen instead of what you *don't* want. You must rely on love, not fear, to motivate yourself and your children. When you learn to love yourself, you will be ready to teach your children to love themselves and one another.

This is a radically different approach from the one summarized in the original rhyme, which goes like this:

There was an old woman who lived in a shoe,
She had so many children
She didn't know what to do.
She gave them some broth
Without any bread;
She whipped them all soundly
And put them to bed.

Have you ever manipulated your child with food like Mother Goose did? ("If you behave while I shop, I'll take you to McDonald's.") Have you ever, in desperation, spanked your child? Unsure of how to proceed, have you sent your child to his room, or put him in "time out"? How often have you felt like the tired "old woman" (or a tired old dad) after surviving a day with your children, fighting battle after battle? The house really can feel as cramped as a shoe with laces tied too tightly.

How would tomorrow feel if you did know what to do? When your children tormented one another, you would be able to teach them how to resolve their conflicts, rather than resorting to playing "bad cop." When your children refused to clean up, you would know how to help them move past resistance and toward cooperation, rather than turning to nagging, punishment, or doing the task yourself. When your children lost control, you would know how to help them calm down and reorganize themselves, rather than out-shouting them. Imagine knowing exactly what to do!

TIMES HAVE CHANGED AND SO MUST WE

When it comes to describing our social situation, "Times have changed" is an understatement. There have been many shifts in our society, yet none so profound as the shift from roles to relationships. Building steam in the late fifties, society began to enter bold new territory. Collectively, we decided that the roles of the past were too limiting. The roles of husband and wife had been explicitly defined. The role of child (to be seen and not heard) and the role of parent (as boss) had been clearly articulated. Relationships were based on these prescribed roles. As long as everyone performed their ordained duties, all was well. Yet in the comfort and safety of these roles, we felt something missing, especially in the case of those who were relegated to the subservient roles. The powerless group (women, people of color, people with disabilities, children) rebelled. Consciousness expanded and people boldly demanded more. We wanted relationships, companions, and closeness based on equality of worth rather than on hierarchical, prescribed roles demarcating the powerful from the powerless. Sadly, however, we did not have the relationship skills or social competence to make these new relationships work. Divorce rates skyrocketed. Businesses instituted shakeups in search of employees who could take more initiative and who had the necessary people skills. Children became demanding, and parents felt at a loss as to how to respond. We placed ourselves on new ground. As we continue to seek meaningful relationships with one another, we must also learn the skills of interaction that promote respect. We must obtain new tools for new times. *Easy to Love, Difficult to Discipline* is a skill-based book to help parents build respectful relationships with themselves, with each other, and with their children.

All parents demonstrate or model a code of conduct and a value system. This is done through their day-to-day interactions with others. Until we become conscious of these patterns of interaction, we will not be able to guide the morality of the next generation. Most of us model respect when we are calm and when life is going our way. However, what happens to our values when we are stressed and life becomes complicated? How do we behave when traffic is backed up, when our children forget their permission slips, when our spouse fails to stop by the grocery store again, or when our mother-in-law keeps harping about our parenting choices? What happens to treating each other with respect during these times?

Easy to Love, Difficult to Discipline relates to us all. Every one of us at times is easy to love, and every one of us at times is difficult to live with. It is easy to love our children when they do what we ask, when we ask. It is easy to love our spouses and partners when we agree on how to raise the children. It is easy to love ourselves when we live up to our personal expectations. This book is about the other times. The times when life does not go as we had planned. When others don't act as we had hoped. And when our own actions are not something we want to write home about.

Easy to Love, Difficult to Discipline presents a framework of discipline called loving guidance. This framework is built on the premise that how we perceive a situation dictates the actions we will take. In order to change behavior, we must focus on our perceptions as well as on our actions. Loving guidance imbues parents with the *Seven Powers for Self-Control*. These powers are perceptual skills that enable you to become proactive rather than reactive in conflict moments, allowing you to stay in control of yourself and in charge of children.

Self-control must be the first priority of all parents. Self-control is not pretending to be calm in difficult moments. It is the ability to reach out and empathize with others, to accept and celebrate differences, to communicate feelings directly, to resolve conflicts in constructive ways, and to enjoy feeling close and connected to others. It is the ability to embrace conflict as a teaching opportunity rather than viewing it as a disruption. The *Seven Powers for Self-Control* are ways of perceiving and thinking. If we adopt these ways of seeing difficult times, we remain self-disciplined enough to begin the process of disciplining others. Each of the Seven Powers has a slogan to help you remember to use that particular power in times of conflict. The *Seven Powers for Self-Control* and the slogans that support them are as follows:

1. The Power of Perception: No one can *make* you angry without your permission.
2. The Power of Attention: What you focus on, you get more of.
3. The Power of Free Will: The only person you can *make* change is yourself.
4. The Power of Unity: Focus on connecting instead of trying to be special.
5. The Power of Love: See the best in one another.
6. The Power of Acceptance: This moment is as it is.
7. The Power of Intention: Conflict is an opportunity to teach.

From these *Seven Powers for Self-Control* emerge the *Seven Basic Discipline Skills*. These are the *only* skills you need to constructively respond to any difficult moment. Parents who draw upon the *Seven Powers for Self-Control* and use the *Seven Basic Discipline Skills* create a home that models the *Seven Values for Living*. This will happen automatically. As parents change their attitudes and behaviors, so will their children. Each of the *Seven Basic Discipline Skills* has a slogan to help remind you what you can expect from using the skill. Listed below are the slogans and the values that you will be modeling and teaching your children.

1. Composure: Living the values you want your child to develop. This teaches *integrity*.

2. Encouragement: Honoring children so they will honor you.
   This teaches *interdependence.*
3. Assertiveness: Saying no and being heard.
   This teaches *respect.*
4. Choices: Building self-esteem and willpower.
   This teaches *commitment.*
5. Positive Intent: Turning resistance into cooperation.
   This teaches *cooperation.*
6. Empathy: Handling the fussing and the fits.
   This teaches *compassion.*
7. Consequences: Helping children learn from their mistakes.
   This teaches *responsibility.*

TO DISCIPLINE AND TO TEACH ARE THE SAME ACTS

This book is about parents teaching their children how to behave, not about parents controlling their children's behavior. Discipline situations with children occur over conflicting needs. The conflict may be between adults and children, or between children. You actually teach your child to resolve his own conflicts with the corrective discipline tools that you use. Your discipline tools evolve into the interpersonal skills your children adopt and then carry with them into all their future relationships. When you look at discipline in this way, you can see that your guidance system involves much larger issues than getting your children to finish their chores or go to bed on time. Your approach to discipline demonstrates conflict resolution for your children, and it teaches them how to get their needs met for the rest of their lives.

Through discipline, you teach your children how to resolve the conflicting needs of different people.

Adults are wracked by conflicts. These conflicts can be within ourselves, with a spouse, or between neighbors or countries. The divorce rate today is about 50 percent. In the twentieth century, warfare has claimed 150 million human lives. The United Nations Children's Fund estimates that in the last decade alone, wars have killed 1 million children, disabled 5 million others, and left 12 million children homeless. Clearly, people need a better way to resolve conflicts.

LOVING GUIDANCE: THE BETTER WAY

Historically, when a child's needs collided with an adult's needs, the needs of the adult took clear precedence. Parents considered any strategy that made the child give up his own needs a success. Parents maintained discipline by negating their child's needs, usually through some form of coercion. In sum, powerful adults dominated powerless children.

Recently, the trend has reversed. Powerful, strident children seem to dominate powerless adults. Parents who know that they do not want to repeat the patterns that governed their childhoods, but lack a better approach, have simply flipped the equation. They have negated their own needs and let the children rule.

There is a better way. It moves beyond issues of control, or power. When you use loving guidance, you teach your child to meet his needs in a socially acceptable manner without either denigrating himself or attempting to dominate others. "Socially acceptable" means that the self-respect and safety of everyone involved is preserved. Loving guidance empowers you and your child, instead of pitting you against each other. It strengthens your entire family.

Teaching is about giving. Control is about getting.

To teach your child to respect limits, you need three essential ingredients. First, you need the *Seven Powers for Self-Control*, to change how you perceive a conflict situation. Second, you need the *Seven Basic Discipline Skills*, to change how you respond to the conflict. Third, you need to understand how children develop. With these three ingredients, you can respond calmly to any challenges your children offer. You will learn and practice them in the chapters that follow.

Teaching is about giving, while control is about getting. Earlier methods of discipline suffered from a lack of emphasis upon teaching. By learning the methods of loving guidance, you will discover how *both you and your child* can get your needs met in a socially acceptable fashion.

WHAT ARE YOU TEACHING?

I have been teaching for twenty-five years. I have taught children of all ages, and I have taught adults in parenting classes, at universities, and through my work with families in crisis. Teaching has led me to far-flung places, and introduced me to people of many cultures.

Ida, a medicine woman with whom I worked in New Mexico, taught me a profound lesson. Ida used the words "learning" and "teaching" interchangeably. At first, I thought she spoke English poorly, but eventually I came to realize that her synonymous use of these words contained great wisdom. Ida taught me that we fool ourselves when we pretend that learning and teaching are separate activities, with the teacher giving something to the learner, and nothing to himself or herself. Moreover, we have mistakenly treated teaching as a special activity that we do only at designated times. I've found that teaching and learning occur continually, and that teaching is a constant process for everyone, not just for those whom we call "teachers" or "students." I have come to realize that whatever I teach, I learn. At every moment, you teach other people *and* reinforce in yourself your sense of who you are, and what other people mean to you. Teaching and learning are actually the same.

If you scream at the driver who cuts you off in traffic, you teach that you are better and wiser than the other driver, and that "inferior" people deserve no respect. You teach that judging others as adequate or inadequate is your role, and that people who make mistakes must be condemned. Think of the many lessons we teach our children as we interact with life. You can teach them to fear, hate, and struggle against things that don't go their way. Or, you can teach them to be open to life, with all its mystery and unpredictability. You can decide to teach your children to treat other people with love, respect, and trust even when things do not go the way they "should." Your methods of discipline impart these lessons, because the need for discipline arises at times of conflict, and conflict arises when life refuses to go as you had planned.

THE JOURNEY FROM FEAR TO LOVE

This book will take you on a journey from fear to love. Nothing holds more power than love, yet love has been neglected as an element of discipline, and many hurtful things have been done in its name. I define love as an action that has the following four results:

1. **Love increases security and provides safety.** You might bark at your child, "Get over here or you'll get lost!" But wouldn't it feel better to say something like, "Stay close to me in the store so I can keep you safe. If something happened to you, I would be sad. I love having you with me." Fear separates, love unites.

2. **Love travels from the worthy to the worthy.** When we feel good about ourselves, we tend to focus on the beauty in our own lives and the goodness of others. When we feel bad about ourselves, we tend to criticize and judge others. If you want to teach your child, rather than blame him, for problems that arise, you must first rediscover and accept your own worth. To extend love to others, you must love yourself. Fear judges, love enjoys.

3. **Love looks for the highest and best in people and situations.** Imagine that you are having lunch with your child in a restaurant and your waitress has bungled your order. Instead of saying, "She is totally clueless, and ought to lose her job," give her a break. Say, "We all have off days. Let's help her by giving smiles and kind words." Fear focuses on what is missing; love sees the best of what is.

4. **Love accepts what is.** Fear looks to blame because things are not going as they "should." Love looks for solutions as it accepts what is. Instead of shouting, "Should the newspapers be spread all over?" calmly say, "Put the papers in the recycling bin." Fear looks for blame, love seeks solutions.

Loving guidance is based on these definitions of love. Its goal is to teach children to express themselves honestly while acting responsibly within a safe environment. The times that problems arise are when children feel entitled to express themselves freely, but do not temper this freedom with a sense of responsibility, or when children grow up feeling responsible for everyone and everything, squelching their own desires in a constant, hopeless search for approval. You can raise children who feel both free *and* responsible, but in order to do this, you must first feel free and responsible yourself. You cannot teach skills you do not possess.

There is a way to raise children to be both free and responsible.

THE PHYSICAL AND EMOTIONAL COST OF RELYING ON FEAR

The journey from fear to love will both fascinate and challenge you. Most of our own parents relied on fear-based discipline. As children, we feared punishment. ("Clean this mess up now, or else!") We feared the loss of their love. ("If you act that way, you'll be sent to your room.") We feared that we were not good enough. ("I work hard to keep this house neat. Why can't you do your part? All I ask for is a little assistance. Is that so much?") The worst fear instilled was the fear of abandonment. ("If you are not ready when I count to ten, I'm leaving without you. One. Two. . . . I mean it!")

Raised on fear, we now rely on fear with our own children. The use of fear may be blatant, as in the above examples, or it may be more subtle.

Several so-called modern approaches to discipline still rely on fear. One such approach is the use of rewards and punishments. ("If you behave, I will buy you a candy bar," or, "If you don't clean that room, there will be no Little League practice for you.") Children fear being deprived of treats or missing cherished activities.

Reasoning with children is another "modern" discipline method that is actually rooted in fear. Parents probe their children with questions such as, "Why did you hit her? Was that nice?" or, "How would you feel if I hit you?" These questions imply that the child is mean or stupid, and can leave him fearing that he is a failure. Parents often ask their children to resolve conflicts without teaching them how to do so. ("Talk to each other and work it out. If I have to get involved, you will both be sorry.") Children reasonably fear being unable to find solutions because they lack the social skills needed to "work it out."

Fear-based discipline focuses both you and your child on what was not done or on what was handled the wrong way. Fear-based tactics can be loud ("Do you call this room clean?"), or soft-spoken ("Come on, honey, remember to finish what you start"). When you constantly focus on what your child has done wrong, you highlight his imperfections and they come to take an exaggerated place in your child's self-concept. The result is children who grow up to feel they are "not good enough." Every adult I know battles with his or her own worth in some way. Some adults become arrogant, trying to prove their worth to others. Some overachieve, while others underachieve. Many adults eat or drink to excess, and some push their children to excel in order to overcome their own sense of failure.

When you rely on fear-based discipline, you trigger physical stress responses in your child that *hamper* his ability to learn from you. When your child experiences stress, stress hormones are released. One of the chemicals released is called *cortisol.* High cortisol levels can damage brain cells in an area called the *hippocampus,* which plays a major role in memory and learning. You want your child to understand and remember the lessons you try to teach, yet how often have you heard him say, "I don't know," or "I forgot"? When you rely on fear, you impede the hippocampus and actually derail your discipline goals. Research has shown that fear-based discipline actually fosters the behaviors that parents are trying to eliminate. Such strategies teach children to be more resistant to parental authority and may alter their brain chemistry for life. Nature provides the construction materials to build the human brain and nurture serves as the architect that designs it.

Your interactions with your children literally shape their brains.

It's likely that fear tactics were programmed into you during your childhood. Unless you become conscious of how subtle and manipulative fear can be, you will unconsciously teach your children to feel they are "not good enough." When you instill feelings of powerlessness in your children, their relationships with you and others inevitably become riddled with power struggles.

Love's goal is to develop healthy relationships which naturally inspire cooperation. With these relationships in place, children are more likely to choose to improve their behavior and are more amenable to learning social skills. Conflict occurs when you proceed without first eliciting cooperation.

Throughout the book I will be offering you examples. The wording in the examples may seem awkward at first. You may wonder, "Why didn't she use 'please' or 'thank you,' or other common phrases in the examples?" The answer will come. For now, read with an open mind and open heart. Shifting from fear to love requires that we change how we talk to ourselves and our children. I offer specific language suggestions to get you started. Ultimately, of course, you will adapt the wording to your own personality. In the following examples, which parent would you prefer to be?

The situation: Two boys are sitting outside eating pizza. Carter, age four, adores John, age ten, whom he is visiting. Carter spits on John's pizza. John rushes inside "to tell."

◆ **If the parent uses fear:** John's mom comes out and commands, "Carter, stop spitting! How would you like John to spit on *your* food? That's nasty! If you don't stop, you will have to sit alone and eat. I know you two can get along. Don't make me come out here again." John sneers, "I didn't do anything." He plops himself down at the picnic table and gives Carter an irritated look. After John's mother returns indoors, Carter spits on John's food again. John pushes Carter off the bench and Carter starts to cry. John's mom returns and sends John to his room and Carter home.

◆ **If the parent relies on love:** After John says, "Mom, Carter is spitting on my pizza," Mom responds, "Go outside and tell Carter firmly, 'I don't like it when you spit on my pizza.' I will go with you." They walk outside and John says to Carter, "I don't like it when you spit on my pizza. Stop spitting." Carter sits quietly. John's mom then says to Carter, "You want John to pay attention to you and talk to you, don't you?" Carter smiles and nods in agreement. "You didn't know what to do, so you spit on his pizza." "Yes," Carter says softly. John's mother responds, "You may not spit on John's food. John does not like it. Listen to him. When you want John's attention, start talking to him. You both like trucks. Ask John about the truck he saw yesterday." The boys then started to discuss forklifts.

These examples show fear-based and love-based discipline in action. The parent who used fear tried unsuccessfully to dominate the situation and eliminate the conflict. The parent who used love taught the children new skills so that they would know how to resolve the conflict.

CHOICE VS. FORCE

I conduct many workshops and lectures nationwide. Again and again, I'm asked questions that begin with, "How do I get my child to_____?" I usually respond, "I don't know; have you tried duct tape?" The audience laughs, and we talk about how tempting it is to fall into fear-based discipline. Fear-based discipline has as its foundation the belief that adults can "make" children behave. When you ask yourself, "How can I make my child_____?" it's a cue that you are seeking a control strategy based on fear, force, or manipulation. Remember, if you use these tools on your children, they will use the same skills to influence people in their lives, *including you!*

> **If you try to direct your child's behavior through fear and manipulation, he will learn to use the same strategies—on you.**

Love-based discipline is built on the belief that children choose whether or not to behave. The basic question you ask yourself when you use discipline-based love is, "How can I help my child to be more likely to choose to_____?"

WHAT YOU THINK IS WHAT YOU GET

If you ask yourself for evidence proving that your spouse is a jerk, your brain will search its data files, retrieve all instances of "jerk-like" behavior, and give you a printout within seconds. With this printout, you can convince yourself that you married the world's greatest moron. If, however, you asked your brain for documentation of how wonderful and loving your spouse is, your printout would read like an ode to his or her virtues. My point? To get new answers, you must ask new questions. Catch yourself when you start to think, "How do I get my child to_____?" Stop right there and change your mind-set by asking instead, "How can I help my child to be more likely to choose to_____?" Changing the question is critical. Loving guidance requires you to discipline your mind first using the *Seven Powers for Self-Control* and your child's behavior second using the *Seven Basic Discipline Skills.*

> **Change requires motivation. The motivation can come from fear or love. The choice is yours.**

I once worked with a kindergarten teacher who was struggling with a very active five-year-old boy who could never stand in line without fidgeting and pushing. She said she had tried everything to "make" him stand in line properly. She had taken away privileges, put him in time out, and sent notes to his parents. She had lectured, reasoned, and promised him rewards. All of her strategies were attempts to force the boy to stand "nicely." None had worked.

I asked this teacher if she had asked the child for his suggestions. She had looked for guidance from his parents, the school counselor, and a behavioral specialist, but not him. I know that you cannot "make" someone do something they do not want to do so I asked the boy, "What would help you stand in line with your feet still, like mine are now?" The boy looked at my motionless legs and said, "You would have to nail down my shoes."

I realized how hard it was for him to stand still and plotted a strategy to help him succeed. I had the child trace his shoes onto construction paper and then cut out the shoe shapes. Then we taped them to the floor at the spot where he would line up each day. As he successfully met his teacher's expectations, her joy in him returned. It sustained and fueled their relationship; and teacher and child felt successful.

Manipulative methods do not work because the belief that underlies them is wrong. How many times have you tried to make your toddler stay in his bed at night? How often have you tried to make a miserable person happy? Isn't it futile and exhausting?

If you believe you can "make" your child mind, then you will resort to tactics that you will hate yourself for using. You will cajole, coerce, bribe, beg, force, threaten, give up, and give in. You may even resort to violence if your child defies your will. (The underlying belief in this case is that if your child ignores your will, then his will must be broken.)

Your job as a parent is to strengthen, not break, your child's will. That will has a vital role to play in ensuring his safety and the fulfillment of his potential. It may drive him to write beautiful novels, master a sport, invent a computer program, or enter politics. His will can give him the strength to choose healthy foods and relationships, and to think positively. It can empower him to refuse dangerous drugs and peers, and avoid premature sex. He will need his will to control his impulses when he is angry so as not to injure others or himself. Your child's will can only serve him if it is left strong and whole, not if it is weak or broken.

The following chart shows the beliefs that underlie fear-based discipline and the values we teach children when we adhere to them. Remember that since teaching and learning occur simultaneously, when we use fear-based strategies, we are also reinforcing these values in ourselves.

Belief	Value It Teaches Children and Strengthens in Us
◆ It is possible to make others change. Failure to make others change equals failure on our part.	When others don't do what you want, you must try to bend them to your will. Might makes right.
◆ When we succeed in making others behave, we have power.	Power comes from overruling people.
◆ When we fail to make someone obey, it is their fault. We are entitled to blame them and others.	If someone does not do things your way, he or she is bad and lazy and deserves hardship.
◆ If others would change (do as we say), we could be happy and peaceful.	Blaming others for your upset is justifiable. Other people are responsible for your behavior.
◆ Children must feel bad in order to learn how to behave better in the future.	Revenge is the answer to life's upsets.
◆ Conflict is bad, disruptive, and must be eliminated.	If you are good enough, conflict will never trouble you.
◆ Fear is the best motivator for learning.	Fear is more powerful than love, and coercion is stronger than cooperation.

Are these the values you want to teach your children? More to the point, are these the values on which you want to base your own life? Are these not the values that contribute to a violent world? The belief that drives fear-based discipline is that *if* you could control the world (and all its people, institutions, and events), you could avoid all upsets and conflict. In reality, controlling others creates more conflict and, even if it didn't, it is very hard work. There is a better way.

DISCIPLINE BASED ON LOVE AND THE VALUES IT TEACHES

The following chart shows the beliefs that underlie discipline based on love, and the values that loving guidance teaches children and reinforces in us:

Beliefs	Value It Teaches Children and Strengthens in Us
◆ Changing ourselves is possible and, as parents, it is our choice to decide whether or not to change.	You are in charge. You can become the person you want to be.
◆ By choosing to control ourselves instead of others, we will feel empowered.	Power comes from within.
◆ When things don't go our way, we will seek solutions.	You are responsible for your own feelings, thoughts, and actions. Your choices have an impact on others.
◆ In order for children to learn how to behave, they must be taught.	You must teach others how to treat you. You cannot expect them to magically "know."
◆ Conflict is an essential part of life, and it presents us with an opportunity to learn a missing skill or let go of a limiting belief.	Conflict is a part of life and mistakes offer us opportunities to learn.
◆ Love is the best motivator for learning and growth.	Love is more powerful than fear, and cooperation is better than coercion.

To teach is to demonstrate by example.

MOVING BEYOND QUICK FIXES

Shifting from fear to love requires you to move beyond relying on quick fixes. It is helpful to understand that misbehavior plays a useful role in your children's development. It's not necessary to squelch every misdeed, so slow down, and enjoy the journey. If you promise a three-year-old child a cookie for sitting quietly in the grocery cart, you probably will have an angel in the aisles. If you threaten your child with a spanking, he will probably suck back tears, repress his feelings, and straighten up. But the calmed-by-cookies child may grow up to be obese because he soothes himself with food. The threatened-by-spanking child may grow up to be so distressed by emotions that he threatens to leave his wife whenever she becomes angry, because he considers her to be hysterical.

Parents have been seduced by the notion of quick discipline fixes long enough. In our society, people expect quick fixes for all sorts of problems. If you have a headache, take a pill. If you are tired in the morning, drink some more coffee. If your child seems out of control, naturally you want a trick or easy technique to control him. But, with maturity, we come to recognize that there are no "magic bullets." If you are tired or headachy, or feel out of control, there are reasons. Assuming they are not medical reasons, their solution may involve changing certain habits. This book is about lasting inner change for you and your child. Such change demands time, effort, and persistence.

THE ROLE OF MISBEHAVIOR IN YOUR CHILD'S DEVELOPMENT

If you were going to Tibet, how would you learn about Tibetan customs? You might read a book, talk to people who have been there, or carefully observe the people you met when you got there and hope you interpreted their behavior correctly. However you prepared, you would make mistakes, and your best lessons would come from your errors.

Misbehavior actually serves many wonderful purposes in your child's development. It would be misguided to try to stop misbehavior. Your goal is better framed as preventing the likelihood of misbehavior being repeated and becoming habitual. You can do this by responding to misbehavior wisely when it happens.

Babies enter human society unable to read or talk with those who have more experience than they have, and they have only limited abilities with which to interpret what they observe. For children, a huge amount of learning comes from making mistakes. Adults often call these mistakes "misbehavior," yet they serve a vital function for a child. Children learn the meaning of yes by declaring no. They learn the meaning of yours by proclaiming mine. Likewise, they grasp the concept of fairness by perceiving unfair actions, and the concept of patience by making constant demands. Misbehavior serves children as a communications system. Adults must learn to read children's signs.

APPRECIATING MISBEHAVIOR

Misbehavior serves these seven essential functions:

1. **Through misbehavior, children learn what is safe and what is not.** No child is born knowing to stay on the sidewalk or to say no to peers who suggest dangerous experiments. The only way children learn these lessons is to run toward the street and feel peer pressure. From your response to these situations, your child starts to figure out what is safe and what is not, and how to behave toward other people who are pushing the limits of safety.

2. **Misbehavior teaches children how to communicate in order to get their needs met.** Megan, age four, and her mom were in the grocery store when Megan dashed away from her mother, down the aisle where the toys were shelved. Fury overcame her mother. After she found Megan, she grabbed her shoulders and said, "Never leave my side in a store. *Never!*" Tears rolled down Megan's cheeks as she pointed to a doll. Her mother rolled her eyes and began walking away. Megan grabbed the doll and pursued her mother, who said, "No, you have a hundred dolls." Megan began whining, "Not like this one." Finally, her mom said, "Okay, but that is all you get today." Mom has now taught Megan how to get what she wants. She must: 1) run off to locate it, 2) ignore her mother's comments, and then, 3) beg. All misbehavior offers an opportunity to teach and to learn. Our responses to misbehavior teach children how to get their needs met.

3. **Misbehavior helps children learn what thoughts, feelings, and behaviors are appropriate to have toward others**. Zachary ran into the house, shouting, "Drew is a butt-head, and I hate him!" A parent could respond, "Is that nice? We don't talk about people like that in this house." This judgmental response teaches Zachary nothing about appropriate ways to express frustration. It leaves Zachary with three choices: 1) stop feeling frustrated, and pretend all is well when it is not; 2) learn to be passive (say nothing), aggressive (say bad things about people but not to your parents), or passive-aggressive (get back at your friends subtly); or, 3) doubt your right to have certain feelings ("I shouldn't feel like this"). Do any of these options sound familiar to you?

Children vent their frustration with others as well as they can. Parents need to teach them better ways to express themselves. A parent might say, "What happened? You seem so frustrated." Once the child has told his tale, his parent can teach him the coping skills he needs. Zachary might say, "Drew was cheating at checkers. He took too many turns." The parent could then say, "You didn't know what to say to make sure you got your turn. So you called Drew names and came home. If that happens again you could say, 'Drew, I don't like it when you take double turns. I want my turn.' Let's practice now."

4. **Misbehavior teaches children how to say yes to healthy things and no to unhealthy things**. We all need this skill. Saying no is powerful. Learning to say no also involves learning to accept no from others. Discipline has a great deal to teach children about no. If you cave in when your children plead, you fail to teach them how to accept or give a meaningful no. (Think about how important saying no will be when your child reaches his teens.) If you hurt children when you say no, you teach them to hurt others with their noes.

Yes and no define relationships. You cannot really know who you are until you can say no to another. If you cannot say no, you will live through the other person, trying to be the person you think he or she wants you to be. Saying no defines who you are and is therefore a positive force, not a negative one. Saying no strengthens character. It is a shield against manipulation, and it can educate other people about you. Saying no literally teaches others how to treat you. Children learn about no through the type of discipline they experience.

5. **Misbehavior defines for children what is their business and what is not their business.** When conflicts arise, you have an opportunity to help your child learn his job description in life. "April made me do it!" your child exclaims. "Is April your boss? Can she tell you what to think and feel and do?" you might respond. "I had to do it because April said . . . ," retorts your child. "You had other choices, but you couldn't think of them at the time," you might explain. "Your job is to think and ask yourself, 'Do I want to do this? Does it feel right to me, or am I doing this so that others will like me?' *You* control your choices, not April." An adult or child who is upset often needs to be empowered by being reminded that he controls his own thoughts, feelings, and choices.

6. **Misbehavior teaches children responsibility.** Responsibility is the ability to respond to the moment. Children who misbehave are clearly saying, "I do not know how to respond appropriately to this moment." If they did, there would be no misbehavior.

7. **Misbehavior provides children with opportunities to learn self-awareness and self-discipline.** Children can only learn to establish, maintain, and regain self-control by losing control, and so each of these out-of-control moments is a teaching moment for you. Children learn self-discipline in three stages. First, they find the limits by experimenting with them. Second, they retest their findings by repeatedly doing what they were told not to do. In this way, they test whether the limit is firm. If a child senses indecision, he will keep testing until he achieves clarity. To further solidify their findings, children may tease and provoke others, which gives them more information about what is permissible and what is not. Finally, children internalize the limits.

DISCIPLINE IS A LIFELONG JOURNEY, NOT A TECHNIQUE. ENJOY IT!

Again, the goal of this book is not to help you eliminate conflict—although it will occur with less frequency after you've mastered the powers and skills—but rather to teach you how to respond to it constructively. If you diligently apply the powers and skills of loving guidance, you will be astonished at the results. However, to reach your destination, you must not obsess about the outcome. Instead, enjoy the process of personal work and growth. Paradoxically, the less you focus on the desired result (a happy, respectful, responsible child), the more easily it will come.

A fable demonstrates this point. A young boy journeyed far from home to study with a sage. When the boy met the teacher he asked, "How long will it take before I am as wise as you?" The sage answered, "Five years." Stunned, the boy said, "That is a long time. What if I work twice as hard?" The teacher then responded, "Ten years." "That is crazy," shouted the boy, "what if I study all day and all night?" Calmly the sage replied, "Then it would take you fifteen years." "I don't understand," said the young boy. "Every time I promise to work harder to reach my goal, you say it will take longer to achieve. Why?" "The answer is simple," replied the sage. "With one eye fixed on the goal, you have only one eye left to guide you on your journey."

Relax. Enjoy this book and the process of change. Be willing to let your old beliefs go and let new ideas enter. Do the exercises. Practice the skills. At the end of the book, in chapter 12, there is a seven-week program that summarizes all the essentials of loving guidance. After you have read the book, pondered its principles, and practiced the skills, commit yourself to doing the seven-week program. Let yourself move from being willful to being willing, and watch how your children follow your lead. The journey starts in the next chapter, with learning the *Seven Powers for Self-Control*.

2

The Seven Powers
for Self-Control

One day, while driving down the freeway, I became obsessed with pulling over to buy some chocolate. Although I toyed with the notion of letting go of this compulsion, I gave in and pulled off the highway, searching for a convenience store. I figured I would find one just off the exit ramp, but I ended up driving for almost five miles before I found what I was looking for.

In the store, I encountered a mother and a young child who were screaming at each other. The boy, who was about six, was throwing a fit because his mother had denied him candy. The mother turned to me and said, "I have had it. These kids are out of control. It's just gimme, gimme, gimme. You'd think he could listen when I say no."

She was talking to *me,* a person who had just driven five miles for M&M's because she could not say no to herself. I nodded and laughed, but I realized that there was no difference between me and that child, and wondered what to do about it.

This was one of several events that launched me on a personal journey. I realized that my focus had been misdirected. I had long believed that others needed to change. But now I realized I had to become the person I wanted children to be. I wanted to become a "wonderful woman" as described in the nursery rhyme at the beginning of chapter 1. In order to do this, I needed to develop self-control.

WHAT IS SELF-CONTROL?

Self-control is mind control. It is being aware of your own thoughts and feelings. By having this awareness, you become the director of your behavior. Lack of self-control turns your life over to people, events, and things as you career through life on remote control, either unconscious of yourself or focused solely on what other people are thinking and feeling. On the freeway that day, I turned my life over to a bag of M&M's.

Ultimately, I came to the realization that I believed if I could predict how others would react to me, I could keep myself safe, and control events around me. So I devoted an enormous amount of energy to trying to read the minds of others in order to please them. When I finally became honest with myself, I realized that I was working to figure out what others wanted so I could use that knowledge to manipulate them to give me what I wanted. I grew up never realizing that there was another way. Up to that point, my self-worth had been rooted in winning other people's approval and in attempting to make the world go the "right" way—*my way.*

Self-control is an act of love and a choice you must make again and again.

Becoming aware of your own thoughts and feelings is a major accomplishment. Most people don't have a clue what they are thinking. Ask them. Usually their answer is "Nothing." Yet psychologists know, and your own observations can confirm, that inner speech runs continually in our heads. Experts estimate that each of us has more than 77,000 thoughts per day. Where are your thoughts right now? My mind wanders so much that sometimes while I am reading, I realize that all I am truly thinking about is my to-do list. The irony is that I don't know what I have read, nor have I finished any of my tasks. In effect, my cluttered mind leaves me mindless and out of control.

Becoming aware of your own thoughts and feelings is a major accomplishment and the first step toward self-control.

It is time to retrain our minds so that we will no longer be slaves to our impulses and insecurities. With self-control, you are self-disciplined. Self-discipline will allow you to be the parent you want to be. It is an essential prerequisite for disciplining children. Remember: You cannot teach skills that you do not possess.

As I began making the shift from using fear to using love to guide my own behavior and that of children, I was often discouraged by how often I would slip back into using fear tactics. I became a reactive, screaming nut (as I had sworn I never would), and more often than I cared to admit. I realized, though, that I must be holding some underlying beliefs that were fueling my insanity. When I was calm and peaceful, I could see that screaming at clerks in stores would not motivate them to resolve a problem. I could see that getting children to feel bad would not elicit their cooperative spirit. What were these misguided powers that had a grip on me? How could I transform them into something more loving and more effective?

I had always heard that in order to discipline children you must "be firm but fair, more positive than negative, treat children with respect, hold them responsible for their own behavior, be consistent and predictable, and model self-control." Yet I had never learned *how* to do all these fine things. How do you exhibit these shining qualities with children who are acting wild, disrespectful, and irresponsible? How is an adult supposed to remain calm when a child is screaming, "I hate you," or throwing a fit because pizza isn't on the menu, or in agony because she can't stay up to watch the *Late Show with David Letterman*?

My search for alternatives led me eventually to the *Seven Powers for Self-Control.* They can foster self-control in both adults and children.

Parents who have mastered self-control are able to do the following:

◆ Focus on what they want the child to accomplish.

◆ Celebrate the child's successes and choices.

◆ See situations from the child's perspective, as well as their own.

◆ Creatively teach the child how to communicate her wishes and frustrations with words, in an acceptable manner.

◆ Hold the child accountable to those teachings.

An out-of-control adult cannot do any of these things. Out-of-control adults focus on what they don't want to happen. ("Stop that this minute!") They see only from their own point of view. ("You are driving me nuts!") They punish rather than teach. ("Go to your room!")

When you lose self-control, you lose your ability to discipline yourself and your children. For this reason self-control—the peace of mind that comes through the awareness of your thoughts and feelings—must be your first priority as a parent. Only when you possess self-control can you offer loving guidance. To stop the "Do-as-I-say-not-as-I-do" syndrome, which we all hated when we were growing up, you need self-control.

Self-control must be your first priority as a parent.

THE *SEVEN POWERS FOR SELF-CONTROL*

The *Seven Powers for Self-Control* shift your focus from blame to solutions, from guilt to action, from punishment to teaching, and from reasoning to results. Here they are:

1. **The Power of Attention:** What you focus on, you get more of.
2. **The Power of Love:** See the best in one another.
3. **The Power of Acceptance:** This moment is as it is.
4. **The Power of Perception:** No one can *make* you angry without your permission.
5. **The Power of Intention:** Conflict is an opportunity to teach.
6. **The Power of Free Will:** The only person you can *make* change is yourself.
7. **The Power of Unity:** Focus on connecting instead of trying to be "special."

The Seven Powers will allow you to look at life through a lens of love rather than through a lens of fear. When you can do this, you will be able to exercise true self-control. As you can see, each of the Seven Powers has a motto that you can use as a reminder. Repeating the motto to yourself shifts your mind from fear and anger to love. Once your mind-set is loving, you cannot help but acknowledge your free will and your child's free will. Then you can offer loving guidance to your child. Remember, loving guidance is about helping children to be more likely to choose to be cooperative. It is about choice, not force.

Sadly, few of us use these Seven Powers enough to build loving relationships with our children. So many of us wander around being miserable in a world full of love. We have given up connecting with others as the result of our failed attempts to control them. It is time to change.

In this chapter, each power is discussed separately, but love is unity. Love cannot really be divided, so there is an interdependence among the powers that I cannot emphasize enough. Still, in practical terms, it helps to focus on one power at a time. When you fully internalize the beliefs behind the *Seven Powers for Self-Control,* you will have the mind-set you need to use the *Seven Basic Discipline Skills,* which you will learn about in later chapters. The Seven Basic Skills, in turn, will empower you to handle any conflict with your children.

Proceed through this section slowly, and do the exercises. I avoided challenging myself in this way for years, waiting for some magic to make everything better. When I finally found that magic, I discovered that it was within me.

The Power of Attention: What You Focus On, You Get More Of

I am going to describe two scenarios in which a parent comes home from work to find children playing in the family room, with dirty dishes in the sink. Parent A enters the house, sees the messy kitchen, and launches into a diatribe: "Who left these dishes here? It's not such a big deal to put them into the dishwasher. Why do I have to do everything around here? I hate coming home to a mess. Am I the maid?"

Parent B enters the house, sees the children playing, and greets them with hugs. When she notices the dirty dishes she says, "Jessica, it is your week for dishes. Please rinse them and put them in the dishwasher."

Angry Parent A chose to focus on what was wrong; calm Parent B focused first on the joy of seeing her children. Her response to the dishes was simple: She focused on the action needed to solve the problem. Which parent would you rather be? What do you want to focus on: the error, or the answer? Both are present in each moment. The choice is yours.

What you focus on, you get more of.

Before you can teach children what you expect of them in a given situation, you must clearly define for yourself what you want to have happen. Often we carry on about the things we want children *not* to do, or to *stop* doing, or what we will *not allow*, instead of on what we *want*. Do these commands sound familiar? "Stop whining." "Don't hit." "Quit pestering me."

Learning to focus your attention on the outcomes that you desire will bring you enormous power. It is probably the most important technique you can learn for living peacefully with children (and with other adults), and for finding joy in life. Focusing on what you want lays the foundation for all the skills you will learn in this book, because it creates the opportunity from which change can occur.

Many people have tried to change their behavior without success. New Year's resolutions are great examples. "I will stop smoking," ". . . eat less junk food," and ". . . spend less time at work" are common resolutions. Usually, people keep these commitments for only a few weeks before backsliding. Why?

The main reason is that we try to change behaviors by focusing on what we do not want to do. If I told you, "Don't think about a purple alligator," what would pop into your mind?

Or watch a toddler. If you say, "Don't touch the lamp," what does the child do? She will look at you, look at the lamp, point at it, touch it, and then look back at you—usually with a big smile. Her brain heard, "Touch the lamp," so she looks at you proudly as if to say, "Hey! I did it! I touched the lamp!" Imagine her confusion when you growl, "What did I tell you?" and push away her little hand. No wonder we all need therapy.

Instead of focusing on what you don't want, you could redirect the child. When she spots the lamp, you could say, "See the pretty lamp? Put your hand in mine and I will show you how to touch delicate objects that might break." Or perhaps you do not want to teach the child how to touch the lamp. In this case you could say, "You see the pretty lamp. Now let's look at this truck. I will roll it to you. Whee!" Then push the truck over to the child. Have fun with the alternative you choose—because children, like all of us, respond to enthusiasm.

As an adult, you probably make the connection between a negative command ("Don't hit") and a positive alternative ("Talk through your problems"). Children younger than five or six simply cannot make this conceptual leap.

Focusing on what you don't want actually pits your body chemistry against your willpower and undermines your chances for success. Let's say that you want to eat fewer sweets. You may tell yourself, "That's it, no more sweets for me. I'm not eating them, at least not after seven o'clock at night." In saying these words, you are focusing on sweets. Your brain hears the word sweets, and, believe it or not, the region of the brain that regulates your body chemistry (the hypothalamus) adjusts your body for an influx of sugar. Your blood sugar actually drops, and your insulin levels change, in anticipation of that luscious sweet.

So this is how you begin your diet, your mind focused squarely on no more sweets, your body chemistry urging you to run to the next vending machine. As the week drags on, you feel increasingly lethargic. Eventually, to get your adrenaline pumping again, you may become self-righteous and start lecturing friends on the harmful effects of sugar. By the end of the week, you are likely to feel exhausted and tell yourself, "I've been good all week. I deserve a little treat." At this point, a hot fudge brownie appears and hits the spot. Full of remorse, you swear off sweets again. The next day your blood sugar plummets, launching you on yet another week of denial followed by wild excess.

What does this all have to do with children, discipline, and loving guidance? To find out, read the following scenarios and determine what each parent's focus is.

SCENE 1: "Robby, why did you hit Kelsey? Would you like someone to hit you? Hitting hurts. Go to your room and think about your behavior. Then come back and be nice."

PARENT'S FOCUS: _____

SCENE 2: "Crystal, you can't sleep with Mommy and Daddy."

PARENT'S FOCUS: _____

SCENE 3: Think about the last discipline encounter you had with your own child or children.

WHERE WAS YOUR FOCUS? _____

In scene 1 the parent's focus was on hitting. In scene 2, the parent's focus was on sleeping with Mommy and Daddy. Where was your focus in the situation you recalled? Remember, what you focus on, you get more of.

This week, pay attention to the many occasions when you tell yourself what *not* to do and what you *don't* want. Then consciously began to redirect your attention by focusing on what *to do* and what you *do* want. Do this in every arena of your life—when you select the food you eat or the video you rent, or discuss the behavior you want from your spouse. Remember the universal principle: What you focus on, you get more of. If you focus on stopping your child from sleeping with you, you create more opportunities to fight at night. If you focus on your child staying in her bed, you create an opportunity for change.

You may be thinking, I think I *do* tell them what to do most of the time. A second principle can help you realize just how often you are in fact focusing on what you don't want rather than on what you do want. The principle is: When you are upset, you are always focused on what you don't want. Think about the last time you felt upset. Bring the scene fully to mind. As you re-create that moment, I assure you, you will see that you were focused on what you did not want. You badly wanted someone to stop doing something. To focus on what you do want, you must be a calm model of self-control.

When you are upset, you are always focused on what you don't want.

When I discuss the Power of Attention with parents, they listen, laugh, and nod their heads as if they can really relate. Invariably, though, when I finish explaining this power, some parent will ask, "How will this help me make my two-year-old stop hitting my five-year-old?" Again, I guide them toward an awareness of their focus by saying, "Think about what you want the two-year-old child *to do.*" Their usual response is, "Stop hitting." So many of us have this deeply ingrained habit of focusing on outcomes that we do not want. In these cases, I continue to walk them through the process. I'll ask, "What skill do you want your two-year-old child to use to get the older child's attention? Do you want her to say his name, or ask him to play?"

Be specific and assertive when you tell your children what you want.

Focus on the *specific action* you want your child to take. Focusing on what you want her to stop doing is like going to a carpet store and telling the clerk, "I want to replace my carpet." The clerk would ask how much carpet you needed. Would you respond, "I don't want to get home and not have enough"? This sounds absurd, but this is how we handle our children day after day. Be clear when you tell your children what you want. Specificity and assertiveness are essential when you address children.

We all get upset. Your goal is to regain self-control once you have become upset, before you deal with your children. You must discipline yourself first, and your children second. To that end, this week practice what I call "pivoting." Pivoting is a wonderful about-face during which you shift your focus from what you don't want to what you do want. When you feel frenzied, stop, take a deep breath, and talk to yourself. You might say, "I feel upset. If I am upset, I am focused on what I don't want. Do I want more of this in my life?" If the answer is no, shift your mind to what you do want and calmly proceed. If the answer is a loud "I don't care!" go ahead and act like a nut, but remember to forgive yourself later.

Practice the Power of Attention by taking these steps:

◆ Consciously pay attention to your focus. Are you focusing on what you want to have happen, or on what you don't want?

◆ When you are upset, *pivot*. Say to yourself, "Okay, I'm upset. If I'm upset, I am focusing on what I don't want. Do I want more of this in my life?" If the answer is no, breathe deeply. Then tell your child what you do want him to do, and why.

◆ Remind yourself at least five times every day, "what I focus on, I get more of." Remind yourself of this when you wake up, at meals, at bedtime, and whenever you are upset.

The Power of Love: See the best in one another

Imagine yourself at a welcome-to-the-neighborhood party, at which you are the newest person on the block. You enter the room wondering how the other guests are judging you, if they are sizing up your clothes and hair, or deciding whether or not you pass muster. How would you feel? You would probably be squirming with discomfort.

Now change the scene in your mind. Pretend you have come to a party believing that all the people there will welcome you warmly. How would you feel now? Probably quite happy. In real life, who decides what you think other people are thinking about you? The answer is good news. You do! You get to make up what you think other people are thinking. You can decide that they find you "good enough," and then feel good enough, or you can decide that they judge you to be "not good enough," and feel not good enough. One decision plants the seeds of peace and the other plants the seeds of conflict. The choice is yours.

What you offer to others, you experience within yourself. This is a guiding principle to remember. Another way to look at this is that what you see in others you will strengthen in yourself. To grasp this further, stop reading for a moment and think of someone you love. Silently, and with a full heart, wish that person well. If no one comes to mind, just take a moment to be grateful for some aspect of your life: your home, health, job, or whatever. Now notice how you feel inside. If we wish others well, we tend to "well up" inside with warm feelings of comfort. If we offer gratitude, we tend to feel grateful and blessed.

If you offer others love and gratitude, you will feel warm and blessed.

The same kind of mirroring occurs when we look at the world and focus on what is wrong with it. The parent who walked into her house and focused on dirty dishes unconsciously chose to feel inadequate. It's a paradox, but it is true: Your sense of self-esteem does not come from how other people see you, but from how you see other people. If you choose to see what's missing, lacking, and not good enough, you not only inhibit change from occurring, you also destroy your sense of your own value. Feeling powerless, you are primed to blame others for your discomfort.

When you approach life fearfully, you actually install the "buttons" in your brain that you then blame your children for pushing. You assume your tantruming child is trying to make your day difficult or is just mean. You see intentional acts of meanness instead of innocent mistakes. Alternatively, you could assume your child is hurting inside, needs some love, or is misbehaving because she lacks better skills for getting what she wants. Again, the choice is yours. If you choose to attribute positive intentions, you will feel peaceful inside and can use that inner stability to form your response. If you choose to attribute negative intentions, you will feel inadequate yourself and bring less patience to your handling of the conflict.

Years ago, a boy and his dog, a black Labrador, got lost in Florida's Ocala National Forest. Fortunately both were found the next day. Television news reporters announced that the dog had stayed with the boy to keep him warm. I wondered who interviewed that dog. Soon after, sales of black Labrador puppies soared in Florida as parents bought them to protect their children. If we are going to put intentions into people's heads, why not put in noble ones? We did it for a dog.

What we offer to others, we give to ourselves.

Love sees the best in people. Being determined to find faults in children simply means that you are unwilling to change yourself. When you give people credit for having good intentions, you will have far more good days than bad, and you will keep your self-esteem high. You will also highlight for your children the best aspects of themselves and others. That is powerful!

Love sees the best in people—including children.

Practice the Power of Love by taking these steps:

◆ Wish people well. Do this silently from your heart while you are driving, standing in lines, or passing people on the street. Notice how you feel when you do this.

◆ When you make a mistake, or others do, attribute a positive intent. Instead of chiding yourself with "I can't believe I forgot to pick up the laundry," reframe your thought. Say, "I wanted to get home in time to greet the children when they got off the school bus, so I forgot the laundry. I will pick it up tomorrow." When a car pulls out in front of you, resist yelling, "You stupid idiot!" Reframe it. Say, "Boy, is he in a hurry." Practice seeing the best in one another.

◆ Affirm to yourself, "What I offer to others, I give to myself." Do this five times a day for at least one week. Put the saying on your refrigerator as a reminder.

The Power of Acceptance: This moment is as it is

We have been programmed to believe that in order to change something, we must resist it. When something happens that contradicts our beliefs about how things *should* be, we automatically try to make what happened be different than it is. Often we will state that the event or problem never should have happened. When we say, "This shouldn't have happened; people shouldn't act like that," we are saying that this moment is not good enough; that this moment would be better—and we would be better—if things had only gone the way we would have preferred. It is a huge responsibility to know what is best for the world. Of course, in judging the moment to be not good enough, we reinforce our feelings of personal inadequacy.

You cannot negate a particular moment and call it not good enough without also attacking the people who are present in that moment. Shouting "Where should you be? What should you be doing? Should you have hit her?" is an attack on your child. Questions like these imply, "You dummy, don't you even know where you should be or what you should be doing?" Other phrases parents use to negate troubling moments are "We don't talk like that in this house," or, "We don't run in this house," said after the cursing or running. An impartial observer might note, "Yes, you do. I just heard them curse," or saw them run. When you negate a moment, you negate the child involved. So many adults carry around this denigrating message we heard growing up. I call it the "stupid message," because it left us feeling hopelessly stupid. We fight that feeling through overachieving, trying to be perfect, blaming others or ourselves, or eating too much or too little. The list goes on and on.

Resistance does not bring about change—it just plants the seeds of conflict. Change only comes about through acceptance. Once you can accept what is and own it, you have the power to choose to stay with the *status quo* or to make a change for the better. Imagine walking down a sidewalk and seeing a car approaching on the sidewalk. You can continue to walk along, and declare, "That car shouldn't be on the sidewalk," or you can accept the fact that the car is where it is and jump away to avoid being hit. The choice is yours.

Acceptance means recognizing that people, situations, and events are what they are. Each moment simply is as it is. Acceptance does not mean that we approve of the moment, only that we recognize that what is happening at a certain moment is in fact happening. Each moment is as it is because the entire universe is as it is. When you struggle against the moment and say, "You shouldn't be hungry; you just ate," you are struggling against the universe. No wonder you feel tired!

The moment will be the way it is regardless of whether you accept it or not. The fact is that your child is not dressed, the room is not clean, and the bath has not been taken. Instead of choosing to be upset and focusing on the problems, acceptance allows you to start responding to your children, creating moments you will enjoy much more. Responsibility is the ability to respond.

This week, practice being present in each moment. Instead of wearing yourself down over what you should have done or what you need to do, practice being where you are. If you are washing dishes, feel the water, notice the color of the detergent, experience the pressure of steel wool on a pan. If you are walking with your child, feel her small, warm hand in yours. Feel the softness of her skin. Listen to the pitch of her voice. Tonight, when you put your child to bed, try a new nighttime ritual. Touch her eyebrows and, as you touch them, say, "I'm going to say goodnight to your eyebrows." Repeat this process with her ears, forehead, hair, shoulders, arms, legs, and feet. Really look at your child, and really touch her. You can do the same thing with your spouse. It is great fun. As you go about your day, practice noticing trees, clouds, birds. Shift your attention from judging things to be pretty, good, ugly, or bad, to simply noticing what is. If you start to become upset, breathe deeply and remind yourself, "This moment is as it is." In any given moment, relax and respond.

When you resist what is, you become upset. Remember, when you are upset, you are focused on what you do not want. What you focus on, you get more of. By focusing on what is not good enough, you will feel not good enough. When you feel inadequate, you will tend to blame others for your internal upset. Avoid this trap by internalizing the Power of Acceptance.

Practice the Power of Acceptance by taking these steps:

- ◆ Practice being in the moment by noticing things. Do this by describing what you see to yourself. Make no judgments.
- ◆ Add the "goodnight ritual" to your bedtime routine.
- ◆ If you start to become upset when things are not going the way you think they should, breathe deeply and affirm, "This moment is as it is, and I can relax."

The Power of Perception: No one can *make* you angry without your permission

"Look what you *made* me do." "Don't *force me* to send you to time out." "You are driving me nuts." Have you ever heard anything similar come out of your mouth? When you resort to these angry exclamations, you send a message to your child that she is responsible for your upset. When you place someone in charge of your emotions, you place that person in charge of you. If you believe that standing in a long line drives you nuts, then you have given your power to a line. If you believe your spouse is driving you to drink, then you have given your power to your partner. If you believe your children are *making* you scream at them, you have placed them in charge of you.

Wouldn't you prefer to be in control of your life? To do so, you must be prepared to own your own upset. Pretend you and I were dating and I brought you roses. When you opened the door and saw me with a bouquet in hand, you might marvel at how thoughtful I was. If you had this perception, you would probably experience joy at receiving the bouquet. What if I brought flowers again the next night? This time you might think, "What are these for? It is not my birthday." With these kinds of thoughts, you would no longer feel happy, but would feel suspicious instead. Did the flowers make you happy or suspicious? Did I make you happy or suspicious? Or did your thoughts about me and the flowers create the emotions? It wasn't me, or the flowers. Your thoughts created your emotions.

Each of us carries around an image of how we think the world should work. We are conscious of some aspects of this image and unconscious of others. Do you have an expectation about what constitutes a *good* school? Do you have an ideal for a *good* marriage? Can you picture what a *good* morning would be? You probably have images for all of these, but don't often think consciously about them. You also have an image of how *"good children"* ought to behave.

We see the world not as it is, but through a lens of our judgments about how we think it should be. This lens alters everything we see. When your children's school or your spouse fails to meet your expectations, you become upset because the world did not work as you thought it should.

Amazing as it may seem, this is the same reason a toddler throws a fit when you take away the markers she is using to color the living room walls. To the toddler, coloring is what should happen. To you, drawing on walls is something that should not happen. So you both become upset, overcome by the feeling of being powerless to run the world according your plan. Neither of you *caused* the other person's upset. It was *triggered* by the other person, but she was not its *cause*. Upset is an inside job. You are never upset for the reason you think you are.

You are never upset for the reason you think you are.

When you feel powerless, you are likely to blame someone else. Through blame, you try to make others suffer for what they have done to you. This is a form of attack, and it does not create a secure-feeling home. You create danger anytime you try to make someone else feel responsible for your upset. Your upset indicates that you have perceived the situation as an attack. Ask yourself, "Is there another way of seeing this person or event?" You will do yourself and your family a huge service if you decide to take responsibility for your own emotions.

Whenever you feel upset this week, start owning your own emotions. You need them. They are navigational instruments to guide you through life. If your feelings create a sense of peace, your worldview is loving. If your feelings create discomfort, your orientation has shifted from love to fear. If you are upset, you are resisting what is: You are either focusing on what you don't want, attributing negative motives to others, or blaming others for your upset. Remember the Power of Attention: What you focus on you get more of.

This week, ask yourself, "Do I want to own my own upset and maintain self-control, or do I want to give my power away and blame others for taking it?" The choice is yours, and the choice never goes away, so you can draw on this power at any moment. To own your feelings, say "I feel upset [angry, sad, etc.], and it's okay. I am safe and I can handle this."

Practice the Power of Perception by taking these steps:

◆ Notice how your thinking creates your feelings. If you are feeling angry, sad, or anxious, check to see what you are thinking and where your mind is directed.

◆ Listen to how often you blame others. Carefully note any "make me" language. Notice how often you disempower yourself by saying, "Don't make me," or, "You made me." Replace "Don't make me" statements with "I'm going to _____." For example, instead of saying, "Don't make me have to stop this car," say, "I'm going to pull over until you two put your seatbelts on."

◆ When you are upset, say to yourself, "I feel angry, and it's okay," or, "I feel anxious and it's okay."

◆ Affirm to yourself, "When I put another person in charge of my feelings, I put them in charge of me," and take back your power. Ask yourself frequently, "Where is my power?"

The Power of Intention: Conflict is an opportunity to teach

Do you view conflict as bad? Most people do. They see conflict as disruptive, and as a problem to be avoided. Many parents also equate disobedience with disrespect. Such parents consider a child who does not follow their wishes disrespectful. A messy room seems to them to be the result of a child who didn't listen, as opposed to a child who got distracted by toys or friends. Such parents might take a refusal to bathe as a defiant act, rather than acknowledging that the child simply prefers to play.

As a parent, when you equate disobedience with disrespect, you create a link between your child's behavior and your own competence. Although this connection is not valid, your belief in it can

cause you to lose control quickly, especially if your child's disobedi-
ent act occurs in public. Has your child ever thrown a fit in a store
when you said no to buying a toy? You would react one way if you
chose to see your child's tantrum as intended to humiliate you. But
your reaction would be quite different if you saw your child as overwhelmed by the many temptations. Adults who equate disrespect
with disobedience forget that children do not yet have all the emotional and intellectual abilities of grown-ups. Toddlers say no for a
reason. They are beginning to define themselves as being separate
from you. Seven-year-old children appear deaf to adult requests for a
reason. Their entire focus is inward, as they concentrate on making
sense of life. It's easy to take children's self-absorption personally, but
in fact it is simply a necessary part of their development.

Still, we cling to the belief that if only we were perfect
enough, our homes would be free of conflict, and our children
would be models of obedience—they would do what we said to
do, when we said to do it, and they'd smile as they did it. But
would you really want a child who was totally subservient to others? Such a child would lack creativity, be unable to think for herself, and say yes to everything. Imagine her as a teenager loose on
the streets.

If you think conflict is bad, when it arises you set out to nail the
"bad guy." ("Who started this?") You seek a culprit so you can
decide who must be made to feel bad for causing your upset. You
would never want to punish the innocent, unless you were so worn
down by the bickering that you felt too tired to identify the "bad
guy." In such instances, you would treat both children as irritants.
"That's it!" you might yell. "Both of you go to your rooms! I don't
care who started what."

When you view conflict as bad, you search for a magic bul-
let—some all-powerful disciplinary technique—that will banish it
from your home forever. You may bribe your children to be good, or
you may plead and bargain with them. At other stressful times, you
may have screamed to let off steam or reasoned with the little ones
and tried to be understanding. At some point, most parents take

away privileges. To avoid more drastic measures, you may have even put yourself in time out.

We pretend that we can eliminate conflict, but it is a part of nature. Nature embraces conflict. A worm crawls out of the dirt only to be scooped up by a bird. For the worm, this was a bad day. However, taking the larger view, the worm played a necessary part in the functioning of nature's system.

Conflict also plays a positive role in human relationships. Through conflict, we learn to establish healthy boundaries between ourselves and others. Conflict serves such a vital purpose, it behooves us to embrace it rather than search for ways to eliminate it.

Every conflict offers an opportunity to teach.

From this moment on, change your view of conflict, and your relationship with it. When conflict occurs, breathe deeply and say, "Here is an opportunity to teach and learn." Then, begin the process of teaching your children. If they ignore you and the conflict persists, say to yourself, "Here is another opportunity to teach," and try again. If your best efforts still do not resolve the conflict, I suggest you step back from the event entirely. Breathe deeply, bow your head, and say, "Thank you for all the teaching opportunities I have had today." Having observed this moment of reverence, you can re-enter the scene with a new sense of appreciation for life's many complexities.

Every conflict presents you with a choice. You can choose to view conflict as an opportunity to teach or as an opportunity to blame and punish. If you set out to punish the "bad guy," you will destroy your own self-esteem and that of your children. If, instead, you use times of conflict as teaching opportunities, you will enhance your own self-respect and allow your children to maintain their sense of worth. You will also increase the chance that, when future conflicts arise, the children will be able to resolve them without you.

Practice the Power of Intention by taking these steps:

- ◆ Whenever conflict arises, breathe deeply and affirm, "Conflict is an opportunity to teach, and learn."
- ◆ Ask yourself: "What is my intention in this situation?" Do you intend to make your child feel bad, or help her succeed? Do you intend to teach or punish?
- ◆ Focus on responding to conflict rather than trying to eliminate it. Ask yourself, "Am I looking for blame or solutions?" Blame attempts to prevent future conflicts from happening; solutions seek to teach answers to future conflicts.

The Power of Free Will: The only person you can *make* change is yourself

I find it difficult to acknowledge free will in myself and others. I keep making two mistakes. First, I continue to believe that others can make me choose certain things in my life. You can hear it in my speech. I hear myself saying, "I have to exercise," or, "I should call Sarah." But I don't have to. These are choices. I could just as easily have said, "I am going to exercise," or, "I will call Sarah." My second mistake is to believe that I can make others choose to act in the ways that I want them to.

These mistakes are two sides of the same coin. If I believe that people can make me act in a certain way, then it is reasonable to assume that I can make others act in a certain way. But both beliefs are false. Still, they are widely held and cause great trouble in relationships and in our handling of discipline.

The belief that adults can *make* children mind and *get* them to change is as common as air. In fact, most people consider it the responsibility of parents to *make* children behave. These people further believe that parents have failed in their duty when their children misbehave, and that the parents must be inadequate. These beliefs have come down to us through the generations. No one seems to question these false, hurtful assumptions.

We must rethink these beliefs. Can we force children to mind, or behave in a certain manner? Can we make anyone, regardless of her age, do something that she is set against doing? Is it possible to make a child who refuses to do her homework finish the assignments? It seems impossible to make others go against their own wishes. In fact, the only way to do it is to rely on force. Our strong-arm tactics teach children that it's legitimate to use force to influence others. Through force, we attempt to remove other people's choices. By removing their choices, we remove their self-esteem and their ability to make commitments.

Practice the Power of Free Will by becoming aware of how often you think others are making you do things. Is the screaming infant making you get up at night, or did you choose to give birth? Notice how often you use the words "have to" and "should." Practice changing "shoulds" into "coulds." If you hear yourself saying, "I should pick up some milk," change your approach and say, "I could pick up some milk." Then decide whether you are going to do it or not. Once you change your "shoulds" to "coulds," you will be more willing to help your child make choices that are acceptable to both of you.

Practice the Power of Free Will by taking these steps:

◆ If you catch yourself saying, "How can I make my child _____?" change the question to, "How can I help my child to be more likely to choose to _____?"

◆ Change your "shoulds" to "coulds." Then make a choice.

◆ Practice allowing others to have their own thoughts and feelings. Resist the urge to try and *make* others happy or convince them you have all the answers.

The Power of Unity: Focus on connecting
instead of trying to be special

Years ago, Miami experienced the awful devastation brought on by Hurricane Andrew. The entire state rallied to support those needing help. During the recovery period, traffic patterns in Miami shifted as populations redistributed themselves. Yet, in a way, the traffic jams were pleasant. Drivers kindly let others change lanes. Everyone took care of each other. As the crisis passed, though, horns began honking, and merging became impossible again. Everyone drove normally—thinking mainly of themselves.

Around the same time, the Orlando Magic basketball team made it to the national finals. Unity reigned in Orlando as people joined forces behind the team's quest to beat the Chicago Bulls. "Magic" bumper stickers plastered buildings and vehicles. Clerks were pleasant and strangers chatted as bonding occurred behind the common goal. In both of these cases, the stimulus of a common threat (a hurricane in Miami, the Bulls vs. the Magic) prompted unity. If threats were the only effective unifiers, families would need constant crises, or an omnipresent "black sheep," in order to stay together. But threats, thank goodness, are not the only unifiers.

Unity can also arise from a sense of security—that is, freedom from threat. It can arise through complete trust and shared vulnerability with another person. It comes from letting go of the need to compare oneself to others, and choosing instead to connect through a sense of equality. We all need to belong and to feel connected to something larger than ourselves, and, further, to feel that we contribute to the well-being of that whole. We want to feel valued and connected. The Power of Unity is about this feeling that we are each bound to one another, and, at the same time, have unique contributions to make. When we truly connect with something or someone other than ourselves, we are transformed into caring, compassionate, self-disciplined individuals. In oneness, there is no one to fight.

This power is truly the mother of all the other powers, encompassing them all.

Ask yourself: "Do I want to be special (i.e., right), or do I want to connect?"

How can we raise our children so that we connect with each other through love and unity instead of through fear and identifying common enemies? To access the Power of Unity, we must relinquish the need to be special. This runs against the grain of American culture, which places a premium on being special. To stand out here, you must wear certain clothes, weigh a certain amount, or achieve a certain level of economic success. We base our feelings of specialness on comparisons that we make, through which we convince ourselves that some people lack what we have. If being special matters a lot to you, you will constantly be judging yourself to see if you are better or worse than others. Such judgments render feelings of equality and true union impossible. In any given moment, ask yourself, "Do I want to be special, or do I want to connect?"

If you must feel special to feel worthy, you will push your children to be special, since your children reflect you. One way parents commonly pressure children to be special is through the words they choose to praise and encourage them. When you judge your children, rather than noticing their efforts and accomplishments, you push them to be special. Driving youngsters to stand out will fill them with loneliness and a sense that they do not, and cannot, fit in. These feelings of loneliness and inadequacy can fuel addictive and compulsive behaviors. Unable to truly connect with other human beings, people may bond instead with work, drugs, alcohol, exercise, or pets.

You could say that a parent carries around a yellow highlighter all the time. With this imaginary pen, you highlight those aspects of life you deem important for your children to notice. Let's say you look at your child's report card and say, "All A's. Fantastic! You're so smart, and we're so proud of you." You just took your yellow high-lighter and spotlit the importance of grades. What if you wanted to highlight the value of learning? You might say, "These grades show me that you put a lot of effort into learning. What did you learn that you really loved?" Both responses celebrate the child's success, but they do it in different ways. The first response fosters specialness, the second one supports connecting. The choice is yours.

Practice the Power of Unity by taking these steps:

◆ For five minutes or longer every day, just be with each of your children. To do this, you must let go of the clutter in your head about what needs to be done. Let go of any pre-conceived outcomes you might have about your time together. When you do this, you will be truly present with your child. The activity of reading, cuddling, or playing is secondary to your *total presence*.

◆ In stressful situations, ask yourself, "Do I want to be special, or do I want to connect with this person?" Another way of saying this is, "Do I want to be right, or do I want to be happy?"

◆ Celebrate your successes in changing your behavior. Decide upon two things you want to accomplish in a day (only two). After you accomplish them, honor yourself by saying, "I did it." Then *describe* (not judge) to yourself what you did.

These *Seven Powers for Self-Control* put you in charge of yourself. Har-nessing these Seven Powers will change your life, and, as your own life changes, you will be equipped to help your children change their lives for the better. Change begins with you and extends to your child. Remember: what you focus on, you get more of. When you are upset, you are always focusing on what you don't want, and you are resisting the moment as it is. Negating the moment negates both you and your children, for what you offer to others, you strengthen within yourself. Change comes from acceptance, not resistance. Be willing to accept the moment by saying, "This moment is as it is." Willingness comes from attributing positive intentions to ourselves and to others. And seeing the best in one another creates unity. Unity is self-control in action.

From these Seven Powers of Self-Control emerge the Seven Basic Discipline Skills. The next chapter introduces these vital skills. With them in hand, you will be prepared to respond to every conflict that will arise with your children.

3

The Seven Basic Discipline Skills

Chris Chenoweth, pastor at the Unity Village Chapel in Missouri, shared in one of his sermons this story of a discipline encounter he faced with his two children. Sitting on the backseat of their large car, each child pressed as closely as possible to his respective door. Despite the considerable space between them, they kept shouting, "He touched me, he's on my side!" Chris said he used the only skill he knew at the time. He spun around and yelled, "Hey! Hey! *Hey!* HEY!" So many of us try to do the best we can by our children, without having the basic skills we need to do the job.

Imagine trying to play basketball without knowing how to dribble. Any activity you undertake involves certain basic skills that are vital for success. This chapter introduces the basic discipline skills you need to guide your children's behavior.

You must approach these discipline skills as you would approach any other new set of skills. You must learn each skill, understand when to use it and for what reason, and then practice regularly. You would not use a screwdriver to hammer in a nail, nor would you grab a hammer to saw wood. When it comes to disciplining our children, however, most of us use the same one or two tools for any misconduct.

The tools most parents use are: time out, removal of privileges, earning of privileges, and reasoning. Some parents also spank. All of these tools (except reasoning) actually involve only one technique— imposing consequences. When you deliver the punishments and rewards listed above, you condition your child to focus on some loss or gain for acting in a certain way. Such consequences do not help children focus on what they must do differently. You might say, "You hit your brother, now go to your room." It's as if you went to work and your boss said, "You filled out this form incorrectly. Now go to the office lounge and sit and think about what you did wrong." The next day at work you might face that same form. Fill it out wrong, and back you would go to the lounge. But how can you possibly learn to fill it out correctly unless someone teaches you?

When reasoning, a more recent discipline strategy, is used from a base of fear, it actually becomes interrogation, with an intent to instill guilt in the child. It is not a true attempt at problem solving. The parent generally focuses on why the child did something wrong: "Why did you hit your brother? You know hitting hurts. It's wrong. Your brother won't want to play with you if you hit. Is that what you want?"

It's as if you kept filling out that form incorrectly at company A until you were fired, so you took a new job with company B. At your new job, you filled out a similar form incorrectly and your new boss said, "Why did you fill it out this way? Don't you know this will cut down on our productivity? If this form is handled wrong, our customers don't get served. They will stop using us and you will lose this job. Is that what you want?" Imagine returning to your desk and again finding the form in front of you. You still wouldn't know how to fill it out correctly. Your colleagues wouldn't help. They would assume that since you are an adult, you should know by now. You would feel a rising panic, mixed with anger at your boss and colleagues, and a nagging sense that maybe you were just too stupid for the job.

The office example is obviously facetious, but the point is serious. You need to develop discipline skills that will help you teach your children how to behave properly. Only after you have taught them how to behave does it make sense for you to hold them accountable for knowing right from wrong. The *Seven Basic Discipline Skills* are the skills you need.

To master new discipline skills, you must learn them, understand them, and practice them.

THE SEVEN BASIC DISCIPLINE SKILLS

To discipline your children in any situation, all you need are these seven skills. As I've noted, each skill evolves from one of the *Seven Powers for Self-Control* described in chapter 2, and each one teaches a basic value. The Powers for Self-Control were presented in an order that would help you internalize the information. The *Seven Basic Discipline Skills* will be presented in a different order, one that helps you use the information. The skills, the powers from which they emerge, and the values they teach are as follows:

Seven Powers for Self-Control	Seven Basic Discipline Skills	Seven Values for Living
Power of Perception	Composure	Integrity
Power of Attention	Assertiveness	Respect
Power of Free Will	Choices	Commitment
Power of Unity	Encouragement	Interdependence
Power of Love	Positive Intent	Cooperation
Power of Acceptance	Empathy	Compassion
Power of Intention	Consequences	Responsibility

When you first start using these skills with your children, you will be imposing them on your children. Ultimately, though, they will become internalized processes that govern your child from within.

THE *SEVEN BASIC DISCIPLINE SKILLS* AND THE VALUES THEY TEACH

Each discipline skill has a motto that describes the results you will achieve by using it.

1. **The Skill of Composure:** Living the values you want your child to develop. This teaches integrity.
2. **The Skill of Assertiveness:** Saying no and being heard. This teaches respect.
3. **The Skill of Making Choices:** Building self-esteem and willpower. This teaches commitment.
4. **The Skill of Encouragement:** Honoring your children so they can honor you. This teaches interdependence.
5. **The Skill of Attributing Positive Intent:** Turning resistance into cooperation. This teaches cooperation.
6. **The Skill of Empathy:** Handling the fusses and the fits. This teaches compassion.
7. **The Skill of Consequences:** Helping children learn from their mistakes. This teaches responsibility.

Many parents are familiar with the Seven Basic Skills mentioned in the chart on page 53. These skills can be used with children from a fear-based orientation concerned with control, or from a love-based orientation based on teaching. The mind-set of the parent is the determining factor. If you use the *Seven Powers for Self-Control* described in chapter 2, you will consciously approach your misbehaving child *lovingly*, so you will be able to connect with him and help him be successful. Without self-control, you will approach your child with the unconscious goal of manipulation. An empowered parent modeling self-control handles situations much differently than an out-of-control parent seeking to make his or her child behave. The following examples demonstrate how the Seven Basic Skills can be used from a base of fear, or a base of love.

> The ultimate goal is to control ourselves and then struc-
> ture situations in which children can succeed.

The Skill of Composure: Living the values you want your child to develop

Most of us grew up hearing, "Do as I say, not as I do." There are several reasons to avoid using this approach with your own children. First, children learn from models, and to believe that children can learn anything without a concrete positive model is crazy. Second, many of us resented the hypocrisy of "Do as I say . . . " and do not want to act as our parents did. Sometimes, though, despite our good intentions, we fall into the patterns we experienced as children.

Composure has its roots in the Power of Perception. This power states, "No one can *make* you angry without your permission." When you choose to reclaim your power by knowing that others cannot make you upset, you can be proactive, rather than reactive, with your children. You can keep your composure when they are losing theirs.

When you react, two things occur physically. First, your adrenal glands send an urgent "fight or flight" message to every cell in your body. At such moments you want to fight with the children who are fighting, or give in to their demands (a form of flight). If you choose to fight, you are modeling precisely the behavior you wish to eliminate. If you give in, you teach the children that those obnoxious behaviors are effective. Don't blame yourself—we all do it. It is a physiological reaction.

> Most of us react to conflict with "fight-or-flight" impulses.
> Both are counterproductive.

A second physical event that occurs during a conflict is a downshifting in your brain. Control shifts from the *cortex*, the conscious and rational region of your brain, to the *limbic system*, the region that deals with emotions and memories. Your limbic system has preserved all the messages you received from your parents, wrapped up in the emotions in which they were delivered. When your brain downshifts, your mouth opens, and out comes your mother's or father's words. When this happens, you are operating on automatic, using "programs" that were installed within you years ago. In essence, you become your mother or father, saying similar words with the same intonations you swore you would never use.

To break the hold of that old reactive programming, you must unhook yourself from your limbic system. You must own your own upset. You can do this by breathing deeply and making a conscious choice to view the situation differently. Draw on the Power of Perception to access the skill of composure. A reactive parent might say, "Look what you made me do. You have ruined this vacation. Are you happy now?" A composed parent would own her own upset by saying, "I feel overwhelmed with all this noise in the car. I missed the exit. I am going to pull over and take some deep breaths and calm myself." The reactive parent modeled the value of blame. The peaceful parent who owned her own upset modeled the value of integrity. The choice is yours.

The Skill of Assertiveness:
Saying no and being heard

Picture your eight-year-old son's room littered with laundry. If you approach him with the goal of control, you might focus on what was done wrong, and ask, "Why are all these clothes on the floor?" Using the Power of Attention (what you focus on, you get more of), you could point out the positive: "Half of your dirty clothes are in the hamper! Pick up the other half and your laundry is ready to go!" Fear focuses on what you don't want; love focuses on what you do want.

When you use the Power of Attention to focus on what you want, the skill of assertiveness comes naturally. Without that focus, you are liable to let your limbic brain take over and be passive (or aggressive) in your limit-setting. An assertive parent would say, "If you want to jump, get off the couch and go outside and jump." If the child continued to jump on the couch, the parent would assert, "I'm going to show you what I want you to do," as he or she assisted the child off the couch and pointed him out the door. A passive parent might plead, "Stop jumping, honey, okay? That's enough! Stop jumping!" As the child continued jumping, the parent would continue pleading. An aggressive parent might shout, "Stop jumping or else! Do you hear me?" If you are passive in setting limits (hoping to *make* your child happy, or avoid upset), you give in to your child or set limits that are easily broken. By letting your child intrude upon the limits you set, you teach your children to allow others to intrude upon them. You can actually create a victim mentality by being too permissive! If you are aggressive in setting limits (hoping to *make* your child mind), you teach children to hurt those who intrude upon them. You may create a bully. In contrast, assertiveness teaches the value of respect. It teaches children how to set limits without denigrating others or themselves.

The Skill of Making Choices: Building self-esteem and willpower

You may think you are offering your child a choice when you say, "You can either finish your homework now, or skip soccer on Saturday." This is not a real choice. It is subtle manipulation. You are trying to *make* your child do his homework. If you control your child's will, he will grow up lacking "will power" of his own. Furthermore, if he believes that he has submitted to you, instead of choosing freely, he will feel ill-used. Fear controls, love structures. Using the Power of Free Will (the only person you can *make* change is yourself), you can let go of the notion that it is possible for you to make your child behave. Instead of asking, "How can I make my child complete his homework?" reframe the question. Ask yourself,

"What would help my child to be more likely to choose to complete his homework?" Within this framework, you might say, "Feel free to finish your homework in your room or in the kitchen. Which works better for you?" Here you have structured the situation to help your child succeed at doing his homework. Either choice is acceptable and your child can exercise his will safely. By helping your child to choose and be responsible for his choices, you have instilled the value of commitment.

Only when you acknowledge your child's free will can he exert it for the good of all.

The Skill of Encouragement: Honoring your children so they can honor you

Loving encouragement comes from the Power of Unity. This is the power that states, "Focus on connecting instead of trying to be special." Utilizing the Power of Unity, you might say, "Look at you! You have made your bed without any reminders! Doing your part helps the whole family." By encouraging your child in this manner, you have paid attention to what he accomplished, and helped him become aware of his value. This awareness strengthens the frontal lobes in his brain, and this area of the brain, if strengthened, can override emotional outbursts. You have also let the child know how his good behavior contributed to the family. This teaches the value of interdependence. Without using the Power of Unity, you might have said, "Thank you for making your bed. You are such a good boy. Here is your allowance." Thanking your child for doing his chores teaches him to do his chores to *please you,* instead of teaching him to do so because he is a helpful, contributing member of the family. Detailed praise is much more effective than a judgmental "Good job," or a material reward such as money. Fear judges, and love notices. Moreover, material rewards often backfire. Children learn to expect "the goods" for being good, and to seek approval rather than wisdom.

Material rewards often backfire.

When a person's energy is geared toward being special, he works for the sake of personal attention, not for the sake of contributing to his family or other group. Feeling connected frees children to give and receive love without the fear of "not being good enough."

The Skill of Attributing Positive Intent: Turning resistance into cooperation

You have just watched your seven-year-old son push his younger sister aside. Attributing a negative motive, you might say, "Was that nice? How would you like me to push you?" The underlying message that your son hears is, "You are thoughtless and mean." At this point, he might become reactive and defensive, thereby escalating the problem. If, however, you attributed a positive intent, you might have said, "You wanted your sister to move. You may not push; pushing hurts. When you want her to move, say, 'Move, please.'" Your son would hear, "You are human. You made a mistake. You can learn from it." Using the Power of Love ("See the best in one another") creates a situation in which your son is more likely to become cooperative.

Your approach to your children's mistakes will shape how they approach mistakes for the rest of their lives. If you blame or accuse your child (by attributing negative motives to misbehavior), you teach him that his mistakes mean that he is bad. Alternatively, you can teach your child that mistakes are just that, mistakes. The skill of positive intent emerges from the Power of Love, which reminds us to see the best in one another. It also teaches that what you offer to others, you strengthen within yourself. Therefore, as you teach your children, "To err is human, to forgive divine," you will also learn to view your own mistakes more lovingly. As you attribute positive intent to others, you model for your children the value of cooperation. You are teaching them that negativity breeds resistance and optimism yields cooperation.

The Skill of Empathy: Handling the fusses and the fits

Empathy is the skill to use to help your children develop emotional maturity. Let's say your son has a daily limit of one hour to watch television. Since you see him watching TV after his hour is up, you tell him to turn it off. "But, Dad, it's a special! Please, can't I watch it?" Your first response might be to hold to the limit by asserting, "No, it's bedtime." He may express his disappointment the best way he knows how by saying, "You never let me watch *anything*. It's not fair." Using empathy, you could reply, "You seem very disappointed about missing the show. Your whole body is slouched." Instead of reacting with resistance, your son might continue, "It's about whales. I love whales." Then you could respond, "It's hard to miss things that are important to you and that you enjoy. I love you dearly and I am going to make sure you get enough rest. Up you go." While walking together toward the bedroom you could say, "I didn't know you were interested in whales. Perhaps we could join Greenpeace." Empathy allows you to listen to your child without attempting to change his feelings. It is crucial to empathize in the spirit of the Power of Acceptance, however. The Power of Acceptance says that this moment is as it is. Your child must go to bed, and he's probably not going to like it.

In the above example, if you had used empathy in order to *manipulate* your child, you might have said, "Your hour is up. I know this is hard, but, next time, read the TV schedule and plan better." This message is "I understand you feel bad, but it is your own fault. If you were not so stupid, your feelings of disappointment would not have had to exist." If you do not accept the moment, you will unconsciously try to fix your child's feelings by stopping them, or trying to get him to be happy again. True empathy would say, "Disappointment is part of life. I will help you through it." This teaches the value of compassion.

Empathy demonstrates acceptance of feelings and teaches compassion.

The Skill of Consequences:
Helping children learn from their mistakes

As with all the basic discipline skills, consequences can be used fearfully or lovingly. Used to instill fear, they punish. Used in a spirit of love, they teach.

Here's an example that shows the difference. If you want to shame your child, you might say, "You know better than to hit your brother. I can't believe what you did. No TV for you tonight." If your intent is to teach with love, you might say, "You have a choice. You can hit your brother to get what you want, or you can say, 'May I have a turn?' If you hit him again instead of talking to him, you will go to your room. Then both of you will be safe. Do you understand what will happen to you if you hit him again? Tell me."

Consequences draw on the Power of Intention: Every conflict is an opportunity to teach. Conflict can be seen as something that is bad, or as a teaching moment. Your intent will dictate whether your children learn from their mistakes, or just feel bad for having made them. When we grow from our mistakes we become ever more proficient at choosing effective responses to the curves life throws us. Consequences thus instill the value of responsibility, the ability to respond to situations.

CREATING A CYCLE OF SUCCESS

Remember, what you offer to others, you strengthen in yourself. Imagine being able to consistently honor yourself and others; learn from your mistakes; have others listen to you; resist the pull of the negative; be able to process your feelings; and handle your own fits. By learning to discipline yourself, you learn how to guide your children. As you guide your children more effectively, you become more self-disciplined. You have set a beautiful, self-perpetuating cycle of love in motion.

In chapters 4 through 9, we'll explore each discipline skill in detail, except the skill of composure. Composure is the skill that derives from the Power of Perception, your ability to own your own upset. All of the *Seven Powers for Self-Control* are concerned, to some degree, with your powers of perception. So, to continually sharpen the skill of composure, review chapter 2 and work on the exercises. Remember, each of the *Seven Basic Discipline Skills* can be used to control your child by evoking fear, or from a position that offers loving guidance. Whenever you choose to shift from fear to love, you will instill positive values in your child. Now, let's learn when to use each discipline skill.

THE ANATOMY OF A "DISCIPLINE ENCOUNTER"

A "discipline encounter" can be triggered in one of two ways. It can start from a parent's need, or from a child's need. Usually the parent's need is for some type of compliance, such as "Get in the car"; "Hug your grandmother"; "Take out the trash." The parent wants the child to do something other than what the child has been doing. A child can trigger a discipline encounter through his lack of information about how to communicate in a socially acceptable manner, needing, perhaps, to learn how to stop someone from teasing him without resorting to name-calling, or hitting. Children need to know how to get what they want without whining, how to be a friend without manipulating, how to obtain help without throwing a fit, and how to handle their feelings. Cues you might hear that indicate they have a need for help include "He pushed me"; "I want candy"; "I hate you"; or, "Nobody likes me."

Often we confuse a child's wants with a child's needs. The child may want candy; but his need may be to learn how to delay gratification and handle disappointment. Parents must address the needs of children, not their wants.

Of these two types of discipline encounters, one is a compliance situation in which *you* have a need; the other is a teaching encounter in which *your child* has a need. Both encounters demand the Seven Basic Skills, but the order in which you will use them may change from situation to situation.

Compliance: A Parent's Need

Compliance situations with children generally unfold in four basic stages. In the first stage, either you want your child to do something he is not doing, or his behavior is out of bounds. At this point, you may well be feeling frustrated. If you are upset, use the *Seven Powers for Self-Control* to regain composure, then grab hold of the Power of Attention—focus on *what you want* to have happen—and access the Power of Free Will. Release the notion that you can *make* the child behave and focus on helping the child to be more likely to choose to cooperate.

In the second stage of any compliance encounter, you set a limit and your child responds. You specify what options are, and are not, acceptable. Do this by using the skills of assertiveness or choices. Your selection will depend on a number of factors that we will explore in future chapters. For now, relax and look at the big picture. Your child will respond in one of three ways:

1. He will *comply* by doing what you said to do when you set the limit.
2. He will *resist* the limit by saying no, verbally or nonverbally. Your child's resistance may be subtle or blatant. Either way, it is still a no.
3. He will *throw a fit* to express his frustration over the limit.

The third stage of a compliance encounter is your reaction to your child's response. If his initial reaction is not to comply, the skills you use when you react will teach your child how to respond when others resist his suggestions.

The fourth, and final, stage of a compliance encounter occurs when your child finally chooses to comply (if he didn't comply initially). Often, by using the skills of positive intent and empathy, you can avoid power struggles. Sometimes, though, children simply will not do as you ask. They will remain, despite your loving intentions, unmotivated to comply. In that case, consequences, delivered with a loving intent, are helpful.

Here is a summary of the four stages of a compliance encounter, and the skills you need for handling them:

Stage 1: The child's behavior is out of bounds. You want your child to do something other than what he is doing. The skill you require is **composure**. Practice using the *Seven Powers for Self-Control* in Chapter 2 *vigilantly.*

Stage 2: You set a limit and your child reacts. You set a limit. The skills you need are **assertiveness** and **choices**. These skills are covered in chapters 4 and 5. The child responds to your limit in one of three ways: he complies, says no, or throws a fit.

Stage 3: You react. You react to your child's response. If he complies, use **encouragement**. You will learn how to use encouragement effectively in chapter 6. If he says no, you can **attribute a positive intent**. Attributing positive intentions is the skill you need to help him transform his resistance into cooperation. This skill is taught in chapter 7. If he throws a fit, you will need to use **empathy**. Chapter 8 teaches you everything you need to know about empathy.

Stage 4: The results. The child ultimately complies with your command or does not. If he complies, **encourage** him. If he remains resistant, use the skill of **consequences**. Consequences motivate children to use skills they already possess. You will learn about consequences in chapter 9.

Of course, compliance is not necessarily achieved in four neat steps. The whole process can escalate, with your child becoming more out of bounds. If that does happen, though, the same four-stage process unfolds again. Your goal is to steer the conflict toward de-escalation rather than escalation. If you consistently use the *Seven Powers for Self-Control,* you will surely witness de-escalation over time. If you lose self-control, escalation is guaranteed.

Discipline situations differ only in detail. They all share a basic anatomy.

Your children will try out all kinds of behavior, and it is your job to clearly differentiate between those behaviors you deem acceptable and those you deem unacceptable. This process parallels the process by which your child learns language. When your child is born, he has the capacity to make every sound that forms a part of human speech. Through hearing adult speech, he learns to develop the sounds used in your native tongue (say, English), and he lets the sounds used in other languages (such as Korean) recede.

Similarly, your child is born with unlimited potential for behavior. He wishes to put *every* object in his mouth, touch *every* item in the store, and attempt in *any way* possible to influence others to do his bidding. Through the behavior you model and the discipline skills you use, you set boundaries on what behaviors you deem safe and acceptable. You set the limits. Behaviors you model and encourage survive, while others disappear.

Teaching Conflict Resolution: Responding to Your Child's Need

Teaching situations, which arise from your child's need to resolve conflict, also pass through four stages. In the first stage, your child wants something he doesn't have, or wants others to act differently than they are. What is happening is not acceptable to your child. Your child's dissatisfaction usually surfaces in the form of fighting, whining, complaining, or general fussing.

In the second stage, your job is to transform this "muddle" into a teaching moment. You will strive to transform resistance and upset into cooperation. You can best do this by using the skills of empathy and positive intent. With these two skills you can move from your child's concrete demands for what he wants, when he wants it, to his more spiritual needs for patience, kindness, trust, and love. To take your child's perspective and offer understanding, you must use the *Seven Powers for Self-Control,* modeling the powers for self-control that he will eventually internalize and use throughout his life.

Your efforts to create a cooperative climate and a teaching moment will generally yield one of the following three responses from the child:

◆ He will become *willing* to learn a new skill or problem-solving strategy to address the conflict in a socially acceptable manner.

◆ He will *resist* your attempts to create a teaching moment and will require more "cooling off" time before he is ready to solve the problem.

◆ He will *pretend* to cooperate to appease you, but will not truly attend to your teachings.

The third stage of a teaching encounter is your reaction to your child's response. If your child is willing to be taught, you must show him specifically how to get his needs met in an appropriate manner. If, for instance, you want him to speak to his friend rather than hit him, you must literally tell him the specific words to use. Do this through using the skills of assertiveness or choices. When the child chooses to use those words, you must encourage him in his choice. Trying new skills is scary. Children need our support to change.

If he is still resistant, a cooling-off period can help. Say, "I see you aren't ready to solve this problem now. Tell me when you are ready for my help." For young children, you will need to provide a specific cooling-off place.

If he pretends to be cooperative, trust is lacking. Your child fears both the loss of your approval and changing. Change comes more easily when love is unconditional. Spend more time connecting with your child. Check to make sure your to-do list has your child's name at the top. Utilize the Power of Unity to build and strengthen the relationships in your family.

In the fourth and final stage of teaching conflict resolution, your child will either: need more practice with the skills you are teaching; begin to use the skills; or resist learning. If you have repeatedly taught your child a skill and he seems unmotivated to use it, consequences can help. Whatever happens, the process continues. There are always new skills to be learned. A child who learns to say, "May I play with your car?" instead of grabbing the toy must next learn which socially acceptable skill to use if the other child says no. Each conflict presents another opportunity to teach. Here is a summary of the four stages of teaching ways to resolve conflict:

Stage 1: Your child wants something he doesn't have, or wants others to do something differently. He usually is upset or is misbehaving. Use the *Seven Powers for Self-Control* to stay calm and model for your child how to stay calm.

Stage 2: You create a teaching moment, exposing your child's need (not want) by using the skills of **empathy** and **positive intent**. Your child reacts to the learning climate in one of three ways: He is willing to learn, resists learning, or pretends to learn.

Stage 3: You react to your child's response. If your child is willing, *assertively* teach him what to do by using the skill of **assertiveness** or **choices**. If he is still resistant, teach him how and where to cool off. If the child is pretending to comply, rebuild your relationship.

Stage 4: Your child responds to your teaching by learning the new skill or "forgetting" to use it. If he tends to "forget," **consequences** will help motivate him to remember.

HOW THE SEVEN DISCIPLINE SKILLS DOVETAIL WITH THE ANATOMY OF A DISCIPLINE ENCOUNTER

One year when I was teaching, I was in my office at the university during registration. A young mother, pushing her infant in a stroller, came to my office to ask me some questions. Soon another mother, with a three-year-old-boy, also entered. The young boy immediately ran to the infant, saying, "Baby, baby." He seemed to want to pick the baby up. His mother yelled, "Stop, don't hurt the baby!" (She focused on what she didn't want.) The more agitated she became about the actions she didn't want him to take, the more excited he became about the baby. Both mothers seemed flustered and my heart went out to them. I approached the three-year-old boy and said, "You wanted to say hello to the baby?" (I attributed positive intent.) He grinned. I continued, "To say hello to babies, you rub their feet like this." (I focused on what he could do.) I took his hand and helped him rub the bottom of the baby's foot. He clearly enjoyed touching the baby. His mother, who had finished her business, asked him, "Are you ready to go?" (She passively set a limit, putting the child in charge of the situation.) He replied firmly, "Baby," indicating he preferred to stay. I then told him, "To say good-bye to the baby, you touch the tops of the feet." I showed him how, and then said, "Give your other hand to Mom, so your hand can say hello to hers." (I used the skill of assertiveness, derived from the Power of Attention: What you focus on, you get more of.) His mother stood there motionless, shocked at how smoothly life was proceeding. Finally I said to her, "Take his hand, and have a good day."

I thought to myself how, without understanding the basic skills of discipline, life can be very frustrating. I had used two discipline skills in my interaction with the boy: assertiveness and positive intent. I used all of the Powers for Self-Control: I used the Power of Attention to maintain a constant focus on what I wanted the boy to do. I used the Power of Acceptance by accepting the moment as it presented itself to me. I used the Power of Intention by viewing this moment of conflict as an opportunity to teach, rather than as a disruption. Helping the child to be more likely to choose to cooperate, I used the Power of Free Will, resisting the temptation to *make* the three-year-old stop. The Power of Unity was used as I joined with the young boy. The Power of Perception allowed me to own my own upset, and not project "badness" onto the mother. Finally, the Power of Love prevailed as I offered love-based skills to the child, and strengthened my own love for myself. I used these skills and powers consciously. That is my hope for you.

THE "WHAT-IFS"

This book guides you through a journey that will change you and your children. Most of us fear change, and our fears emerge as doubts. "What if I say these words and it doesn't work?" "What if I do what you suggest, and the children still fight?"

Ironically, these fears reflect the fear-based discipline we experienced as children. Many of us fear trying a new skill because we dread making mistakes. Unconsciously, and with the best of intentions, our parents made us feel bad in order to improve our behavior. The message we received is that mistakes indicate weakness, a form of inadequacy that could have been prevented with forethought. To avoid these feelings, many of us continue to resist change instead of embracing it. To grow and do better as parents, however, change must occur. To embrace change we have to become conscious of the power of the "what-ifs" to keep us stuck and stagnant.

Let's say I was describing how to change a flat tire to you. I would tell you to pull over to the shoulder when the car ride becomes bumpy. "What if there is no shoulder?" you might ask. I might reply, "Then pull over onto the grass." "But what if the grass is muddy? I could get stuck in mud with a flat." I might advise waving down a car for help. "What if the driver who stops is a rapist?" you might respond. This dialogue could continue *ad nauseam,* and the original goal—learning to change a tire—would be forgotten. Your fears would have kept you from acquiring a valuable skill. When you avoid change to avoid mistakes, you avoid life, and this avoidance reflects how you were disciplined as a child. In order to change, you must push past your fears. As you read, if doubts arise within you, do the following:

◆ **Take a deep breath and relax your body:** This allows old programs in your brain to dissolve. You must quell the "you are not good enough" message in order to begin your healing journey. Physical relaxation helps you to do so.

◆ **Become aware of your anxiety:** Once you hear yourself saying, "What if this . . ." or, "What if that . . . ," let yourself feel the anxiety. Say to yourself, "I feel anxious but I am safe and in charge of my thoughts. All is well." Then notice the next thoughts that arise. These show how you handle anxiety. Do you attack people? ("This is stupid. The author knows nothing.") Do you remember past problems? ("I tried this last week.") Do you concoct future problems? ("If I try this with my child, she will run away screaming.") Do you berate yourself with negative inner speech? ("I am the world's worst parent.") Listen quietly to your thoughts. Become familiar with your language of anxiety. Keep breathing.

◆ **Decide whether you want anxiety to control your life and impede your learning, or whether you want to be in charge.** Ask yourself, "Am I willing to live through some discomfort to learn new skills that will bring more tranquility and joy into my life?" If the answer is yes, continue. If the answer is no, go ahead and close the book.

◆ **Write down your "what-ifs" as you encounter them on the special page at the back of the book.** If after reading the whole book your "what-ifs" have not been addressed, write to me. If I can help, I will.

DISCIPLINE YOURSELF FIRST, THEN WORK ON YOUR CHILDREN

Consider this story about Mahatma Gandhi, the Indian nationalist leader. A mother walked several days on a pilgrimage to see Gandhi. When she arrived, she told him of her concerns about her son, saying, "He eats only sugar—no other food. I have tried everything to get him to eat healthfully, yet he refuses. Please help me." Gandhi told her to go home and return in one week with her son. The woman had hoped to receive his guidance on the first trip, since it had taken three days to reach Gandhi, but nevertheless, she journeyed back to her home. After waiting one week, again she walked three days with her son to see Gandhi, as she had been instructed.

When she arrived, he remembered her. He looked at the boy and said, "Stop eating sugar." The mother, shocked by the brevity of his command, said, "I walked nine days and that is all you have to say? Could you not have told him this last week?" Gandhi responded, "I could not tell the boy to stop doing something that I was still doing. It took me one week to stop eating sugar."

Gandhi couldn't tell a child to stop doing something that he himself still did, and neither can you.

This story tells you that you must saturate your children with direct images of correct behavior. Do your children hear you blaming traffic jams for your upset? Do they witness your rudeness to slow service people? Do they hear you lie to friends on the phone or verbally attack people you love? If your children watch you throw fits when life does not go your way, they will do the same.

The process of learning to discipline children with love is a journey. It involves letting go of old habits and being willing to risk a different world view. At the outset of this process, you must become aware of what you have been doing and honestly assess the effectiveness of your approach. Then you will need to diligently practice these new skills, forgive yourself when you fail, and celebrate your every success. This journey will greatly enhance your relationships and your life. The journey will take you from being controlled by others to self-control, and from shaming to teaching. It will take you from perfectionism to acceptance, and from resentment to forgiveness. Your personal journey from fear to love will change your life, and in the process, will change your children. The voyage begins with setting limits. It is time for you to become assertive and start using the Power of Attention by focusing on what you want your child to do.

4

Assertiveness: Saying No and Being Heard

A colleague of mine—call her Nancy—once lent other professors some of my books, without asking my permission. She simply left me a note that began with the classic words, "I hope you don't mind but . . . ," and went on to explain what she had done.

I was livid. I felt intruded upon. Nancy had clearly crossed a line.

You may relate to my subsequent behavior. Instead of telling Nancy how I felt about her presumptuousness, I complained bitterly about her to three other people. It was as if I reacted to a problem with my refrigerator by repairing my car.

Now the assertiveness plot thickens. When I asked myself, "Becky, why didn't you speak to Nancy?" I answered my question with these kinds of statements: "What good would that do now?"; "I don't want to hurt her feelings"; and, "I don't know what to say." The first response indicated that I felt my voice lacked power. The second response was me lying to myself, since telling the people she also knew about her rudeness would surely hurt her. The third response indicated that I lacked a major communication skill.

Adults seldom tolerate children who behave as I did. Children constantly come to us saying, "He poked me," or, "She took my doll."

In response, we demand that they deal with the person with whom they have the problem. If children do not come to us with their complaints, they fight and bicker among themselves. Children cross boundaries with each other so often that it sometimes seems that fighting is all they do. Adults, in turn, often expect children to know how to deal with these conflicts. Adults actually expect children to possess skills that they themselves have yet to develop! But as I've noted, you simply cannot teach your children skills you do not possess.

Children also engage in conflicts with adults—and often. Your reactions to conflicts with your child set the communication patterns she will follow. If she disobeys you and you scream in response, you teach her to be rude to people who don't do her bidding. If you permissively allow your child to ignore your limits, you teach her to infringe on others and to let others infringe on her. Assertiveness is the heart of discipline: Setting clear limits on your child's behavior is the key discipline skill you must cultivate. Your style of setting limits teaches your child how to set and hold boundaries in all of her future relationships.

In all of our relationships, we actually teach others how to treat us. People who seem doubtful or unsure invite other people to boss them around and "help" them, even when they don't want or need help. Your use of assertiveness lets other people know your limits. Assertiveness lets you set boundaries on what behaviors you consider appropriate, safe, and permissible. Assertiveness enables you to say no to your children and teaches them how to say no to others. Assertiveness also enables you to say yes to interactions that support you, and teaches your children when saying yes is in order. In sum, assertiveness is the medium through which you can teach children the value of respect—of self and of others.

You have a right and a responsibility to say no.

This chapter will help you learn to be assertive and, in turn, teach it to your children. Assertiveness comes from the Power of Attention: What you focus on, you get more of. If you tell your children what *not* to do, you will get many opportunities to repeat your instructions. If you assertively tell children what *to do* in understandable terms, you will maximize the possibility that your child will choose to comply.

THE PASSIVE-AGGRESSIVE FLIP-FLOP:
A NATIONAL EPIDEMIC

Our goal with young children is to teach them that speaking is more powerful than hitting and kicking. You cannot, however, teach your children the power of words until you have learned this yourself. All parents, especially mothers, must find and become comfortable with their assertive voices. Many parents have gotten into the habit of approaching their children from a passive position. They say things like, "Come on, honey, are you ready to go see Grandma?" These kinds of comments are often ignored or answered nonverbally. The child may continue to play, indicating without words, "No, I'm not ready." Parents, thus faced with what they perceive of as disobedience (although it really is not), often flip to an aggressive position. A mother might then shout, "Listen to me. If you want to watch TV later, you'd better get moving now!" After taking such an aggressive position, a parent will often feel guilty. Her guilt will often prompt a switch back to the passive mode: "If you're good at Grandma's, we'll stop for ice cream on the way home." All parents, especially ones who dig themselves into holes like this, need to learn about assertiveness.

BLOCKS TO ASSERTIVENESS

In order to be assertive, you must express your feelings, thoughts, and wishes without diminishing those of other people. This *sounds* simple, but to clearly state your thoughts and desires, you must recognize and own them, and feel entitled to have them. In short, you must value yourself. You must shift your focus from what you assume others are thinking and feeling to consciousness of your own mind's contents.

You can learn assertiveness. It is not a personality trait that some people have and others lack. Like passivity and aggression, assertiveness is learned behavior. To learn it, you must do the following:

◆ **Achieve self-awareness.** Do you tend to interact with your children in a passive way, an aggressive way, or, do you favor the passive-aggressive flip-flop? Or are you already assertive?

◆ **Monitor your own thought patterns.** How do you talk to yourself? Do you use the Power of Attention with yourself? Do you focus on what you want to do, or on what you haven't done? Do you address yourself passively, aggressively, or assertively? Once you learn to talk to *yourself* more assertively, you will naturally use this skill with your children.

◆ **Teach and utilize assertiveness in all your relationships.** By becoming more assertive with yourself and other adults, you will model this skill for your children. When your daughter complains to you, "Emily pushed me," or, "Nathan is looking at me," you will be ready to teach her what words to say in order to assertively state her limits.

SELF-AWARENESS: BEING POLITE AND RESPECTFUL

Early on in life, we internalize guidelines for social conduct, rules about what is "good, polite" behavior as opposed to "rude, bad" behavior. We learn as youths what types of thoughts and feelings are to be shared, and what types are to be concealed. We absorb these rules from parents and other role models.

It is sometimes difficult—but all the more important—to remember that these rules are not cast in stone. We can change them if we consciously decide to do so. To help you become aware of certain beliefs that can block your efforts to be assertive, do this exercise:

ACTIVITY: Read the beliefs listed in columns A and B. Check the statements in column A that remind you of rules you learned as a child that continue to influence you. The extent of your emotional investment in the ideas expressed in column A reflects how often you rely on passive-aggressive behaviors. The extent to which you identify with the behaviors listed in column B shows how assertive you are.

Column A Passive-Aggressive Beliefs	Column B Assertive Beliefs
◆ You should have an appropriate response for every situation.	◆ You have a right to make mistakes.
◆ Mistakes are shameful, especially if someone's feelings get hurt.	◆ Mistakes, not perfection, are part of being human.
◆ It is selfish to put your own needs first.	◆ You have a right to put yourself first sometimes; this models responsibility.
◆ You should not waste others' time with your problems. They have problems too.	◆ You have a right to ask for help and emotional support. This gives others the opportunity to request help and support.
◆ When someone is in trouble, you should always help him or her.	◆ You have a right not to take responsibility for other people's problems. They are strong.
◆ If you cannot convince others that your feelings and opinions are reasonable, then your feelings must be wrong.	◆ You can think and feel the way you want to, and accept your feelings and opinions as legitimate, regardless of other people's reactions.
◆ You should be intuitively sensitive to the needs and wishes of others.	◆ You should not be expected to be able to read minds or figure out other people's needs and wishes.
◆ Always try to accommodate others so they will like you.	◆ You have a right to say no.
◆ You should always be logical and consistent.	◆ You have the right to change your mind.
◆ Knowing that you have done something well is its own reward. People do not like show-offs.	◆ You have a right to receive recognition for your work and achievements.
◆ You should always have a good reason for what you say, feel, and do.	◆ You do not have to justify and defend yourself to others.
◆ If you are criticized, you have been rejected as "not good enough."	◆ You have a right to hear feedback and to filter out that which is of no value to you.

Adapted with permission from *Messages: The Communication Book*, McKay, Davis, and Fanning (1983) Oakland, CA: New Harbinger Publication.

Now, pick two beliefs from column A that you are going to drop. From column B, pick two new beliefs that you are going to adopt. Keep them in mind as you read the sections that follow.

ARE YOU PASSIVE, AGGRESSIVE, OR ASSERTIVE?

The first step toward assertiveness is learning to distinguish between speech or actions that are assertive, aggressive, or passive. Remember that passivity invites aggression, aggression begets aggression, and assertiveness dissipates aggression. Decide to become aware of how you currently communicate with yourself and others. This awareness is a critical first step for change.

Passivity invites aggression. Aggression begets aggression. Assertiveness dissipates aggression.

Passivity

The goal of assertiveness is clarity. When we communicate passively, the goal is not clarity, but to please others. A passive person's speech and actions constantly ask, "Approve of me, love me." A passive parent manipulates and may even plead with her children to behave. In the process, she gives her power over to them. A person's power is his or her ability to have an effect on the world. Passive people relinquish this ability by leaving decisions to other people. "Where should we eat?" is one passive message a wife may send to her husband. A mother who says, "Let me hang up, honey, and then Mommy will talk to you," is asking the child's permission to remain on the phone. By putting another person in charge, the passive person skirts any blame if something goes wrong.

Passive people long to be "perfect" so everyone will like them. They seldom express direct desires for fear that their desires may not be the "right" ones. Instead they drop hints: "Wouldn't it be nice if the family could eat together?" Sometimes they say what they don't want: "I don't want to be another statistic about families who don't talk." They may ask questions instead of making statements: "Don't you think it is important for us to eat together?"

If you surrender your power to your children, you usually hope that the children will take that power and make the "right" choice—to act "nice." If they don't act nicely, you are likely to feel frustrated, and this frustration often begets aggression—hence the passive-aggressive flip-flop mentioned earlier.

Susan, a mother of three, announced to her children that soon they would all go out to run errands. "I need you children to cooperate. Could you try to be helpful?" she said. Her oldest child, Sean, began to whine, "I don't want to go. Can't I stay home alone? Other kids my age do. You treat me like a baby, and it's not fair." He stomped angrily through the house. Susan replied, "You're not a baby, you're the oldest. Can't you just help me? We'll talk about staying home alone another time, okay?" Sean began to plead, "Please, Mom." Finally Susan said, "All right, but just this once."

Susan then turned to the younger children and asked, "Are you ready to go?" She noticed that Amber had just removed her shoes and was drawing. Frustrated, Susan said, "Why did you take your shoes off? Didn't you hear me say we're going? Can you put them on? Let's not start this today, okay?" Ignoring her mother, Amber continued drawing. Steaming, Susan shouted, "Amber, stop drawing! Don't make me send you to time out!" Amber continued drawing. Susan spewed more empty threats, "I'm warning you. This is not very nice. Why are you doing this?"

Susan demonstrated almost all the behaviors of a passive parent:

◆ **You ask your child to accomplish a vague, indeterminate task.** Susan, for example, asked, "Could you try and be helpful?" Often passive parents say, "Try to be nice"; "Try to clean up."

◆ **You ask questions about your child's behavior that fail to communicate what you want her to do.** Susan pleaded, "Why did you take your shoes off?" Other parents might ask, "Where should you be?" or, "Was that nice?"

◆ **You do not follow through on consequences and you adjust your schedule and events to accommodate the child.** Susan adjusted her schedule in response to Sean's whining. Another common passive procedure is to say, "The next time you do that, you're going to time out!" and then a few minutes later, "I'm warning you—just one more time and . . ."

◆ **You give your power to your child, putting her in charge.** Susan did this by asking, "Are you ready to go?"

◆ **You blame your child for your anger and actions.** You might say, "Don't make me ground you," or "You're driving me nuts." Susan said, "Don't make me send you to time out."

◆ **You give your children choices when none exist.** You might say, "Can you hop in the car and put on your seat belt?" Susan used phrases like this, including, "Can you put your shoes on?"

◆ **You ignore a conflict in hopes that it will magically resolve itself.**

Through her speech and actions, Susan taught her children how to treat her. By letting her children control her, Susan lacked self-control, and unconsciously, she modeled irresponsibility. Having given her power away, she found it difficult to regain. She also tried to fulfill her need to avoid upset, at the expense of the children's need for usable information.

Aggression

Aggressive communication aims not to *clarify* but to *win* by over-powering. Winning means getting the other person to do what you want. A sign of an aggressive father, for instance, is that he states his wishes in sentences that begin with the pronoun you. Instead of telling his child clearly what to do while he is on the telephone, an aggressive father might say, "You always interrupt me." "You" statements focus on the other person, not the problem. When a parent makes remarks about his child instead of stating his own feelings or thoughts, the parent is attacking. If a parent says, "You hurt me," a child feels attacked. If the parent says, "I feel hurt," no attack is implied. Because "you" statements focus on the person and not on the problem, the recipient generally feels she must respond defensively. Between adults, we call the resulting exchange an argument. With children, we call it "talking back."

Accusations that start with "you" leave a child feeling attacked, and invite an argument.

Aggressive people often speak for others and act as mind readers. They will describe the other person's viewpoint (often wrongly) but seldom express their own. A mother might say, "You think I'm the maid," or, "You think you're entitled to every toy on TV!"

Aggressive people also use the words "always" and "never" as forms of attack: "You never remember your lunch"; "You always put off big projects." Such extreme statements suggest that you view your child as all good or all bad. By generalizing, you teach your child to generalize about herself and others. Your child may grow up making categorical statements like "I never do things well" or "All teachers are mean."

Any statement about the other person, as opposed to statements about one's own feelings or thoughts, tends to have an attacking quality.

Let's observe an aggressive parent in action. Anne was having a rough day. She saw her three children lounging around the family room and shouted, "What are you doing inside? How many times have I told you to play outside? I don't care if it's ninety degrees in the shade, get up and get out. You never listen." Laura, the oldest, tried to speak to her mother: "Mom, Tara has a video from school we were going to watch—" Anne interrupted, "You are just using that video as an excuse to watch television." "But, Mom—" whined Tara. "Don't you talk back to me, young lady. Now get outside before you make me do something I'll regret. You think you can do whatever you want, but you're wrong. I need some quiet time after working all day. You children are all so selfish." As the children grudgingly began to leave the room, Anne threatened them: "Don't give me those sulky faces. You ought to be grateful for fresh air."

Anne demonstrated most of the characteristics of aggressive people:

◆ **She made "you" statements that focused on the other people, not the problem.** ("You children are all so selfish.")

◆ **She spoke for others, often wrongly describing their viewpoints.** She seldom expressed her own thoughts and feelings. ("You are just using that video as an excuse . . . ")

◆ **She used the words "always" and "never."** ("You never listen.")

◆ **She viewed others as attacking her.** ("Don't you talk back to me, young lady.")

◆ **She used empty, extremely punitive threats.** ("Now get outside before you make me do something I'll regret.")

In addition to the types of behavior that Anne exhibited, aggressive parents often:

◆ **Impose consequences that are overly severe.** ("No television for two weeks.")

◆ **Physically respond to a child out of anger,** shaking or squeezing the child's arm, jerking, threatening to hit, or actually hitting the child.

Assertiveness

The goal of assertiveness is clear communication. When you communicate assertively, you make straightforward statements about your feelings, thoughts, and wishes. It would be assertive to say "I want to go out for pizza." It is not assertive to quiz others ("Where should we go to eat?"); think for them ("You probably want Chinese food. You always do"); or try to control them ("Everyone loves pizza. Why not you?"). You cannot be assertive if you think a lot about what others think of you. Nor can you be assertive if you fret about what somebody will do or say in response to what you might do or say. To be assertive, you must concentrate on your own actions, instead of focusing on what someone else might be thinking about them. By focusing on yourself, you are exercising the Power of Attention.

Assertiveness comes from the Power of Attention: Focus on what you want to have happen.

To be an assertive parent, you must do these things:

- ◆ **State your wants, needs, and expectations clearly and simply.** ("Give me the scissors. These are too sharp. They could cut you. I will get you a plastic pair.")
- ◆ **Match your nonverbal communications to your verbal communications.** If your nonverbal cues are too casual, your child can easily choose not to comply. If your nonverbal cues are too intrusive, your child will resist in self-defense. When your nonverbal and verbal communication match, you let your child know that you mean what you say. Before your child decides whether to comply with a command, she will read your facial expression, tone of voice, and gestures. You increase the chances that she will obey if you appear confident and in control, sound sure of yourself, and use gestures to provide information.

◆ **Give children choices only when they really have choices.** "Are you ready for nap time?" implies that your child has a choice of being ready or not. If you say, "It is nap time, so climb into bed to rest," you leave your child no choice. You have stated plainly what will happen.

◆ **Give commands that contain usable, helpful information** and avoid asking rhetorical questions. Remember, concepts like goodness, badness, and being polite can confuse children. If you say, "Tell Jason, 'Stop calling me names. I don't like it,'" you are being assertive. Asking a child, "Are you being nice?" is not.

◆ **Own and express your feelings to your children.** If you say, "I feel angry when you interrupt me," you are being assertive. Saying, "Look what you made me do" is not.

◆ **Show respect for your child and enforce rules** without teasing, embarrassing, or bullying. Being respectful means you focus on improving behavior rather than on punishing. You might say, "Hitting hurts; you may not hit. When someone pushes you, say, 'Stop! I don't like being pushed.'" If you wanted to be assertive, you would not ask, "Why did you hit her? Is that how we treat people?"

When I first became aware of the differences between assertive, passive, and aggressive behaviors, I began to notice how people spoke. In the halls of elementary schools, I listened to teachers begging, bribing, and even screaming, and I felt their exhaustion. I used to do the same things when dealing with children. The only difference is that I learned to hear myself, and how to change—and that has been a wonderful improvement.

Below is a chart for you to fill out in order to assess your current communication style. Jot these percentages down on a calendar for the next few weeks. Estimate the percentage of time you speak to your children in each communication style. Remember, to be assertive you must use the Power of Attention and clearly tell your children what you want. In chapter 12, the same chart reappears. It will be fun to see your progress.

Week Ending	Passive Communications	Aggressive Communications	Assertive Communications
_____	_____ %	_____ %	_____ %

WHEN YOUNG CHILDREN TURN FEARFUL SITUATIONS INTO A GAME—USE ASSERTIVENESS

Imagine someone cutting you off on the freeway. You might curse with fury, but beneath your rage would lie fear—fear of an accident. When we feel angry with people we love, we are also full of fear. We may fear that if the misbehavior continues we won't know how to respond, or we may fear triggering bigger problems. Anger has its roots in fear.

When you get angry, your child senses your fear and it in turn frightens her. A frightened child may turn a scary situation into a game. Do you remember two year-old Jessica who fell in the well in Texas? Rescuers dug for two days to reach her. When they did, they found her singing. She had turned her dreadful predicament into a game in order to master it. You yourself have seen young children do this. Most children watch cartoons, and cartoons feature about 25 violent acts per hour. Cartoon violence can frighten young children. How do they respond? Often, they beg for toys based on the TV shows. Once they own these figures, they master the fearful situations they have witnessed by manipulating the characters in play.

An aggressive voice sounds angry. Children sense that if a parent is angry, that parent is also afraid. If, on the other hand, you speak passively, you put your child in charge. Being in charge is also quite scary. Children know they are not equipped to be in charge of adults. When young children hear either an aggressive or a passive voice, they feel frightened and turn it all into a game in order to regain a sense of control. Toddlers do this with great panache.

Karen wanted her two-year-old daughter, Christina, to get in the car seat so they could keep a doctor's appointment. Karen said, "Christina, get in your car seat. Over here, honey—here is the car seat. . . . Come, get in." Christina paused for a moment, as toddlers do when they are processing information, and Karen got nervous, perceiving that Christina was dawdling. Her nervousness quickly flared into anger, and she snapped, "Don't start with me. Get over here *now* and get in your seat." Karen was angry because she was afraid they would be late if they didn't leave soon.

Christina could practically smell her mother's fear. In response, Christina ran away, looking back at Karen over her shoulder and giggling as if they were playing tag. Karen chased her daughter, shouting threats. Karen finally caught Christina, gave her a swat, and forced her into the car seat.

Similar problems arise when parents use an aggressive or passive voice to send older children to time out. The children may refuse to go, may go with "an attitude," or may play once they get there. Again, they are turning the fearful situation into a game in order to master it. To a parent, of course, such actions appear to be defiance.

To avoid such problems, use an assertive voice, and keep fear out of your conflicts with children.

USE ASSERTIVE COMMANDS TO GIVE USABLE INFORMATION

Assertive commands tell your children what you expect from them when you cannot offer them a choice. If you are telling your child to wake up, get dressed, and bathe, you will generally expect these things to be done. You are not offering choices about whether or not the child may comply. You expect obedience, and to get it you must issue assertive commands. You may, though, offer your child choices about *how* to complete a necessary task. She can decide which side of the bed she will get out of, which clothes she will wear, and whether to bathe or to shower. However, whether or not to do the task is not a choice. The secret to giving assertive commands is to tell your children what to do and to give them usable information on how to do it.

EXERCISE: Four-year-old Maggie is twisting her sweatpants into a cord instead of dressing. Which of the following statements would offer *usable* information?

1. "Mommy will be late to work if we don't dress quickly."
2. "Do you want me to take your clothes away?"
3. "What's wrong? Why aren't you dressing?"
4. "Do you want to go to outside? Hurry up and we'll go."
5. "Maggie, lay your pants out flat and slide your legs in. I will help you lay them out."

The fifth statement gives Maggie information that she can understand and use. Statements one through four only confuse Maggie and heighten her parent's irritation. Give your children usable information.

HEADS UP! HELPING YOUR CHILD PAY ATTENTION TO YOU

The first step in giving an assertive command is to get your child's attention. This can be a challenge, but several tricks can help. Proximity—getting close to your child—is one such strategy. Here is an example in which an adult used proximity effectively.

Megan was a "spacey" child who was often lost in play and fantasy. Initially, her mother, Katherine, feared that Megan had a hearing problem, but doctors said the girl's ears were fine. Still, Katherine regularly struggled to get her daughter's attention. Speaking or calling to Megan from across a room never worked, so she would crouch down close to Megan and say things like, "Look at me. Mom has something to say. Megan, are you listening?" Katherine might clap her hands in an effort to rouse some sign of recognition from Megan. Often Katherine would end up yelling out of utter frustration, "Megan, are you deaf?"

Katherine's sister Cindy once watched an interaction like this with some amusement. Cindy's laughter made Katherine so angry that she said, "If you can do better, go right ahead." Cindy walked over to Megan, who was busily playing, and got down at the girl's eye level. With her own face about six inches from Megan's face, Cindy waited for Megan to notice her. When Megan looked up and made eye contact with her aunt, Cindy said, "There you are!" With a firm, quiet voice, she stated Megan's name, touched her shoulder gently, and said, "Pick up these puzzle pieces and put them in the box." As she spoke, Cindy pointed to the pieces and the box. Her gestures reinforced her verbal command. Megan began picking up the puzzle pieces.

Katherine, who had been watching, sighed, and observed, "It's easy for you. You're not her mother." It's true. It is easier to deal with other people's children. Even so, an assertive manner improves your chances of being heard even if you are the parent.

Below are the key characteristics of assertive commands which Cindy demonstrated:

- ◆ **Kneel down to the child's eye level and make direct eye contact.** To establish eye contact with a young child, you must adjust the distance between your face and the child's until she notices you. This is a much better starting point than shouting. Restrain yourself and wait for the child to notice you *before* you speak.
- ◆ **When your child looks at you, say, "There you are,"** or the child's name.
- ◆ **Touch your child gently on the arm or back.** Your touch helps your child prepare to organize the words you are about to say.
- ◆ **Tell the child what you want.**

◆ **Match your words with supporting gestures.** Point to all the dress-up clothes scattered about and then use your arms and hands to show where they belong as you say, "Put all the clothes [point to them] back in the basket [indicate exactly where]." Move your arms like a traffic cop.

◆ **Praise or encourage your child for her choice to comply with your command.** (See chapter 6.)

When giving assertive commands to your child, engage as many of her senses as you can. Use vision (eye contact and gestures); hearing (state the child's name and your expectations); and touch (as you touch her shoulder or back). Teaching your child to meet your expectations is no different from teaching her to read. The more senses you engage as you help her learn to read, the more likely it is that she will become an adept reader.

YOU ARE ASSERTIVE, YET THEY STILL DISOBEY

Children will resist, refuse, and oppose you. They have to—it is part of their developmental journey. There are five levels of opposition you will receive. Level one represents the least amount of resistance. The children may ignore you, saying, "I don't want to," or asking why. At level two, which is more intense, they will verbally or nonverbally say no. At level three, children try to pull you into a power struggle. Their behavior seems to say, "Try and make me!" Level four is a full-blown fit, and level five is mute withdrawal.

Each level of resistance demands a slightly different skill from you. Children at level one usually respond well to your repeating the command or saying, "I will show you what to do." After saying this phrase, gently assist them through their resistance with a demonstration. Children exhibiting level two resistance will usually comply if you use the skill of choices (see chapter 5). If your child is trying to drag you into a power struggle (level three opposition), you will need to use assertive commands, choices, and empathy (see chapter 8). Children operating at levels four and five will challenge you to employ every skill this book teaches and all of your intuition as well.

Remember, no matter how much you practice sound discipline skills, sometimes your child will refuse to obey. Your child will say no and you will get angry. You need to learn to express this irritation assertively.

LETTING OFF STEAM ASSERTIVELY

Like all parents, you will at times feel frustrated with your children's behavior and will find it exquisitely annoying. You can express this frustration passively, aggressively, or assertively. The passive and aggressive approaches are indirect, "sideways" methods of venting your feelings. Read the following statements to see if you tend to use indirect or direct methods to express your frustrations:

- **Indirect** (through labeling): "You are rude to interrupt."
- **Direct:** "When you interrupt me, I feel angry."
- **Indirect** (through commands): "Stop running, sit down, and be quiet."
- **Direct:** "When you run through the house while I am trying to work, I feel distracted. I can't think."
- **Indirect** (through questions): "What did you do? What's wrong with you?"
- **Direct:** "Something seems to be bothering you. I feel concerned."
- **Indirect** (through sarcasm): "So, you finally decided to join us for dinner. How thoughtful."
- **Direct:** "Our dinnertime is important to me. When you don't come when I call you, I feel unappreciated."
- **Indirect** (through accusations): "You don't care about anybody but yourself. You should be ashamed."
- **Direct:** "When you keep ignoring me, and what I am telling you to do, I feel furious."

Indirect expressions of emotions attack children; direct expression communicate with them.

Do you tend to express your frustrations with commands, questions, accusations, or sarcasm? Listen to yourself carefully for one week and strive to express your feelings in a direct and assertive manner. To help you do this, I offer a formula. It is called an "I-message," because it helps you share your own feelings and expectations. Use it to respond to your children when they have frustrated you:

"When you _____, I feel _____."

Then, using the Power of Attention, tell your child what you want her to do.

Make sure the word following "feel" is a one-word description of an emotion (such as irritated, annoyed, worried, or upset). Do not say, "I feel like you don't care." That is a thought, not a feeling. When you confuse thoughts with feelings, you will unconsciously and indirectly attack rather than communicate with your child.

WHEN A CHILD LASHES OUT—USE AN "I-MESSAGE"

"I-messages" tell your child that you believe she has infringed upon you. Remember, children are not born knowing the difference between respect and disrespect. They must be taught. I often see children hitting their parents or telling them to shut up. I have seen parents dodging blows, or retaliating by intentionally saying words that hurt the child. I seldomly see assertiveness or teaching.

Four-year-old Nathan and his mom were in a restaurant. Mom was reading the menu while Nathan played with a brochure. Suddenly, he took the brochure and hit her with it. She said, "Why did you hit me? What was that for?" He made a growling sound, balled up his fist, and punched her arm. She responded, "Does Mommy hit you?" He said no and began to cry. As he cried, she asked, "Why are you acting like this?"

This mother forfeited a teaching opportunity. She asked irrelevant questions and failed to offer any usable information. Nathan had been hurtful, and she needed to assertively set a limit by saying something like, "It hurts when you hit me. If you want my attention, say, 'Mommy, I have something to say.'" If Nathan hit her again, she could restrain his hands and tell him, "You may not hurt me or anyone else. I will hold you until I think you are safe and I am safe." If this was too much for her to remember, she simply could have said, "I don't like it when you hit me. Stop!"

Another child and his mother were discussing soccer practice. She said, "You play better when you don't get so angry." The child snapped back, "Shut up, Mom!" and she responded, "You are so rude. Do you want to be grounded?" Her words have taught him to feel bad, not how to express himself in a socially acceptable manner.

Imagine trying to learn division but, still not understanding it, making a mistake, and hearing someone say, "That's wrong, Stupid. Be ashamed. Make another division mistake and you're grounded." This type of response would not help you master division. You still would not see your mistakes, nor would you know how to correct them, and your feelings about math would likely be negative. It works the same way with behavior. When you have been treated with disrespect, you need to respond assertively. If you respond aggressively, you are simply treating your child with disrespect while trying to teach respect. The "soccer mom" could say in an assertive voice, "I do not like it when you speak to me like that. If you disagree with me, you must say, 'Mom, I disagree.' If you say that now, I will listen. If not, I am leaving the room. I will not be treated with disrespect."

Remember, learning useful new skills will not eliminate conflict. Conflict is simply part of life. Embrace it. Once a young father who tended to yell at his child decided to practice calming himself instead and addressing his child with "I-messages." One day his son, who was five years old, was hammering nails with his dad in the garage. The child accidentally hit his thumb and said, "Shit." The father inhaled deeply and said, "Son, I don't like it when you use that word." The child, in all innocence, looked up and said, "I know, Daddy, but *damn*, it hurt!"

"HE HIT ME!"—
TEACHING ASSERTIVENESS TO CHILDREN

"He pushed me." "I had it first." "She said I'm stupid." "He started it." Sound familiar? Children regularly struggle to establish boundaries with other children. If you are passive or aggressive with your children when setting limits, they will be passive or aggressive with each other. You must assertively set limits for your children and teach them to do so with others.

TATTLING: A WONDERFUL TEACHING OPPORTUNITY

When a child resorts to tattling, she is saying, "I'm clueless about how to handle this. Help me." This is a wonderful teaching opportunity that is missed by many parents. Consider this battle over a video game:

"It's my turn to play," proclaims Erin. "It's not! I just started," snaps Tiffany. "It is. Give me the joystick," demands Erin as she grabs it away from Tiffany. To defend her possession, Erin punches Tiffany, who immediately shouts, "I'm telling!" and runs to find a parent, to whom she whines, "Erin hit me." Below are some typical adult responses:

- ◆ "Erin, did you hit your sister? You know better. How would you like her to hit you? Now it's her turn."
- ◆ "You two better stop fighting. I don't want to hear it. Any more fighting and the video game goes on vacation."
- ◆ "What happened?" Tiffany tells her side of the story, to which the parent responds, "You girls take turns. Don't make me say it again."

None of the responses above teaches the children how to handle conflict assertively. The only thing the girls may have learned is that you cannot rely on parents for help (later this generalizes to all authorities). All of these responses foster a sense of helplessness. Or the girls may have learned not to seek help with a problem they can't handle because they may land in worse trouble. Alternatively, if they have learned that the adult always fixes everything, this lesson fostered a sense of dependency. Finally, the children may have learned to just give in to the tirades of others in order to avoid problems. How many times in your life have you let go of something you really wanted just to avoid a conflict? Do you want your children to live this way?

HOW TO TEACH THE TATTLER

Martin says to you, "Logan pushed me." When a child brings you a problem involving a perceived intrusion by another, the first question to ask is, "Did you like it?" This may seem odd, but it is critical for three reasons. First, it helps you to assess how much assertiveness energy the tattler possesses. Assertiveness energy is the level of faith the child has in the power of her words to influence others. Second, saying no has a great deal of assertiveness energy, and answering your question makes that energy instantly available to your child. Third, you have helped your child focus on herself and her own feelings rather than on the other person. This lays the foundation for self-control.

When your child responds with some form of a no, take note: Was it a shake of the head; a loud, firm no; an aggressive no; or a weak, passive no? Some noes (the assertive ones) reveal a high confidence level while others (said in passive or aggressive tones) reveal low confidence.

If the no reveals high confidence, say to your child, "Go tell Logan, 'Stop, I don't like it when you push me.'" Then have your child practice the Power of Attention by telling Logan what he wants him to do. For instance, "You must ask me to move."

If your child demonstrates low confidence with the way she says no, you must teach her the words to say and the tone of voice to use.

A child with a passive temperament must learn to use her "big voice." If you send your child off alone to talk to a sibling in a passive voice, when you leave the room, that child will get hit for tattling. It is almost guaranteed.

You can vary the sophistication of the language you provide for your child depending on her level of development. For young children (say two years old), those with developmental delays, or those with language or speech disorders, you might say, "Go tell Jeremy, 'Stop!'" As children progress in both their cognitive and language abilities, the words you provide must also change.

WHAT ABOUT INFANTS?

While shopping at the mall, I heard a baby crying and looked up to see a mother pushing a double stroller with a four-year-old boy in back and an infant in front. The four-year-old hit the infant's head as if it were a drum and, naturally, the baby continued to cry. To soothe the crying infant, the mother (who was unaware of the hitting) pushed the stroller back and forth. The woman looked exhausted. I walked over, commented on her lovely children, and asked if I could take a closer look. I bent down and looked at the boy, waited for him to make eye contact with me, and then said, "See your sister's face. She is crying. She is saying, 'I don't like it when you hit me. Stop.'" Briefly the boy had an awkward look on his face as if he were processing the information. I could almost hear him thinking, "So *that's* why she's crying."

You must teach the older siblings of a baby to read the infant's face. "Look at Robin's face. She is smiling. Her face is saying, 'I like it when you talk to me and touch my hands.'" When an older sibling hugs a baby too hard, teach her to "listen" to the baby by saying, "See his face. It is red. His lips are quivering. His face is saying, 'I can't breathe when you squeeze my neck; hold me under my arms.'" Guide the child's hands to reinforce your words. As a parent, you must speak for the infant until the infant can speak.

THERE'S NO TIME LIKE THE PRESENT!

Begin your assertiveness journey by practicing the following:

♦ **Listen to yourself talk to children.** Are you passive, aggressive, or assertive?

♦ **Focus on giving children usable information.** Tell them specifically what to do. Use your Power of Attention to focus on what you want to have happen.

♦ **Capture your child's attention before you speak.** Move close to your child, wait for her to look at you, and say, "There you are."

♦ **If your child ignores you, say,** "I'm going to show you what I want you to do." Then guide your child to success.

♦ **When you are frustrated, express your feelings directly by saying,** "I don't like it when you _____" or, "When you _____, I feel _____."

♦ **Teach your children how to handle intrusions by other children.** Start the interaction with the victim by asking, "Did you like it?"

Assertiveness is the *main skill* you will use to set limits for your children. Assertiveness is a very powerful skill that lets you set boundaries with others, and helps you teach your children to set boundaries. These boundaries model and teach the value of respect. In order to be assertive, you must use your Power of Attention, focusing first on what you want, and then expressing your desires in a forthright manner. In a family, in a community, in a democracy, each person must learn to be assertive and stand up for his or her own rights without trampling on the rights of others. Choices, the discipline skill you will learn in the next chapter, is another skill that will help you to set limits.

Choices:
Building Self-Esteem
and Willpower

Jane had been working with her daughter, Mara, to help her get dressed in the morning, so both could leave the house pleasantly and on time. After breakfast, she would go to Mara's room, get down to her level, and wait for her daughter to make eye contact. Then Jane would give an assertive command such as, "Put your toys in the bin, and then get dressed." Jane would point to the bin and to the toys, since nonverbal gestures helped Mara attend to her words. Jane also waited for Mara to begin putting the toys away so she could praise her for choosing to comply with the command. Once Mara seemed focused and on task, Jane left to finish dressing herself.

Five minutes later, Jane checked on Mara. The child had emptied the toy bin and was sitting in it, naked. With a deep breath, Jane reaffirmed to herself what she wanted Mara to do and offered her two positive choices: "Mara, you have a choice. You may climb out of the bin and put your shirt on, or you may climb out and put on your pants. Which do you choose?" Mara began climbing out and said, "Pants first."

With that choice, Mara empowered herself to take action. She had channeled her will and curbed her impulses to continue play-ing. Offering two positive choices is a wonderful skill to have in your parental repertoire. The skill comes from the Power of Free Will, which reminds us to resist the temptation to try and make children mind. It asks us to acknowledge free will in others and structure situations whereby children are more likely to be coopera-tive. When children feel free to make choices, the value of commit-ment is taught.

THE "BLAME GAME"

Every moment of every day, we make decisions. However, we often blame others for choices that were ours to make. "He made me do it," your child might cry. "Don't make me have to tell you again," you might warn. "Now look at what you made me do—I missed the turn!" your spouse might say. These examples show the kinds of words we say when we foist our own reaction or behavior off on an outside situation or another person. We move through most days on automatic pilot, forgetting that we are the ones in charge of our decisions.

In fact, we choose to forget that we are making choices. Life seems to "happen" to us. Have you ever moaned, "Boy, did I have a bad day"? But who decides how your day will go? Does the day choose your thoughts? Have you ever complained, "Traffic today is horrible"? Is it horrible, or are there simply many cars on the road? Traffic is not inherently horrible, but you can choose to perceive it as such. Choos-ing to see a situation as awful, you automatically feel angry.

When you believe a person or an event has caused your feelings, you have put that person or event in charge of you.

I recently stayed in a lovely hotel in Chicago, in a room on the thirty-sixth floor. One morning, I rode the elevator with a woman who was irate because the elevator kept stopping. She was choosing to be driven nuts because the elevator stopped for people. But this is what elevators do. Why did she want to be a nut? Why would any of us want to be a nut? Why do we give our power away to elevators, children, spouses, or institutions? What is so attractive about victimhood? These questions fascinate me.

Whenever you believe that something besides your perception of an event or a person is angering you, you give your power away. You believe the event or person has *made* you angry, happy, sad, or guilty. Whoever or whatever you have put in charge of your feelings, you have allowed to be in charge of you. You lose your Power of Free Will every time you think that others are making you act a certain way, or that you can make others behave as you wish.

Reclaim your choices, and you reclaim your power and self-control. As a consequence, however, you can no longer blame others for your actions. If you say, "Don't make me have to take away that yardstick," you have given your power away to your child. You have put the child in charge by telling him that he is making you respond in a particular way. You can reclaim your power by acknowledging that your feelings and actions are created by your own free will. By reclaiming your power, you will also reclaim responsibility and, in turn, model both of these for your child. You might then say, "If you choose to poke Jordan with that yardstick, I will take it away. You can measure things with it or play with it alone. What is your choice?" In saying that, you maintain your control of the situation and send the message to your child that you are in charge of your choices, and he is in charge of his. You have utilized the Power of Free Will (the only person you can *make* change is yourself), and modeled how to responsibly direct and use free will. You have given him usable information.

This chapter will show you how to use choices as a discipline skill, thereby fostering the development of self-esteem and willpower in your children. By assisting your children in making choices, they learn how to commit to certain actions and outcomes. You will be teaching them the value of commitment.

RECLAIMING YOUR PARENTAL POWER:
MAKING YOUR OWN CHOICES

Generally, parents give their power away to firstborn children, and the children try not to abuse their reign. When you say, "Don't make me have to speak to you again," these firstborns straighten up and immediately try to regain your love and approval. Second-born children, though, often respond differently. When a parent says to them, "You're making me angry, so behave," they seem to take this information and experiment with it. It's as if they are thinking, "If this make her angry, what would it take to make her cry?" When you give your power away to children, you never know what response you will get. You may have a little Stalin or you may have a Mother Theresa.

Below are some phrases commonly used by parents that give their power to children. Each one sends the false message that the child controls the parent:

- ◆ "Don't make me have to speak to you again."
- ◆ "You are pushing me over the edge."
- ◆ "Look how you made your mother [sister, friend] feel."
- ◆ "Don't make me put you in time out."
- ◆ "You are ruining this meal."
- ◆ "I can't believe what that child is putting me through."

Most of us grew up hearing these statements, and after years of such messages we felt an overwhelming sense of inadequacy. If we controlled our parents, why couldn't we make them happy? Why couldn't we make them get along with each other? Why couldn't we be better and make everything better? Of course, the reason was that we never really were in charge. We were simply given that false message by our well-meaning parents.

Before you can offer empowering choices to children, you must first learn to make choices yourself. Here are assignments to help you:

1. **For one day, give up the attitude, "I don't know, and I don't care."** It allows you to avoid making choices. For one day, act as if you do know. If a friend asks where you would like to go for lunch, state your preference clearly: "I'd like Chinese food."

2. **Transform your "shoulds" to "coulds" and then choose.** When you hear yourself saying, "I *should* pick up the dry cleaning," catch yourself. Own your choices and say instead, "I *could* pick up the dry cleaning." Then decide whether you will or will not. There are no "shoulds," "have-tos," or "oughtas," only choices. Start choosing and committing.

3. **Convert your "make me" language into choices.** Use the Power of Free Will to remind yourself that you are in charge of your thoughts, feelings, and actions. Instead of saying, "Don't make me stop this car," say, "I am going to stop the car until you have your seatbelt on." Instead of saying, "You are driving me nuts," say, "I feel crazy. Too much is happening at once." Then assertively tell your children what to do. "You sit here, and you sit there, while I think."

"WIN-WIN" DISCIPLINE—
GIVING TWO POSITIVE CHOICES

Young children, who are developing a sense of their own autonomy, often need to assert themselves when they hear an adult command, which can lead to a face-off. Instead of giving an assertive command, you can offer your child two acceptable choices. These choices allow your child to comply with your wishes while also giving him the "last word." Offering your child two positive choices can help him do the following:

- ◆ Attend to the task you deem important.
- ◆ Comply with your wishes.
- ◆ Learn decision-making skills and the value of commitment.
- ◆ Feel empowered, thereby reducing power struggles.
- ◆ Redirect his behavior, and learn impulse control.
- ◆ Establish and maintain self-control.

FALSE CHOICES

When I broach the topic of choices with parents, they often roll their eyes as if to say, "Yeah, we know about choices. Let's move on to a new topic." They don't realize that they have been failing to use choices *positively*.

Most of us have been raised with what I call "false choices." "You can mow the grass, or be grounded." "You can go to sleep now, or never have another sleepover." I call these false choices because the parent is presenting one preferred (good) choice, and one negative (bad) choice, with the intent of coercing the child. In the example of Jane and Mara on page 97, Jane offered two positive choices to Mara about how she could get out of the bin. Both of them focused Mara on the necessary task. Jane might have told Mara, "Get dressed or go to time out," but her decision to offer two positive choices allowed both her and Mara to feel successful.

When you offer a false choice, you set your child up to believe that when he thinks, feels, or chooses differently than you do, he is bad, wrong, or disrespectful, instead of simply having made a choice.

Another way in which a parent may give a child a false choice is with words that seem to put the child in charge of situations which he does not actually control. "Put your pajamas on, okay?" "Could you please get dressed?" "Let me finish the dishes and then I will help you." "Shall we go shopping now?" Parents do not really want their children to dictate their own bedtimes, decide whether to dress or not, or determine the day's schedule. False choices give an illusion of control by seeming to place one person in charge of another. This destroys free will. The illusion bursts when your child behaves differently than you thought he would, or should, and then you threaten punishment. Parents who offer false choices are afraid to say what they really want, or don't know what they want. Such parents lack the skill of assertiveness (see chapter 4).

GIVING AGE-APPROPRIATE CHOICES

All children can benefit from being offered two positive choices, but the choices must be age appropriate. It would be foolish to offer young children unlimited choices. If you tell your child to pick out one toy in the store, you may be there until closing. Then, too, your child might pick a toy costing $69.95, while you planned on spending about $5.00.

Parents must structure choices for children because too many decisions are overwhelming to children. You *must* stay in control of yourself and in charge of your children. In giving your child choices, consider his age, temperament, and the specific situation. The following guidelines will help you provide children with choices:

1. **Offer children under the age of five a choice between two predetermined events or objects.** It works like this:

- ◆ **Clothing:** "You have a choice: You may wear the blue shirt or the red shirt."
- ◆ **Food:** "You have a choice between orange juice or milk."
- ◆ **Activities:** "You have a choice: You may build with blocks, or draw."
- ◆ **Compliance:** "You have a choice: You can pick up either your clothes or your toys. Which do you pick?"

Never offer a young child a choice about the daily schedule ("Are you ready for bed?"); adult activities ("Could Mommy leave you with Daddy now and go shopping?"); relationships ("Would you like to spend Christmas with your dad or your mom?"); or situations that put the child or others in danger. The following example demonstrates a parent offering an inappropriate choice.

Tasha's mother repeatedly requested that Tasha come visit so she could spend time with Hunter, age six, her grandson. On the phone, Tasha's mother often made guilt-inducing comments such as, "You'd think we lived a thousand miles away by how seldom you visit me. I suppose I will see Hunter at his high-school graduation." To relieve her guilt, Tasha decided to visit her mother on Saturday. She and Hunter arrived in the morning so they would have ample time with Grandma. Hunter was excited to see his grandmother and to learn that they would go to the park. After three hours, Tasha asked Hunter, "Are you ready to go home now? Mommy has to do grocery shopping."

With her question, Tasha put Hunter in charge of the schedule. What if Hunter was not ready to leave? Did he truly have a choice? Adults often use children as pawns in situations in which the adults fear to say what they want themselves. This creates tremendous problems. Tasha offered Hunter a choice—staying with Grandma or leaving. She did it because she was afraid to decide for herself and risk incurring her mother's disapproval again. You must give children choices to foster their own development, not to compensate for your own lack of maturity.

2. **Some children need more limited, structured choices than others in order to stay focused and on task.** Mara, who decided to get naked in the toy box, needed more direction than other children her age might need. Because she needed more guidance, her parents could easily fall into the trap of giving her too many commands, such as, "Mara, get out of the toy bin"; "Mara, listen to me"; "Mara, put your toys away"; "Mara, eat your breakfast." Needing structure from adults, Mara might miss out on some of the decision-making practice other children more readily acquire. Instead of constantly steering Mara, her parents could use choices to help Mara learn to steer herself. Choices would give her the structure she needs, while allowing her to practice decision-making. Ultimately, choices could help build her self-esteem while she learned to operate successfully within a given framework.

3. **With children over the age of five, you no longer have to structure their choices with two predetermined options.**

Usually, a school-age child can handle as many options as commands. Let's say you tell your son to take out the trash, wash his hands, call his brother, and set the table. If he can successfully complete this four-part command, he is ready for wider choices. Watch your children to see how much structure they need in order to be successful. If your child cannot handle multiple commands, continue to provide more structured, limited choices.

4. **As your child gets older, he can also contribute to a discussion about rules, routines, and daily schedules.** However, it is vital for you to realize that these ultimately remain adult decisions.

5. **Anxious or overwhelmed children respond better to assertive commands than to choices.** Think about a time when you felt overwhelmed. The last thing you wanted to do was make a decision—even choosing between a doughnut and a bagel might seem too taxing. When children feel overwhelmed, choices are just another problem they feel they can't solve. At such times, clear, assertive commands will be soothing. If you woke up feeling overwhelmed, would you rather hear, "What do you want for breakfast?" or, "Here are some pancakes. Eat them and you will feel better." When your child is out of control, tighten the reins, reduce the choices, and take over until he bounces back.

Here is another success story. Carol's four-year-old son was playing at a friend's house. She went to pick him up, dreading the moment she would have to tell him it was time to leave. They had already suffered through many power struggles about ending play dates. On this occasion, though, Carol chose to try a new approach. She had literally rehearsed what she would tell her son. She began by assertively telling him it was time to leave. Then, before he began to complain, she said in an upbeat voice, "You have two choices. You can leave through the front door or through the back door." Her son immediately replied, "Can I ring the bell if I choose the front door?" She said yes, and they went home in good spirits.

THE STEPS IN DELIVERING TWO POSITIVE CHOICES

In order to deliver two positive choices to children on a regular basis, you need two things:

1. **You must think in positive terms about what you want your child to do.** Draw on the Power of Attention: What you focus on you, get more of.

2. **You must give your child a true choice.** Utilize the Power of Free Will, recognizing that people choose how they will behave. Offer two positive options, either of which is acceptable to you.

The following steps will help you deliver two positive choices:

Step 1: Breathe deeply. Make a conscious decision about what you want your child to do.

Step 2: Tell your child, "You have a choice!" in an upbeat tone. Your positive attitude will lighten up the situation, especially if your child seems resentful.

Step 3: State the two choices you have created to achieve your goal. Say, "You may_____, or you may_____."

Step 4: Complete the process by asking your child for a commitment. You might say, "What is your choice?" If your child hesitates, you may want to repeat the options. Simply say, "Pants or shirt?" If your child says, "Play more," repeat the two choices again calmly but assertively: "Pants or shirt?"

Step 5: Notice your child's choice. If he chooses the pants, then comment in an encouraging voice: "You chose to put your pants on!" Be sure to make this final comment. It is critical because it brings awareness to your child about his choice. Awareness of oneself strengthens the frontal lobes in the child's brain. Again, the frontal lobes have the capacity to override emotional outbursts and are critical to self-control. Remember, most people make their choices unconsciously and end up feeling controlled by life. If you raise your child with an awareness of his choices, he will not only *feel* less controlled, he really will have a greater command of himself, both psychologically and physiologically.

For older children you might say, "Seems to me you have a couple of options. Feel free to_____, or _____. Which would be better for you?"

PRACTICE, PRACTICE, PRACTICE

Below is a scenario in which you might elect to use the discipline skill of two positive choices. First, use the Power of Attention to think of what you want the child *to do*. Then offer two choices that will allow him to achieve that goal. Express these options to him in an upbeat manner. Remember the basic formula to use when you present the choices to your child:

Younger Children	**Older Children**
1. "You have a choice!"	1. "Seems you have a couple of options."
2. "You may ____ or ____."	2. "Feel free to ____, or ____."
3. "What is your choice?"	3. "What would be better for you?"
4. "You chose ____!"	4. "Looks like you decided to ____."

SCENE: PLAYING WITH FOOD. Nathan (age 3) is busily squeezing his mashed potatoes through his fingers. Breathe deeply. Think about what you want to have happen. Now decide which choices you will offer to Nathan. You will say:

_____

_____

"WHAT-IFS"

By now I'm sure that "what-ifs" are running wildly through your head. "What if my child doesn't choose either option?" This is probably your biggest anxiety. Hold on, keep breathing, and keep reading.

CHOICES AND SELF-ESTEEM

A person's ability to make choices and to accept responsibility for those choices is a measure of self-esteem. In order to really make a choice, you must make a decision and accept the consequences of that decision. This is called commitment. Therefore, it is vital to help children who have trouble making choices and/or accepting the consequences of their choices. You can only help your children if you choose to help yourself first. Listen in on this conversation and see if it sounds familiar.

"Where would you like to have lunch?" asks Pat. "Wherever, it doesn't matter," responds Sheryl. "Doesn't matter to me, either. Really, Sheryl, whatever you like is fine," says Pat. "You're driving, you decide," answers Sheryl.

In our society, women are socialized to please others. It is impossible, though, to make your own choices and simultaneously please others. As a parent, you cannot set a limit and take care of your child's feelings at the same time. Those of you who are passive must pay special attention to this idea. Write the following words down and post them on your refrigerator:

You cannot set a limit and take care of another person's feelings at the same time.

HELPING CHILDREN WHO HAVE TROUBLE MAKING CHOICES

Children who have trouble making choices fall into three groups:

- ◆ Those who refuse to make a choice.
- ◆ Those who resist the given structure. Given a choice of A or B, they pick C.
- ◆ Those who change their minds. Given a choice of A or B, they pick A, then switch to B, then switch back to A, and so on.

Before reading further, think about yourself. Have there ever been times when you refused to make a choice, or changed your mind a thousand times, or balked at the options life offered? By reflecting on yourself, you will better understand your children. On many levels, especially the emotional one, you are not that different from them.

Helping Children Who Refuse to Choose

Lisa, age seven, was given a choice—to put her backpack on a shelf in her cubby, or to hang it on a hook. Lisa stood staring at her teacher and then suddenly burst into tears. For Lisa, the decision was overwhelming.

Perhaps you can relate to Lisa. Have you ever felt under so much stress that you felt you simply could not handle one more thing? Tremendous anxiety is brewing within those children who find decision-making very difficult. This difficulty is their way of saying, "My world is overwhelming." These feelings could arise from developmental issues. Imagine the length of your arm changing daily, or your vocabulary doubling in a month—so much rapid change would be tremendously taxing. Anxiety such as Lisa's may have its roots in major life stresses—in a move or a death. It may also stem from everyday aggravations—a child's disappointing his parents or himself, changing teachers, fighting with friends, or having been teased by a sibling. Depending on temperament, some children get overwhelmed easily. Others seem to roll with life like a surfer on a wave. Don't fight your child's temperament. Instead, learn how to best respond to it.

To assist children who have trouble making choices, do the following:

◆ **Point out to the child the many choices he makes every day.** For instance, when he decides to color with crayons, say, "I see you chose to draw today." Whenever possible, show your child how he is always making choices. The child may look back at you as if to say, "Duh!" That is great—it means that he is aware of his actions. The frontal lobe of his brain is maturing.

◆ **Offer your child small choices that involve closeness with you.** For example, say, "Marvin, hold my hand to cross the street. You can choose my left hand or my right hand. Which do you pick? You chose my right hand! I like holding hands with you." Making choices demands autonomy and, for some children, at certain times, autonomy is scary. To ease your child toward independence, use warmth as a starting point. Once he can handle choices within your relationship, offer further choices. Say, "Do you want to invite Maya or Justin over to play this afternoon?"

◆ **Model acceptance of mistakes.** Children who refuse to choose may fear disappointing others or being wrong. Model the fact that everyone slips up. Your child needs to see you make a mistake, forgive yourself, and then choose a different strategy (that is, learn from your error).

You can use the "think-aloud" technique to model this skill when you have made a mistake. When you think aloud, you speak your inner thoughts aloud, which allows your child to hear how you process your mistake.

Here is a scenario: A father says, "Where is my screwdriver? You kids always borrow my tools without permission. Who took it? Speak up! I have had it—I don't lose your things. It's important to respect other people's property. That movie you wanted to see is out of the question now."

"But, Dad—" his daughter says, and he snaps back, "Don't 'But Dad' me; you should know better—what's gotten into you?" Then his son says, "Dad, you took those screwdrivers to Grandma's house when you went to fix her cabinets." The father realizes that he has made a serious mistake. He has not only blamed his children, he has attacked them. He realizes that this is a perfect time to use the "think-aloud" technique.

Speaking his thoughts out loud, he says: "Well, I made a big mistake. I was angry about the missing screwdriver. Actually, I was really upset because my boss yelled at me today. I felt so rotten about work that I took it out on you two. I blamed you and tried to make you feel as rotten as I felt. I owe you an apology. Kids, I am sorry for my behavior. Next time I feel upset I am going to breathe deeply and think before I talk."

By thinking out loud, this father modeled constructive handling of mistakes: He modeled learning from a mistake, and making a commitment to change his behavior.

Many children are taught that, no matter what you do, an apology will eliminate the problem. Children must learn that, while it is important to express regrets about misdeeds, you must also (and more importantly) change misguided behavior.

Helping Children Who Resist the Given Structure: Developmental and Learned Opposition

Some children will use the structured choices you offer as an opportunity for a power struggle. Such children, when offered two options, consistently create a third option in order to try to maintain control of the situation. Asked to pick A or B, they select C. You might say, "Sweetheart, you have a choice. You may walk next to me in the mall, or hold my hand. Which is your choice?" At this point, your resistant child might simply bolt off. Or, given a choice between milk or juice, a resistant child might request soda.

Before we discuss how to handle resistant children, you need to understand why control matters so much for them. What events in a child's life can prompt him to oppose all structures created by adults? There are two explanations for children who *habitually* resist structure—developmental reasons or having been taught such behavior.

Developmental Opposition

All young children go through a process that researchers call "individuation separation." This process transforms a helpless, dependent infant into a socially competent person with a separate identity. The child begins this journey toward selfhood by defining himself as "that which is 'not mom' or 'not dad.'" Thus, any assertive stance from an adult prompts the child to react with the opposite behavior. Children in the oppositional years often show their resistance by ignoring the structured choices an adult presents. These children are testing—but not to make you angry or to see what they can get away with. They are testing to figure out who they are (where *they* end and *you* begin), and to discover their uniqueness.

To assist a child who resists structured choices for developmental reasons, do the following:

◆ **Realize that if you allow yourself to be dragged into a power struggle, you have allowed your focus to shift from love to fear.** You will then be operating from a negative basis, trying futilely to make your child do something. To avoid this trap, take a deep breath, become conscious of your thoughts, and decide to shift from fear to love. Consciously choose thoughts that put you in control of yourself, not your child. Use the Power of Perception to own your own upset, or use the Power of Acceptance to tell yourself, "This moment is as it is."

◆ **Once you are in control of yourself, recognize that your child will choose to operate within your framework, or not to.** Coercion by you or the child is the problem, not the answer. Consciously choose to rely on the Power of Free Will. You both have a choice of how to behave. You can control your actions, but not your child's.

◆ **Use the parroting technique.** This involves repeating the options you have presented to your child in a calm, assertive voice.

> **Parent:** "Joseph, it is time to put away these toys. You have a choice—you can begin by picking up small blocks or large ones. What is your choice?"
>
> **Joseph:** "No!" He begins throwing the blocks.
>
> **Parent:** "Joseph, it is time to clean up. You have a choice—you can begin by picking up small blocks or large ones. What is your choice?"
>
> **Joseph:** "You can't make me. I hate you."
>
> **Parent:** "Joseph, it is clean-up time. You have a choice—you can begin by picking up small blocks or large ones. What is your choice?"

As you continue to calmly repeat the choices, one of three things is likely to occur. Joseph may start to put away the blocks. He may do this grudgingly, yet may still begin to clean up. Alternatively, he might escalate in his verbal assault on you and might resort to physical aggression (e.g., hitting you). Third, he might attempt to escape the situation through a temper tantrum or by running away.

If your child chooses to cooperate with you, celebrate his choice. Recognize how much willpower and energy the child harnessed in order to transform his negative response into a positive one and to engage in the clean-up process. "You chose to put the small blocks in the bin first!" This is close to a miracle, so celebrate it.

What's so miraculous about your child obeying you? Think about yourself. Have you ever been so upset that your negative thoughts about another person or situation pushed you to the point of outrage? Surely you have felt unfairly treated. Have you ever felt determined to prove that your point of view was correct? Think about how much strength it takes to stop a landslide of blaming, anger, and self-righteousness in order to become cooperative again. The child who chooses to comply has just completed a difficult process, one adults struggle with mightily. From the depth of your heart, praise your child, and celebrate his victory of love over fear. Your words will be perfect if your intention is to show true thanks for his gift of choosing cooperation over opposition. Any leftover huffs and puffs your child may mutter are just the bleeding off of the adrenaline that was rushing through his body during the conflict.

If Joseph escalates in his opposition, you will need the skill of empathy discussed in chapter 8 to help him move through his fit and return to a cooperative state.

Permissive parenting always follows feelings of guilt. Permissive parenting yields power struggles.

Learned Opposition

The second type of child who resists structured choices has learned that this is an effective way to get his needs met. Children can learn this lesson in three basic ways: through permissive parenting; from parenting that fails to meet the child's needs; and from family troubles.

Permissive parents either cave in to their child when he becomes upset, or try to dance around an issue in order to avoid upsetting him. These kinds of actions teach a youngster to fight limits and misbehave to get his way. They also teach him that adults don't mean what they say. The sad part of this is that when a permissive parent looks at the child and says, "I love you," the child can't believe that, either.

The second way children learn to resist structured choices begins in infancy, and has to do with the way in which the baby's needs were met, or not met. When a baby has a need (hunger, warmth, comfort), he enters an aroused state. When an adult fulfills the baby's need, a relaxed state is produced. If the parent responds to the baby, but cannot soothe him (due to colic, premature birth, or other physical problems), the baby will remain in an overly aroused state. From the infant's perspective, his needs were not met. That baby may come to believe that he must attempt to run the world in order to have his needs met. As he grows, the child will become controlling and will resist imposed structure. He will expend a great deal of energy trying to steer the world his way because he believes that this is his only chance for survival. Such children do not resist structure to test the boundaries of their power. Instead they try to control others in order to feel safe. They have a low tolerance for frustration.

One last way a child learns to oppose structured choices is through the experience of serious family trouble (for example, through divorce, death, or a depressed, drug-abusing, or alcoholic parent). Such troubles create enormous stress for a child, and leave him feeling overwhelmed and thus unable to make choices. It is hard for parents to admit that such problems color their child's life for fear that they will be perceived of as bad mothers or fathers. So long as a parent denies such problems, however, they cannot be addressed. Although it takes courage, a parent must admit to the presence of situations that may hurt his child's emotional health. Only then can the parent be responsible and address the problem.

To assist a child who opposes structure, do the following:

First, keep in mind that although an oppositional child will challenge your patience, you *must* maintain self-control to help him. Diligently practice all the techniques of loving guidance outlined in the book. If your child is typically willful and controlling, he is not likely respond to the old fear-based approach to discipline, so it's best for all concerned to shift to a loving guidance approach. Regardless of the discipline style you use, however, power struggles may be common.

You will need to follow the steps listed below to enable both you and your child to heal spiritually after a power struggle has occurred.

◆ **Forgive yourself.** Since all power struggles end in someone getting hurt, after the dust clears you will probably feel guilty, and guilt can lead to permissive parenting. Permissive parenting leads to the creation of demanding, willful, oppositional children. Stop the cycle by truly forgiving yourself. Forgiveness takes place in three steps, which I call the "three R's of forgiveness." First, *recognize* and accept your feelings. Tell yourself, "I feel angry and anxious, and that's okay." Second, *reframe* the experience. Forget about finding a good guy and a villain. Admit that, given your states of mind, you did your best and so did your child. Third, *request* help. Calmly ask your child to work with you in forging new patterns of behavior. Here is an example of what you might say: "Last night at bedtime, I screamed at you and spanked you. I did those things because I lost control, not because you are bad. Sometimes I think you want to be my boss. I am your mother and I am in charge. I am going to be a better parent. I am going to work on expressing anger differently— with words spoken firmly."

The three R's of forgiveness are: to recognize your feelings, reframe the experience, and request help from your child.

◆ **Engage your child in solving problems.** Together, forge a plan for the future that will help your child do a better job of obeying you. You might say, "Bedtime is a problem for us. I don't like yelling at you. What would help you get to bed peacefully at 7:30?" If the child has reasonable suggestions, try them. (Don't change the bedtime, though.) For children under the age of six, putting the bedtime routine in pictures can help. Put the pictures in order from left to right in a visible place and have your child review them often. The pictures might show his bath, pajamas, toothbrush, a book, saying goodnight to all the body parts, a kiss, and lights out. At bedtime, show your child what he is doing and what he will be doing next.

◆ **Help your child feel powerful.** Do this by giving him the chance to participate often in activities that he enjoys and at which he can succeed. Point out the many decisions he makes each day.

◆ **Play with your child regularly.** If you concentrate on playing with young children for at least five minutes a day, you may reduce power struggles by as much as fifty percent.

Helping Children Who Change Their Mind

Kaitlin's dad asked her to choose between milk or juice for snack. She selected milk. When he brought the milk, Kaitlin pushed it away and said, "No, juice." Dad then passed her some juice and Kaitlin said, "I want milk." Understandably, Dad was ready to dump both drinks on her head.

Children like Kaitlin may have self-esteem problems. At such indecisive moments, they may be feeling down on themselves or their world for any number of reasons. She could be tired or stressed by a serious family problem, or she might just be having a rough morning. Through indecisiveness Kaitlin is trying to control her dad and her environment. Children who pick C after being given a choice between A or B are launching into a direct confrontation. You could call them aggressive. Children like Kaitlin, on the other hand, could be called passive-aggressive. They use passive rather than direct means to control others.

Helping these children begins with a diagnosis. The first question Kaitlin's dad could ask himself is whether this is a developmental issue or a learned behavior. Is this indecisiveness a new behavior for this child? Is this wishy-washiness occasional or chronic?

When an inability to choose appears from nowhere and occurs only infrequently, the child may be temporarily overwhelmed by stress. Developmentally, when children are stressed, they regress (that is, they revert to behaviors you would expect from a much younger child). When children regress, they need assertive commands, not choices. Dad could say, "Kaitlin, you are having trouble choosing for yourself this morning. Here is the milk. Drink it if you like." Commands teach children what they are to do, whereas choices teach them how to make decisions and keep commitments. Teaching decision-making to a six-month-old infant would be silly, and the same is true for highly stressed children who have temporarily regressed.

If this is a chronic problem, there is a good chance that it is a learned behavior. The child gets more attention by changing her mind than she does for being cooperative. If you live in "hurry-up" mode, slow down, be with your child, and celebrate her choices to be cooperative. Use your Power of Attention, which states, "What you focus on, you get more of."

If you play with your child regularly, power struggles will diminish.

EXERCISING THE POWER OF FREE WILL

Becoming aware of our choices as adults and passing this awareness on to our children is a wonderful gift to them. You can become conscious of your choices as you *interact* with your children, or you can opt to remain unconscious of your choices and simply *react* to your children. Once you accept that you are constantly making choices, you can take charge of yourself and realize that your power lies within you, not in your ability to manipulate others. You can become a conscious choice-maker, or you can remain, or be, controlling—it's up to you. Remember to use the Power of Free Will by embracing the notion that the only person you can make change is yourself. Ask, "How can I help my child be more likely to choose to be cooperative?"

THERE'S NO TIME LIKE THE PRESENT!

After you close this book today, give your children two positive choices. Use the following formula as a guide for children five years old and younger:

1. "You have a choice!"
2. "You may ＿＿, or you may ＿＿."
3. "What is your choice?"
4. "You chose ＿＿!"

For older children say, "Feel free to ＿＿＿＿, or ＿＿＿＿. Which would be better for you?"

When you set a limit with an assertive command or two positive choices, two outcomes are possible: Your child may choose to comply with the limit, or he may refuse to comply (or even throw a fit out of frustration). Either of these two outcomes requires you to use another one of the *Seven Basic Discipline Skills.*

If your child complies, you would use the skill of encouragement. If your child becomes resistant and upset, you would use the skill of empathy and positive intent. Chapter 6, which covers encouragement, shows you how to celebrate your child's choices in a healthy manner. Chapters 7 and 8 show you how to employ the skills of positive intent and empathy. These skills will help you teach your child how to manage and work through difficult feelings.

6

Encouragement: Honoring Your Children So They Can Honor You

I give many presentations every year around the world, and I ask participants to evaluate them. Ninety-nine percent of the evaluations are highly positive, with generous praise for content, style, and speaker (me). Sometimes, though, I receive negative feedback, and it amazes me how large such criticism looms. In the face of it, I find myself tending to discount all the praise I have received. This really makes me wonder.

Why am I so fixated on the negative opinions? What forces in my life led me to enlarge criticism and minimize praise? Why, in the midst of so much encouragement, do I nonetheless discourage myself? I know that I am not alone. Many of us process the world this way.

This chapter will explore this common, harmful tendency. It will also show you the difference between effective and ineffective praise, and will examine the value of rewards. I will show you encouraging ways to acknowledge your children, their efforts, and their accomplishments. You will learn to praise your children in a way that supports their feelings of self-worth and security, and builds unity in your family.

WHAT YOU DO UNTO YOURSELF,
YOU DO UNTO OTHERS

Use the skill of encouragement to show your child that you celebrate her decision to operate within your limits. Most adults encourage children through the use of praise. In fact, however, praise can be either discouraging or encouraging, depending on the form it takes. My goal is to help you move beyond praising your children to get them to behave or to bolster their self-esteem, so you can achieve a bigger goal—the creation of an encouraging environment.

Encouragement comes from the Power of Unity, and it can help you stay connected to your child. It says, "I honor, celebrate, and acknowledge you and your choice." By using encouragement as taught in this chapter, you will instill in your child the value of interdependence. Only when your child can wholeheartedly celebrate herself can she also celebrate other people. Through this celebration of self and others, a sense of belonging grows.

Remember, the way you treat yourself is the way you will treat your children. One weekend, I visited a friend who has a young son. My friend and I went to a party together. Upon our arrival, I noticed that she looked tense. When I asked her why, she said, "I'm wondering why I chose this awful dress—I look dreadful. I'm so stupid." The next day, at her house, she told her son to clean his room. He started right in and finished quickly. As he was about to leave the house with his friends, his mother called him back, and she asked, "Do you really consider this room clean?" He stood there silently. "Throwing your clothes in the closet is not cleaning. It looks dreadful. You can do better—you're not that stupid!" Her words to him echoed the words she had spoken about herself at the party. In both cases, she offered harsh discouragement.

My friend has lots of company. The National Family Institute reported that the average American child spends 12.5 minutes each day communicating with her parents. Of that time, 8.5 minutes are spent on corrections, criticisms, or arguments. A University of Iowa study revealed that on average, a child hears 432 negative comments daily, compared to 32 positive ones (Hochschild, 1997). This area of family life clearly needs attention.

CREATING ENCOURAGING ENVIRONMENTS

Do you tend to encourage or discourage yourself? The following quiz can help you pinpoint your tendency:

1. During the course of one day, I tend to focus more on:
   (a) my assets and strengths
   (b) my liabilities and weaknesses
2. Typically, I:
   (a) accept myself as I am
   (b) focus on what is wrong and needs changing (too fat, too thin, too something)
3. I generally talk to myself in a way that:
   (a) builds self-confidence
   (b) makes me feel confused or inadequate
4. During the day, I tend to think about:
   (a) what I currently am doing
   (b) what I should be doing
5. I notice:
   (a) my efforts and improvements
   (b) that I am not where I think I should be
6. As life unfolds, I tend to:
   (a) judge events as good or bad
   (b) notice the turn of events without the need to judge

If you selected more A answers than B answers, you are probably good at encouraging yourself. If you selected more B answers, you may tend to discourage yourself. If you routinely discourage yourself, you will unconsciously discourage your children. Since change begins with you and then extends to your children, decide today to be kinder and more encouraging toward yourself.

To begin the change process now, say the following affirming statements out loud:

- ◆ I will recognize and honor my own contributions to a better world.
- ◆ I will allow myself to make mistakes and I will forgive myself.
- ◆ I will encourage myself to be successful.
- ◆ I will accept praise other people offer me because I know I am a valuable human being.
- ◆ I will suspend my judgments long enough to allow my love to shine through.

If you change how you treat yourself, you will naturally change how you treat your children.

The skill of encouragement is rooted in the Power of Unity, which, in turn, encompasses all of the other Powers for Self-Control. Here is how it works. In order to become encouraging, you must:

- ◆ Accept both yourself and your situation as they are, not as you think they should be (the Power of Acceptance).
- ◆ Focus on what you want rather than on what you don't want (the Power of Attention).
- ◆ Own your own upset (the Power of Perception).
- ◆ Attribute positive intent to yourself and to others (the Power of Love).
- ◆ Acknowledge the only person you can make change is yourself (the Power of Free Will).
- ◆ View conflict as an opportunity to teach or learn (the Power of Intention).

As you can see, self-control and encouragement represent two sides of the same coin. Encouragement allows you to deeply connect with others and to fully appreciate their unique qualities. It lets you drop your self-centeredness so you can reach out, rejoice in others, and focus on giving rather than getting. Encouragement affords a deep sense of belonging.

Self-control and encouragement are two sides of the same coin.

The payoff for encouraging children takes several forms. A family gains psychologically when its members have a strong sense of belonging. An encouraging environment also builds your child's self-esteem. It leads to easier days with children because they are much more likely to cooperate. An encouraging atmosphere also offers neurological benefits. It actually sculpts your child's brain for a lifetime of healthy adjustments. Discouraging homes shape brains that are prone to depression, violence, addictions, and impulsivity. In order to foster an atmosphere of encouragement, you *must* practice the *Seven Powers for Self-Control*. As you master the powers, your capacity to offer encouragement will grow.

CAN PRAISE BE DISCOURAGING?

It seems logical that praising children would foster enhanced self-esteem. However, two decades of research have shown that this is not always true. Certain kinds of praise are actually dangerous. They inhibit a child's self-esteem.

I will tell you more about this research below. First, let's examine several forms of common, but damaging, praise. (Then we'll explore healthy, constructive forms of praise.)

◆ **Giving too much general, all-encompassing praise can unduly burden your child, so she feels pressured to live up to unrealistic standards.** Perhaps you grew up hearing, "You are *always* so sweet and helpful." Hearing this again and again left you with two options: You could try to live up to the perfect image that adults had bestowed upon you, or you could "act out," hoping that your parents would see the "real you." Many families who overdo general praise wind up with one "perfect" child and one "demon." The perfect one excels at school and, as an adult, strives to be the perfect employee, model spouse, and ideal parent. The other sibling seems to intentionally bollix up everything she touches. Her life is a continual psychodrama and she provides her family with plenty to talk about during the holidays.

◆ **Giving too much praise that relies on value judgments teaches your child that "good" equals "pleasing others," and "bad" equals "displeasing others."** Many of us praise children by imparting value judgments: "What a good boy you are!" or, "What a great job." Young children think simplistically. We often suggest to children that they are good if they do as they are told, and they come to believe us. By extension, they also figure out that when some action an adult has requested is not accomplished, they must be bad. Children who absorb this message can grow up feeling guilty when they slip up, as all human beings do. They may also grow up to be very judgmental and critical of others who fall short. They may feel that people who disappoint others or who make mistakes are bad. Have you witnessed how critical and rude some adults are toward store clerks? "How dare you make a mistake while ringing up my purchase! You have ruined my day."

Praise based on judgment has another side effect. Children can become "judgment junkies." They will anxiously ask, "Is this good? Did I do this right?" I have taught college students who became extremely anxious when I did not give them exact instructions for an assignment. They might ask, "How many pages do you want?" If I reply, "As many as you need to express yourself," they come back and ask, "Could you check this to see if I'm on the right track?" If I reply, "Only you can decide that," they look as though they might need some Valium in order to complete the semester.

◆ **Praise that focuses on what *you* think or feel about the child's behavior teaches your child to seek approval.** If you praise your children to get them to behave well, your praise will actually backfire because it is a form of getting, not giving. You might say things like, "I like how you behaved yourself in the grocery store," or, "I am proud of you when you do well at school," in hopes of future good behavior or performance. But that tells your child, "I like you when you please me." She may well conclude, "I am only lovable when I please my parents," and that when she misbehaves, you will not like her.

Many of us have internalized the belief that if we disagree with people or refuse them, we will not be loved. We struggle to please others, living as we think "they" want us to live, rather than following our own hearts' desires. Sadly, many of us do not even know who "they" are anymore, nor do we have a clue what our own hearts do desire.

◆ **Only praising your child for well-done, completed tasks teaches her that effort does not matter—only accomplishments do.** Many adults only offer praise when commands are carried out. When the toys are all put away, you may say "Good job." Imagine how boring a football game would be if the fans sat in silence until their team completed a touchdown. Football fans jump and shout throughout the game to encourage the players. If we treated our children the way we treat our favorite athletes, my guess is that we would create a true "home court advantage." Children need to learn that the process counts as much as the product. To do this, you must focus on your children's efforts and the small steps they take, not only on the touchdown.

If you praise only finished jobs, done well, you teach your child to devalue effort.

◆ **Praising your child by comparing her to others teaches her that in order to be valuable you must be special.** "I'm so proud of you. That was the best story ever." "You got all A's. No one in our family has ever done that." Such comparative statements say "I want only the best."

When you compare one child to another, you promote competition. A mother went shopping with her school-age son and preschool-age daughter. The mother said to the little boy, "See how nicely your sister is behaving. You act like that." The boy immediately changed his behavior to please Mom. Then the mother said, "I like how nicely you are behaving now." Competition and comparison build conflict in the home, not cooperation. This mother solved the immediate problem, but unconsciously promoted future sibling rivalry. There is a difference between trying to do well and trying to beat others. One is ultimately encouraging and the other is ultimately discouraging. When you compare one child to another, you promote competition. Competition divides people. Remember, encouragement comes from the Power of Unity, which asks us to use as many opportunities as possible to bring people together.

I'm sure that many of these examples of misguided praise and their outcomes are familiar to you. You may know people who desperately seek the approval of others or seem obsessed with winning. Perhaps you have friends who strive to be perfect and deny mistakes they make. Maybe you fear being who you truly are for fear of losing the love of your dearest ones.

You may be amazed that all this damage can result from hearing damaging types of praise as a child, but I believe it often does. Most of us have been praised at home or at school in the harmful ways I have described above, and now are repeating the errors with our own children. It's not that we are bad or uncaring adults—we are simply using the forms of praise with which we were raised. The issue now is your willingness to change. If you are willing, you can learn a better way.

HOW TO OFFER HEALTHY ENCOURAGEMENT

At this point, you may be thinking, "What else can I say?" or, "I have ruined my children." Hold on! Channel that energy into a willingness to learn a healthier approach.

Awareness is the first step of change.

Awareness is a necessary precursor to change. To learn how to constructively encourage, you must first understand the ways in which your usual dealings with your child are discouraging. To let in new habits, you must first let go of old ones. The Power of Unity reminds us to connect rather than seek to be special. In order to use encouragement that promotes a healthy sense of belonging, two major ingredients are needed. You must:

1) Notice your children rather than judging them.
2) Link your child's actions to enjoyment and satisfaction rather than to tangible rewards.

NOTICE, DON'T JUDGE

How many times have you heard a young child say, "Look at me!"? A million times? If she is standing on one foot you might hear, "Look! I am standing on one foot!" If she is jumping into a swimming pool, you will hear, "Daddy, watch me jump!" As soon as she has climbed out, again you will hear, "Daddy, watch me jump!" This can go on for a *very* long time!

Children want and need to be seen. Your attention is greatly encouraging *by itself* and your parental role is quite straightforward. You can respond simply with, "Yes, I see you," and your child will be tickled. If you want to foster her language development, you can expand on her words and say, "Wow! You are balancing on one foot." All you really need to do is describe for your child the efforts or accomplishments you see. In effect, you become your child's mirror.

Children ask to be seen, not judged. But adults tend to judge rather than see. Your child might say, "Watch me on the monkey bars." Instead of replying, "Look at you climbing so high," you might say, "Good job, honey." Instead of describing your child's action, you have judged it. If you replace seeing with judging too often, the excited four-year-old child who shouts, "Watch this!" grows into an anxious eight-year-old who asks, "Did I do this right?"

Noticing children is an excellent way to encourage them. Describe what you see to your child and leave her free to make her own evaluations of her efforts or accomplishments.

Every Christmas, a municipal fire truck comes through my town carrying Santa Claus. Families wait outside their homes, listening for the siren that announces Santa, so they can greet him and catch the candy he throws. Caroline and Brittany, two six-year-old girls in my neighborhood, are deeply exploring the concept of "best friends." I saw Caroline catch several pieces of candy and carefully divide them between herself and Brittany. To encourage this behavior, I said, "You gave half of your candy to Brittany!" She smiled broadly. Later, I overheard her tell her mother, "I'm a good friend to Brittany." By noticing what Caroline had done, I brought her actions to her consciousness, which allowed her to judge herself.

THE NEUROLOGICAL BENEFITS OF NOTICING

To raise a peaceful, happy, creative child who can make wise decisions and be responsible for them, you must stimulate frontal lobe development. The brain, like a muscle, is a use-it-or-lose-it organ. Adults lose more than ten thousand brain cells daily through deterioration or lack of use. The frontal lobe (your "reasoning" brain) has the capacity to regulate the *amygdala* (your "emotional" brain). Consider this example: You have told your child four times to get ready for bed. She ignores you until you snap and start screaming. At that moment, you can pivot by summoning your frontal lobe to help you become calm. If your frontal lobe is well-developed, you will be able to regulate your emotional brain and calm yourself. If it is poorly developed, and the emotional part of your brain is overdeveloped, you will keep yelling and escalate your attack.

In truth, the *Seven Powers for Self-Control* are all frontal lobe exercises for parents. With children, too, we want to encourage frontal-lobe development. You do this by helping them to become conscious of their actions. You actually stimulate their frontal lobes when you highlight their achievements and kindnesses. You also stimulate their frontal lobes when you let them make their own judgments. The strength of your children's frontal lobes will determine the amount of willpower they can muster, and their ability to manage emotions and maintain self-control under stress.

Inescapable stress alters the landscape of the brain.

LEARNING TO NOTICE

When you judge your child, you tell her who you think she should be. Her perceptions of life become separated into categories of good and bad and her perceptions of herself do too. Judgment underlies *conditional love*—love that makes demands. Encouragement is about accepting your child for who she is. Acceptance notices and describes that which exists. Noticing joins you, your child, and the moment. It unites. Acceptance underlies *unconditional love,* which makes no demands. Here are some examples of the differences between the two:

Judging	Noticing (describing)
"Good job, Erica."	"Erica, you put your toys in the bin and your clothes in the drawers. You have cleaned your room so you can find things when you want them!"
"You are such a good boy."	"You showed your friend Cody how to butter his bread without tearing it. That was helpful."
"That was a great slide!"	"You did it! You came down the slide feetfirst and landed right in my arms."

Here are some guidelines to help you notice children rather than judging them:

◆ **Start your sentence with the child's name or the pronoun "you." Alternately, start with "You did it!", "Look at you!" or "I noticed_____."** This is an important step in breaking the judgment habit. Judging statements generally start with "Good," "Great," and other general terms. Work on "you" statements instead, such as, "Corey, *you* climbed into the car and fastened your seat belt"; "Max! *Look at you skip!*"; *"You did it!*—you dressed your doll."

◆ **Next, describe exactly what you see.** Pretend you are a camera. Before you speak, ask yourself, "Can a camera record what I am about to say?" If not, then you are still judging. You might be about to say, "Thank you, Greeley, for being so kind." A camera cannot record that, so rephrase the statement. Say, "You found Mia's blanket and gave it to her. That was helpful." This description is judgment-free—a camera could record it.

General praise such as, "You do such good work," offers a child no specifics about what good work entails. Children process information in images, so offer them images that their minds can record. To do this, speak specifically. "You finished all your homework and double-checked your answers. That's good work." You have given your child your definition of good work. This helps her start to construct her own definition—one she will use for a lifetime.

Acceptance notices what exists and describes it. Acceptance is the cornerstone of unconditional love.

◆ **End your description with a "tag."** In the example above, "That's good work" is a tag. Tags can help as you wean yourself from making judgments of yourself and others and move toward acceptance. At first, you may feel as though your words are not complete without a "Good job" or "Good for you." If so, use those phrases as tags. For instance, "Chris, you emptied the dishwasher; good for you." Beware, though, of judgmental tags. Instead, use tags that describe attributes of your child or values you admire. Eventually, try dropping the tags entirely.

◆ **Tags that judge—use sparingly:**

"Good for you!"

"Good job, honey."

"Doesn't that feel great?"

◆ **Tags that describe attributes—use regularly:**

"That took determination."

"That was gutsy."

"You sure are organized."

◆ **Tags that describe values—use lavishly:**

"That was helpful."

"That was thoughtful."

"That was kind [caring, loving, etc.]."

WHERE YOU SHINE YOUR LIGHT

Remember the Power of Attention: What you focus on, you will get more of, and will strengthen within yourself and in others. Giving praise is like turning on a flashlight in a dark room: The places you point your flashlight at indicate what you value. If you focus your children on being "good," you teach them to please others in order to feel worthy. Your goal, you're implying, is for them to feel "special." To feel special they must outshine others. It creates a "better than/less than" orientation in them. By devaluing equality, we remove our children's ability to truly join and connect with each other. Haven't you wondered why a teenager with the "best" grades, or the one who is very popular, or who is the "exceptional" cheerleader with the "perfect" family, feels so isolated that she commits suicide to erase the pain of loneliness?

If you accentuate children's strengths, you teach them about their abilities. If you encourage their contributions, you teach them how important it is to share their gifts. Encouragement grounded in the Power of Unity reminds us to connect people with each other and their accomplishments. Through joining, children learn that we are all connected. Interdependence is valued.

Below, I offer some categories of what you might notice in your child, along with examples for doing so. As you read, notice how the phrases begin, the specificity of the descriptions, and the tags, if there are any. (Remember, tags are optional.)

◆ **Notice your child's assets and strengths. Bring them to her attention.**

"Ashley, you planned the tasks involved in making that diorama. That took organizational skills. You have them."

"Look at you! You are eating with your spoon."

"At the game, I noticed how you were looking up while you were dribbling and passing the ball. Great game."

◆ **Notice your child's efforts, progress, and accomplishments. Bring them to her attention.**

"You've been working on your science project all week. You are putting in a lot of time and concentration."

"You did it. You went potty on the big potty. Good for you."

"You hung up all the clothes that had been thrown on the floor. I bet that will give you more space in your room."

◆ **Notice a child's contributions to others. Highlight these contributions publicly.**

"Casey, you held the door for Grandma. That was helpful."

"You offered Molly a cookie. That was thoughtful."

"You played quietly and let Mom and Dad sleep a while longer. That was considerate."

If you want kind, caring children, notice the helpful acts your children perform and announce their contributions publicly as well. This can be done in several ways. Here are some suggestions, but be creative and make up your own:

◆ At dinner, take time to share one way that each person in the family was helpful that day.

◆ Keep a list on the refrigerator that says:

"I noticed _____."

Any family member who sees a caring act could write it down or have someone else write it down for him or her.

Before bedtime, the family can read these contributions together.

◆ Once a week (or month) have a loving family party and play "Kindness Charades." Family members can act out kindnesses they received from others and the observers can try to guess who the helpful person was.

Here is the basic formula you can use to begin noticing your children's kind and thoughtful acts:

"You _____ [describe the child's actions]. That was helpful."

If you do this regularly, you will train yourself and your children to see the positive aspects of their world. Just as you label objects for a baby who is learning to speak ("Spoon. Mommy has a spoon"), so too must you label helpful actions. When your child learned to say spoon, you smiled. When your child grows into a compassionate human being, you—and the world—will feel blessed. There is one other act to be sure to notice in your child:

Notice your child's willingness to cooperate when you set limits. Set limits for your children with an assertive command or two positive choices (you learned these skills in chapters 4 and 5). If your child chooses to obey, celebrate her choice by noticing her actions.

Here are some examples:

Clearing the table: Mom moves close to Cary, waits for her to look at her, and says, "Cary, take your dishes off the table and put them in the sink." Cary stacks her dishes neatly to take them to the sink in one trip. Mom notices this and encourages her by saying, "Look at you! You stacked your dishes carefully so you could take them in one trip. That is efficient." (If you must add some form of judgment, use a tag such as, "Good for you!" It's best to forego the tags, though.)

Going to the hardware store: Emily was busy playing with her Barbie doll. Dad knelt down beside her to engage her attention, but she kept playing. When Dad moved closer, Emily made eye contact. Dad then said, "It is time to go to the hardware store. You have a choice. You can bring Barbie or leave her here. Which will you do?" Emily said, "I'll take her." Dad commented, "You decided quickly. I get to travel with *two* girls. Lucky me!"

WHAT ABOUT SAYING PLEASE AND THANK YOU?

Whenever your child chooses to obey you, praise and encourage her for her cooperation. Many of us say things like, "Emily, please stop playing and get in the car. I need to go to the hardware store. Emily, did you hear me?" If Emily ignored us, we would command, "Get up now and get in the car." If she whined but reluctantly moved toward the car, we might say, "Thank you."

Many parents say thank you after the child complies with a command (rather than offering praise). They may say, "Please take out the trash. Thank you." This is another subtle way in which a parent teaches a child that pleasing others is a priority. This kind of communication is not encouraging.

Please and thank you are words we use when we make a request of another person, or when someone does something for us. "Please pass the salt" is a request. If the other person passes it, we say, "Thank you." "Please take this glass of juice to your father" is a request. If your child chooses to comply, thank her.

There is a big difference between commands and requests. Requests imply that the child has a choice: "Please do this for me." If the child does what you have asked, you would say, "Thank you." Commands are firm expectations that leave the child no choice. You create confusion when you begin a command with please, or end it with thank you. Your message is: "Do this *for me*." You are subtly saying, "Clean your room *for me*." "Use the potty *for me*." When your children are angry at you or at the world, they will not want to do things *for you*. Furthermore, when you imply that your child's achievements are done for *you,* you rob her of her own accomplishments. And how will she behave when *you* are not there for her to do it for?

Obey the commands below. Then feel the difference in my response to your obeying my commands:

- **Command to you:** "Stop reading this book and look out the window."
  My response: "Thank you."
- **Command to you:** "Stop reading this book and look at the door, then look back at the book."
  My response: "You did it! You looked at the door and back to the page. Good for you!"

Can you feel the difference? One response says, "Please me," while the other one celebrates you. If you were a child, which kind of response would you prefer?

PRACTICE, PRACTICE, PRACTICE

Start noticing your children right away. In order to notice, you must be present in the moment. You cannot describe what your child is doing while thinking about your work or what to serve for dinner. You can judge a child without paying much attention. You can reward a child with a toy and not connect with her. In order to notice her, you must be *with* her. You must be attentive and giving. I believe that many children have trouble attending to others because they receive too little real attention in the form of their parents' noticing them. How can they tune into you, when you do not teach them how to do this by tuning into them?

ENCOURAGING CHILDREN DURING HARD TIMES—
HAVING FAITH

On her television show, Oprah Winfrey once said that author Maya Angelou taught her one of the most important lessons she ever learned. Oprah had phoned Maya, distraught about some occurrence that Oprah felt was unfair. Maya told Oprah, "Stop crying right now and say 'Thank you.'" Oprah was crying so hard, she said, that it took several moments for her to hear her friend. She also said it took years to understand Maya's message. Maya was teaching Oprah to have faith in life. Faith comes from knowing that there is a bigger picture and that all is well. We don't know enough to judge, and events that are hard for us can prove to be turning points.

When your children are having a hard time obeying you, they need to believe that you have faith in them. They need to sense that you have confidence in them before they can develop confidence in themselves. Here are some encouraging phrases you can use to convey confidence and faith in your child:

- "I have confidence that you will figure out another way of handling this."
- "You'll figure out a way to be helpful. I know that you do not like to be hurtful."
- "We all make mistakes—what could you do now that would be helpful?"
- "You can do it."
- "You'll make it. You have a lot of love to help you along the way."

Encouragement is basically a dose of hope, and people need hope to feel safe.

REPLACING ENCOURAGEMENT WITH REWARDS

Many of us were raised by parents who praised us by giving us gifts. We may have earned money for good grades. Recently, many educators have also sought to replace praise and encouragement with tangible rewards such as stickers and candy. Instead of teachers saying, "You located a pencil for your friend so she could complete her work. That was thoughtful," students are now more likely to get a toy or a piece of candy out of the "treasure box" for good behavior. Sadly, in many cases giving these tangible items has replaced giving affection and encouragement. Advertising drives this trend towards material reinforcement. Think of all the commercials that suggest that a product can say, "I love you." In reality, however, Gummy Bears can never replace connecting with other people. Over time, material rewards either become meaningless or teach children that their value depends on the things they acquire. When adults rely on material rewards, they teach children to value things more than relationships. This lesson has tremendous side effects.

THE SIDE EFFECTS OF REWARDS

Alfie Kohn, a former teacher turned author and lecturer, wrote an enlightening book called *Punished by Rewards*. In it, he stated that rewards cannot produce lasting changes in behavior, because they do not affect the recipient's beliefs or emotional ties. Kohn noted that rewards actually have undesirable side effects for the following reasons:

1. **Rewards decrease the** *quality* **of a child's performance, although they may increase the** *quantity.* In recent years, many schools have offered reading incentives to children. One popular program was designed in such a way that if the children read enough books, they would earn pizza. Research on these types of programs found that rewards did encourage children to read more books. However, the programs also changed the kinds of books children selected. The youngsters chose short picture books so they could read them quickly and arrive at the number needed to attain the reward. The focus was not on reading, but on the reward.

Children need your presence, not your presents.

---

2. **Rewards damage relationships.** While punishments train children to fear adults, rewards train them to please adults. Rewards put power in the hands of one person and leave the other person powerless. Such skewed relationships create children who crave

approval excessively. Training children to please others may seem beneficial, but when the same children become teenagers and continue to please others, the others they please are no longer their parents.

3. **Rewards discourage children from giving their all.** Research shows that when people work toward a reward, they only do what is necessary to get it, and no more.

4. **Rewards change how people feel about what they do.** External rewards undermine people's internal motivation. The focus shifts from, "Look at what I have done," to, "What do I get if I do it?" How often do you hear your children ask, "What do I get?" or, "If I clean my room, will you take me to the movies?" These phrases indicate that you have relied too often on rewards and that it is time to shift to offering encouragement.

Your use of rewards negatively influences your child's values. Let's say you use a formula such as: "When you _____, you will get _____." Whatever you have put in the first blank loses value and whatever you have put in the second blank gains value. If you say to your child, "When you eat your broccoli, you will get ice cream," broccoli will become a demon while ice cream will reign as the supreme treat. You might say, "If you are nice at Grandma's, you will get a new toy." Here, being nice has been devalued and materialism has been overvalued.

EXPRESSING APPRECIATION, LOVE, AND PRIDE

When your heart swells with parental pride and love, you will want to let your children know. Your words expressing sincere thankfulness for their presence or actions are a priceless gift, and your children need to hear them. When you express pleasure to your children, however, be careful that your underlying goal is not critical. If you say, "I appreciate your help with dinner," in hopes that they will do more chores, you are being manipulative and your goal is to get, not to give. However, if you look at your child and say from your heart, "I am so proud of you," you have given a most precious gift.

NEVER SAY "GOOD JOB"?

You may ask, "Can't I ever tell my child that she did a wonderful job?" Of course you can, but don't overuse that kind of general, judging praise. Such comments are like antibiotics—when overused they can cause serious long-term problems for individuals and society.

BALANCING THE FLOW OF GIVING AND RECEIVING

At the beginning of this chapter, I wrote about some of my own difficulties receiving praise and encouragement. I am happy to report that I have grown a lot in this respect. I am now much more receptive to encouragement. When I am down, I am blessed with friends who help me carry on. One friend, in particular, says, "Relax, Becky. God knew what he was doing when he asked you to take on the task." I delight in the love she offers.

I have found that when I can stop judging others, I also stop judging myself. When I no longer need to judge, I stop splitting the world into two camps, "the good" and "the bad," and love flows both ways. In the unity of our world, criticism no longer seems attractive. I can give and receive praise comfortably.

THERE'S NO TIME LIKE THE PRESENT!

Start right now to use the skill of noticing to encourage yourself and your children. It will take practice and persistence to break the judgment habit. In order to be successful, do the following:

◆ **Notice your tendency to judge your child.** At least three times per day, catch yourself before you issue a judgment. Instead, make a comment that shows your child that you have noticed her.

◆ **Choose a way to publicly highlight your family's helpful acts.**

◆ **Consciously notice and encourage your child at least five times every day.** Use the following formula to get started.

1) Start your sentence with one of the following: Your child's name, "You," "Look at you," "You did it," or, "I noticed. . . ."
2) Describe exactly what you see.
3) Add a tag if desired. Use one of the following: "That was helpful," "Good job," or, "Good for you."

◆ **After giving your child a command, praise your child if she chooses to obey you.** Start the praise with, "You did it!" Then describe what she did. Praise her even if you had to repeat the command five times. She still decided to cooperate. It just took longer than you thought it *should*. Cooperation, no matter how long it takes to get it, deserves celebration.

Encouragement is the skill you will use to help your child choose to operate within the limits you have set. When your child chooses to obey you, honor her choice with specific praise. This will teach her to honor you. Encouragement is the discipline skill you use to highlight and teach acceptable behaviors during peaceful times. How do you teach your child to behave in the midst of conflict? When your child is out of bounds, how do you seize that moment as a further opportunity to teach your child how to function successfully? That is the next skill you will learn: the skill of attributing positive intent to *every* one of your child's actions.

Positive Intent:
Turning Resistance
into Cooperation

Imagine you are a five-year-old boy having a birthday party at your home with four friends about your age. Your mom walks over to the table and places a tray holding five cupcakes before you. *She* thinks she's providing one cupcake for each child. *You* think it is your birthday and they are all for you (since you are five now, five cupcakes is just right). You pull the tray toward you and lock your arms around it. Your eyes dart to the other children, daring them to touch your cupcakes.

Suddenly events unfold that make little or no sense to you. The child beside you starts to cry. Another calls out for his mom. The guest opposite you folds his arms across his chest, glares at you, and says, "You're not my friend anymore." The remaining guest simply leaves the table and goes to play. All this brouhaha about *your* cupcakes is baffling.

Your mom approaches and you sense an atmosphere of increasing fear. You hold the tray tighter to safeguard your cupcakes.

Your mom says, "Mark, the cupcakes are for all the children. How would you feel if someone had a lot of cupcakes and wouldn't give you one? Don't you want to share with your friends?" If you could talk to yourself in your head, you would probably say, No, I want them all. Does it look like I want to share? But since, at the age of five, children have not developed inner speech and communicate mostly through actions, you turn your back on your mother and hold the tray tighter than ever.

Your mom then says, with increasing irritation, "You don't need five cupcakes! What should you do with those cupcakes? We share in this house! That's not nice. Now, give each of your friends a cupcake." You bend over to protect the cupcakes, in fear that she may grab them from you. For extra safety, you put the tray in your lap.

Completely frustrated, your mother shouts, "Give me those cupcakes!" You ignore her. (That's what she does to you when she wants you to go away.) She becomes even more irate and shouts, "Do you want all your friends to leave? Do you want to go to time out on your own birthday?" You don't care where you go as long as the cupcakes go with you, so you stand up and walk off with the tray. Your mom, totally embarrassed in front of the other parents, runs after you and tries to grab the tray from your hands. You try to hold on. In the struggle, the cupcakes fall on the floor. With your cupcakes ruined, you begin crying wildly out of frustration, confusion, and disappointment. You hit your mom as she tries to get you to behave more acceptably—by offering more threats. Finally your mother carries you to your room, sobbing and out of control.

In this vignette, the mother began each attempt to persuade Mark to share by unconsciously assuming that his motives were negative. When you attribute negative intent to others, you subtly attack them. Your attempt to make them feel bad about themselves and their choices is a form of assault. You actually implant a feeling of danger in others every time you try to make them feel bad, wrong, or responsible for your upset, and this sense of being in danger usually creates conflict, as the other person becomes defensive, not cooperative. The conflict mounts if you proceed with your own agenda without inspiring the other person to cooperate. When you learn to attribute positive intent to other people, you possess a powerful skill. It is the skill you need to transform opposition into cooperation.

Conflict escalates when we proceed with our agenda without first obtaining cooperation.

WHY CHILDREN MUST SAY NO

Children will oppose you. Their ongoing development demands that they be negative at certain times and in certain situations (see chapter 10). Children need to say no sometimes to test their limits and the social rules that prevail. At each stage of life, right through to adulthood, people need to resist and oppose.

A two-year-old child is starting to define himself as a unique individual separate from his parents. He does this by differentiating "me" from "not me." He also does this by saying no. Two-year-old children even say no to things they adore. They declare all things "mine" in order to learn what is theirs and what is not. Three- to five-year-old children are learning how to influence other people's behavior. They will try every possible maneuver to persuade others to do their bidding.

Children ages six through eight are learning how to classify. This leads them to view themselves and others comparatively. Comparison can lead to introspection and can result in moodiness, procrastination, and dawdling. Children who are learning to compare often wail, "It's not fair!" This frequent complaint of unfairness rattles around the house like the ball in a pinball machine. Although older children are less defiant than younger ones, they may still complain or be slightly fresh as they comply, reluctantly, with your demands. These stages occur naturally as children develop, but we are all resistant at times. I'm still resisting learning how to program my VCR at the age of forty-five. I dignify my latest round of resistance by giving it a name: my "mid-life crisis."

Resisting and opposing the wishes of adults allows children to define limits and test rules.

Your child, like all children, will behave in a negative, oppositional manner again and again as he moves through the normal stages of development. The nature of your response to your child's negative behavior is critical. Many parents respond in a way that actually teaches children to be *more* oppositional! These parents literally teach their children to put up a fight for what they want. If you usually assume that your child's motives are negative, you unconsciously make matters much worse. By attributing negative motives to him, you also do the following:

- ◆ You attempt to make your child feel bad for his actions.
- ◆ You focus his attention on what he is doing that is wrong or not good enough. Remember the Power of Attention: What you focus on, you get more of.
- ◆ You imply that he is deliberately making your life more difficult.
- ◆ You highlight character flaws that he, in turn, incorporates into his self-concept.

At the birthday party, Mark's mother was unconsciously teaching him to fight rather than cooperate to get his needs met. She did this by *beginning* her exchange assuming that Mark's motives were selfish. When your child's actions are outside the limits of acceptability, your first task is to inspire him to cooperate. Only then can you teach him what to do in order to bring his behavior back within acceptable limits.

The manner in which you *begin* your interaction when a conflict looms is critical. Let's see how Mark's mother, in all innocence, was encouraging Mark to dig in his heels. Pay close attention—it is somewhat subtle because you must "hear the *intent*" of the message.

When Mark's mom first realized she had a problem, she said, "The cupcakes are for all the children. How would you feel if someone had a lot of cupcakes and wouldn't give you one? Don't you want to share?" Her statements tell Mark that his view of the situation is wrong. The cupcakes are not his, as he thinks they are. They are for all the children. His mother implies that Mark is selfish. A kind child would willingly share. Mark confronts two negative choices. He can either submit to her attack and give up the cupcakes, thereby admitting that he is wrong and selfish, or he can defend his honor and resist. Whether Mark submits or resists depends on his temperament, age, and mood. He might have submitted by grumpily pushing the tray toward the middle of the table and then pouting. He might have submitted by relinquishing the tray and staring down at his feet while the cupcakes were distributed to the guests. In either case, his birthday joy would have evaporated. Rather than submitting, though, Mark chose to resist the perceived attack by defending his perception of the situation, holding tight to his cupcakes.

Even if you refrain from a direct attack on your child, your implication and tone can hurt him deeply.

Mark probably did not hear his mother's attack message, but he felt it. You might think, "Doesn't he need to know his behavior was wrong?" Yes, he does. However, your goals are to communicate this information in a fashion the child can hear, and create an environment in which he can maintain his dignity while choosing to be cooperative. If Mark hears repeatedly that he just wants things for himself and doesn't care about others, he will come to view himself as selfish and he will act in a way that confirms this self-image. This is called a "self-fulfilling prophecy." Remember, what you focus on, you get more of.

When her first attempts to influence Mark fail, his mother steps up her unconscious attack. She says, "You don't need five cupcakes!

What should you do with those cupcakes? We share in this house! That's not nice. Now, give each of your friends a cupcake." Her hurtful messages have become more direct. Mom implies that Mark's perceptions are wrong, that he is stupid for not understanding, and that he is downright mean. Mark hears, "What's wrong with you?" and knows his mother is saying that if he were smart, nice, and good, he would know what to do. She is attributing negative motives to Mark, and her unconscious attacks again leave him with two choices—submit or defend.

If Mark submits, he unconsciously accepts the hurtful labels ("wrong, bad, stupid") and incorporates them into his self-concept. Most of you reading this book were probably good little girls or boys; you submitted. Sadly, you are probably still defending yourselves as adults against being wrong, bad, or stupid. Most of us do this through trying to be perfect or through other compulsive, addictive behaviors. Mark, however, chose to defend himself rather than submit, and the cycle escalated.

His mother, frustrated and ashamed, then said, "Do you want all your friends to leave? Do you want to go to time out on your own birthday?" Her message was "Your actions are wrong. You are guilty and deserve punishment." Again, she is attributing negative intentions to Mark. You may think, Well, wasn't he wrong? Didn't he deserve to be punished? I would say no; he was only five years old and still learning how to share. He was trying to influence others and make the world go his way. He was learning that the world does not necessarily follow his rules. This is a difficult lesson—I am still struggling with it.

When the attack/defend process gets rolling, communication and connection break down.

The saddest part of the whole attack/defend process is that when it happens, you lose the ability to reach the person you love. It is also sad that this process leads us to believe that when we make a mistake, we must punish ourselves. We grow up attributing negative motives to ourselves when we make innocent human errors. The blame we heap on ourselves keeps our self-esteem low and robs us of the strength we need to make lasting changes in our thinking and behavior. We often feel bad about ourselves but seem paralyzed when it comes to acting to resolve our problems. If you are over-weight, you can diet and exercise, or you can feel rotten about being heavy. The catch is that you cannot simultaneously feel guilty about your situation and focus on what you must do to change it. The choice between drowning in guilt or improving your life is yours. But a lifetime of being made to feel bad and guilty is very difficult to undo.

You cannot simultaneously feel bad about what you have done and focus on what you must do differently.

ASSIGNING BLAME FUELS THE FIRE

When you attribute negative motives to another person, the attack/ defend cycle usually escalates, unless one person either becomes aware of his actions or surrenders. Suppose Mark gives in to his mother's demands. Then he has submitted his will to hers. This submission diminishes Mark's willpower, the same willpower he will later need to resist dangerous peer pressure. It is the same willpower he will need to say yes to healthy risks, and the willpower we lack when we try to improve our habits (to eat better or to exer-cise) but fail to do so. It's willpower that allows us to overcome obstacles, and propels us toward our dreams. Do you often find you cannot resist chocolate, shopping, or coffee? Do you have trouble keeping commitments you have made to yourself? If you do, you are probably still attaching negative motives to your actions. As a result, you view yourself as incapable of, and unequal to, the tasks life presents. This dim self-image drains you of willpower, the thing you need most in order to succeed.

There is a constructive way to deal with children whose actions are out-of-bounds, a way that allows a child to maintain his feelings of worth and strength while still shifting course. In order to use this approach, you must learn to become aware of your intent when you address your children. You must rely on the Power of Love. This love reminds us to see the best in one another. Furthermore, it states that what we see in others, we strengthen in ourselves. Seeing the best in our children defines both them and us as lovable.

INTENT IS REAL, AND IT IS A POWERFUL COMMUNICATOR

Science has now verified what many people have felt for years. You do not have to be conscious of something in order for it to affect you. All of us have had "gut feelings." Researchers who study the brain estimate that we unconsciously process close to one trillion bits of information per second. However, our *conscious* mind can only process about fifty bits per second. An enormous amount of information reaches us on an unconscious, "gut" level. Part of what affects our responses to other people is that we do "feel" their intent.

Both psychology and physics have proven that the image we hold of other people has a huge impact on them. Psychologists speak of the self-fulfilling prophecy. The labels we give others eventually become their labels of themselves. In many of the examples in this book, the parents did not come right out and call their children stupid, lazy, or disrespectful. But the adults' words and tone implied it, on a much subtler level.

Modern physics proposes that the universe consists of matter floating in a vast ocean of energy that is interrelated and connected. On the energy level, we are all connected. Current research on how plants and people interact has revealed that houseplants can "feel" their owner's thoughts about them over distances as great as seven hundred miles. If a scientist used measuring devices in my house in Florida while I was in Denver thinking, "You cute little plant, keep growing," these devices would indicate that the plant immediately responds to my tender thoughts. Research on tomatoes has shown that the energy field surrounding the vegetable changes as the knife approaches to slice it. This energy field in which we all operate is called the *morphogenetic field* (Brennan, 1987).

Clearly, our intentions are conveyed to one another across the morphogenetic field and affect each other profoundly. Have you ever spoken with someone and simply felt that something was amiss? The conversation may have been completely cordial and no specific problem was named, but you still felt uncomfortable. Perhaps you sensed dishonesty or disapproval. In these instances, the other person's intentions are reaching you on an unconscious level. You can use the same words with the intent of being open, or with the intent of being manipulative. You can speak the same words to children with the intent of punishing them, or with the goal of teaching them. Your intent is actually more powerful than the words you use.

WE MAKE IT UP!

There is a better way to help ourselves and our children handle conflict. Since conflicts arise when you proceed without first winning your child's cooperation, you must do something at the start of a combustible moment to confirm for him that you are allies. That something is straightforward—you must start out assuming that your child's motives are positive. You must vigilantly see the best in your child, instead of assuming that he is bad, or is trying to make your life difficult. You can assume instead that your child is simply trying to achieve some goal but lacks the appropriate skills to do so. When Mark grabbed the cupcakes, what do you think was his intent? Choose one:

- ◆ He wanted to keep the other children from having fun (negative intent).
- ◆ He wanted to irritate his mother to get more of her attention, even if she was angry (negative intent).
- ◆ He wanted to humiliate his mother in front of the other parents (negative intent).

◆ He wanted to make sure he got enough cupcakes on his birthday (positive intent).

Truly, we don't know Mark's intent until we ask him. And even then he probably would say, "I don't know." Most of us (adults and children) are not conscious of our true intent in heated moments. In the meanwhile, we make it up, so we might just as well assume it is positive. Recently I watched Tiger Woods play golf on television. He hit the ball and it seemed as if he were about to make a hole in one. Instead, the ball stopped just inches from the cup. The cameraman zoomed in on Tiger grinning broadly, and the announcer said, "He's thinking, 'I don't deserve this.'" Only Tiger knew what Tiger was thinking, but we all put thoughts in other people's heads.

We are better off if we attribute positive intent to other people. When we do, we define them positively, holding them in high esteem, and this in turn brings happiness to ourselves. When you learn to attribute positive intent to others, you have mastered the Power of Love. This power reminds us that what we offer to others, we strengthen within ourselves. Therefore it behooves us to see the best in one another.

When you attribute positive motives to your child's behavior, you position yourself to teach, and your child to learn. You model the value of cooperation. Again, picture yourself as little Mark. You have just grabbed all the cupcakes. Your mom approaches and says, "Mark, you wanted to be sure you got enough birthday cake. I want you to have enough too. I want you to have the best birthday ever. To do that, give yourself one cupcake and one to every guest. Then we can light the candles." Now, doesn't her approach help you relax? Can't you just feel a sense of cooperation easing through you?

Here are two scenes to show you the contrast between pegging a child with a negative versus a positive intent.

Negative Intent:

Mother: "Adam, hold your brother's hand while we cross the street."

Adam: "I don't want to."

Dylan reaches for Adam's hand. When Adam withdraws it, Dylan grabs Adam's hand. In response, Adam punches Dylan.

Adam: "I won't hold your hand."

Mother: "Adam, what are you doing? Was hitting your brother nice? Stop being so mean. Hold hands and let's go."

Adam grabs Dylan's hand and squeezes it hard. Dylan screams in pain.

Mother: "That's it. I've had it. Adam, when we get home you will not go outside or watch television. Now straighten up or you'll sit in your room all day tomorrow, too."

Positive Intent:

Mother: "Adam, hold your brother's hand while we cross the street."

Adam: "I don't want to."

Dylan reaches for Adam's hand. When Adam withdraws it, Dylan grabs Adam's hand. In response, Adam punches Dylan.

Adam: "I won't hold your hand."

Mom: "Oh, Dylan, that hurt. Adam punched you and you were just doing what I asked you to do. Tell Adam, 'I don't like it when you hit me. Stop!'" (This teaches Dylan to be assertive.)

Mom: "Adam, you wanted to cross the street without holding hands and wanted Dylan to understand this." (This assumes positive intent.) "When he didn't listen to you, you got mad and hit him. You may not hit your brother. Hitting hurts. If someone does not listen to your words, ask me for help." (This offers usable information.) "I will help you find a solution other than hitting." (This teaches Adam to ask for help.)

Mom: "We must hold hands to stay safe while we cross the street. In our family, we look out for each other. Dylan, you hold my right hand and, Adam, you hold my left."

When you attribute negative motives to your children, you will tend to become upset. Then, from an angry and often out-of-control position, you will seek to punish your children with words, tone, or actions. You will be focusing on what you don't want and will tend to escalate your punitive stance. When you escalate, you invite your children to escalate also. They may run from the pain you are causing them, or they may be defensive to protect their self-esteem. They may strike out at you to get rid of the awful feelings of powerlessness, guilt, and inadequacy. In each case, they are seeking a way out of their state of powerlessness. When you assign a negative motive to one child, you also send out a message that defines him for the other youngsters involved. When you label one child as being bad or mean, you actually separate siblings or friends from each other.

When you attribute positive motives to your child, you will stay calm and help your child be calmer because you will convey the message to your child that you know his inner core is good. You also send the message that it is the actions he has chosen that are not helpful. With this as the backdrop, a child is more willing to learn a new skill and listen to adult directions. He feels empowered to be flexible and choose a better course of action.

In the first example, the mother's lecture implied that Adam was "bad." Adam's reaction to this was predictable. When she attributed a positive motive to Adam, she stayed calm, helped the children be calm, and then taught them important new skills.

Dylan learned to be assertive when he had been wronged. Adam learned to ask for help instead of hitting when he felt frustrated. Mom learned to be open to diverse solutions to problems.

THE SECRET TO UNCONDITIONAL LOVE

When do you need the most encouragement? For me, it is when I am feeling unsure of myself, anxious, and inadequate. I have noticed that at such times I make terrible choices. I often choose to be short-tempered and critical toward both others and myself. I may also choose to overeat or find other ways to assuage my feelings of failure. At such times, I need encouragement, not lectures that will only provoke more guilt within me. The same idea applies to children.

You are probably quite comfortable encouraging children when they do what you want them to do: "Way to go, Alex; your room is looking better. Just finish putting the LEGO bricks away and you'll be done." In school, teachers are comfortable encouraging children who sit still, listen to directions, and help their classmates. Most adults accept the premise that when children make decisions that adults like, they have earned encouragement. The underlying message is, "When you do what I want, you earn my love. When you ignore what I want you to do, I will withhold my love." Many adults have internalized this kind of thinking. This explains why so many of us desperately seek approval and try so hard to please. We struggle for approval not because we love others, but because we fear that they won't love us.

How then can we encourage children who have made a mistake, or who are choosing to be hurtful? How can we set limits, yet remain loving? How can we give children unconditional love without being too permissive or seeming to condone misbehavior? The answer lies in attributing positive motives to *all* behavior—actions we judge to be good *and* actions we deem bad. You can reflect back to your child an admirable motive so he can feel worthy owning both his intention and his action. This will define both of you in the highest possible light. When you help a child own his motives and his acts, he is more likely to choose to change his behavior and to accept new strategies.

THE POWER OF POSITIVE INTENT

When you attribute positive motives to yourself and to others, you achieve an amazing number of good ends. Among them:

◆ **You uphold the highest image of yourself and of others.** In doing so you focus their attention on their best qualities. With children, your continual focus on their best selves strengthens their good traits and their self-esteem.

◆ **You foster cooperation by joining with someone to solve a problem.** Your children will view you as an ally.

◆ **You foster a sense of security.** Children who feel secure are more likely to share feelings with you about problems that are bothering them. We are never upset for the reasons we think we are. When we feel secure, we can explore the real upset that hides behind hostility or anger. When children feel secure, they are better able to move from a disorganized internal state (characterized by tantrums or fits) to an organized one (levelheadedness).

◆ **You foster responsibility.** Your child is willing to own his motives and actions because they do not mean he is bad. When he is able to own his motives and actions, then he is able to have responsibility.

◆ **You set your child up for a teaching moment.** Your child becomes conscious of his current actions and of his freedom to choose another course. You can help your child feel safe even while you help him realize the hurtfulness of his actions. He is more likely to be ready to learn another way of behaving than he would be if he felt threatened.

◆ **You convey healthy responses to your child that will help him handle and embrace diversity.** People can look, think, and act differently than you do, and you can still accept them for who they are.

♦ You encourage your child to develop his own will by acknowledging that he does not need to obey you in order to keep your love. You allow your child to discover his own true self rather than steering him toward becoming a person who constantly scrambles for the approval of others.

♦ You model unconditional love.

ATTRIBUTING POSITIVE MOTIVES TO YOUNG CHILDREN'S ACTIONS

Little children convey their wants and needs through their actions. They hit and grab to get what they want. You must teach them to communicate with words. You can achieve this by attributing positive motives to your child's behavior in this way:

Step 1: State the child's positive motive. You can usually do this by completing the sentence, "You wanted _____." This builds security and cooperation. For example, if your older child is playing with his baby sister and turns her head roughly, you might say, "You want Laurel to look at you."

Step 2: State for the child the skill he used to achieve his goal. Make no judgments—simply describe your child's actions. Try to use a phrase like, "so you _____." This builds awareness. In our current example, you would say, "You wanted Laurel to look at you, so you pulled on her head like this." Demonstrate with your own head and hands. This description helps the child become aware of his actions. This awareness strengthens the frontal lobes of the brain and supports reasoning over reacting.

Step 3: State the limit and why it is needed. This gives your child a clear boundary of what is not acceptable. Do this by completing the sentence, "You may not _____. _____ hurts." In this case, you would say, "You may not pull Laurel's head. Pulling like that hurts."

Step 4: Teach your child what you want him to do or say in the situation. Then ask him to do that action or say those words. In this way, your child can start immediately to practice the appropriate way to fulfill his needs. To teach your child a new course of action, use the following words: "When you want _____, say [or do] _____. Say [or do] it now." In the example with the baby, you would say to your older child, "When you want Laurel to look at you, turn your head so your eyes find her eyes." You would show him how to do this, and then say, "Try it now."

Step 5: Praise and encourage your child for being willing to try a different approach. If possible, point out how the new approach proved successful. If you have difficulty praising your child, review chapter 6. As your older child tries out the new skill, encourage him. You might say, "You did it! Laurel is looking right at you. She's laughing. She likes you."

The following examples show how this method works in other situations:

Situation 1: A child walks over and pushes his sister away from a favorite toy.

> **Steps 1 & 2: Describe your child's intent and action:** "You wanted to let your sister know that you didn't want her to play with your toy, so you pushed her away."
>
> **Step 3: State limit:** "You may not push. Pushing hurts."
>
> **Step 4: Teach:** "When you want to tell your sister that it is your toy, say, 'That is mine, get your own toy,' and point to one she can play with. Say that now, and remember to point."
>
> **Step 5: Encourage:** "You told your sister clearly what you wanted and she looked up and listened to you. Showing her what to play with was very helpful."

Situation 2: Your child angrily pushes food away from himself.

> **Steps 1 & 2: Describe your child's intent and action:** "You wanted to let me know you had eaten enough, so you pushed your food away."

Step 3: State limit: "You may not push your food across the table. It may spill."

Step 4: Teach: "When you are done eating, say, 'I'm done. May I be excused please?' Say that now."

Step 5: Encourage: "Yes, you may." Hug your child.

PRACTICE, PRACTICE, PRACTICE

In the situation below, attribute positive motives to the child and teach him another way of reaching his goal. Write your answers.

Situation 1: Your child is just starting to show an interest in dressing himself. He pinches your arm when you approach to help him pull on his pants.

STEPS 1 & 2: **Describe your child's intent and action:** "You wanted _____, so you _____."

STEP 3: **State limit:** "You may not _____. _____ hurts."

STEP 4: **Teach:** "When you want _____, say _____."

STEP 5: **Encourage:** _____ .

How did it go? Was thinking in this manner a challenge? There are many suitable responses. Here is what I might have said.

My Situation: Child pinches my arm as I reach down to help him pull on his pants. First, I would set a limit on the behavior (pinching) because the child intruded in my space and was hurtful. Assertively I would have said, "Ouch, that hurt. I don't like to be pinched." This gives immediate, honest feedback. The child hurt me, so I let him know it. Then I would teach him another way of achieving his goal.

Steps 1 & 2: "You wanted me to know you could do it yourself, so you pinched me."

Step 3: "You may not pinch. Pinching hurts."

Step 4: "When you want to do something yourself, say, 'I want to do it myself!' Say it now."

Step 5: "Look at you, you *can* do it yourself!"

ASCRIBING POSITIVE MOTIVES
TO THINGS CHILDREN SAY

As your children learn to use language to express their wishes, they will sometimes say things that you consider inappropriate. It is then up to you to teach them more acceptable forms of speaking. As with actions, you can do this by attributing a positive motive to your child and teaching him another way. The process is exactly the same as the one you learned to handle unacceptable actions, but this time, it's your child's language that is out of bounds. Here is an example:

Situation: Your child says that he hates his teacher. Eric says: "I hate school! I hate my teacher. Mr. Trumbull is a stupid idiot." Dad replies: "Eric, you want me to know how frustrated you are at school and what a hard time you are having with your teacher. You may not call your teacher or anyone else names. It is hurtful. When you are angry and frustrated with your teacher, say, 'I feel frustrated, it is hard to deal with Mr. Trumbull.' Come over here and say, 'I feel frustrated with Mr. Trumbull,' and let's talk about what is going on at school."

Dad puts an arm around Eric's shoulders and says, "I know it's upsetting to have problems with your teacher, but you can discuss them with me, and you can still be respectful."

SHORT-CIRCUITING CONFLICTS THROUGH
REDIRECTION: REDUCING IMPULSIVITY

You will often find that you can intervene with your children *before* a hurtful situation reaches full-blown proportions. You may see a child start to climb on the table, a child intently reaching for an object his sibling is holding, or a child becoming frustrated with another child's actions. When you sense a conflict brewing, you have a perfect opportunity to redirect your child's energies from hurting to helping. Make the most of such opportunities by eliciting cooperation from your child. You can do this by reflecting your child's feelings to him (see chapter 8 for more information) and by attributing positive motives to him.

The skills needed for redirection are similar to the skills described earlier, but you use them *before* the child actually breaks a limit. The beauty of redirecting children before they misbehave is that you give your child an opportunity to practice impulse control.

Imagine yourself on a diet. In a weak moment, you are heading for the leftover Halloween candy. Your spouse notices and says, "You must really crave something sweet. Remember your desire to eat more healthy foods. How about a banana instead?" Think of the willpower and impulse control you must exhibit to 1) not divorce your spouse, and 2) redirect your desires from candy to fruit. If you succeed, you have increased your willpower, reduced your impulsivity, and increased your self-confidence, as well as the overall love in your home. Children benefit in the same way when they resist harmful impulses.

Kendra was climbing up on the chair, heading for what appeared to be a Magic Marker on the far side of the table. Dad spotted her before she reached the tabletop and said, "You wanted to get the Magic Marker." Kendra looked up at her dad. Her body language indicated his assumption was correct. To redirect her, Dad said firmly, "You may not climb on the table. It is not safe. When you want something from the other side of the table, walk around the table to see if you can reach it." He then demonstrated how she could reach the marker by walking instead of climbing. He assertively told her what to do, "Climb down and walk around the table." As she chose to cooperate, he encouraged her by saying, "You did it! You got off the chair and walked over to reach the marker. Good for you!"

The more often you can redirect your child's behavior *before* she is in deep trouble, the more you will help her develop impulse-control. You can use each moment of conflict (or even potential conflict) as a teaching and learning opportunity. Because of the hectic pace of life today, parents are less and less available to redirect children. Usually a problem has already occurred before parents intervene; this is a contributing factor in the increased impulsivity characteristic of today's children.

FINDING POSITIVE INTENTIONS BRINGS OUT THE BEST IN PEOPLE

Around Christmas, I watched a television show called *Mrs. Claus*. It was the story of a young immigrant girl who lived with her father, but whose mother and baby sister were still in the old country. The father worked constantly to earn enough money to reunite the family, while his daughter spent her days getting into fairly serious trouble.

The pivotal point in the story came after the girl had stolen some eggs. She planned to throw the eggs out the window in hopes of hitting a police officer on the head. Mrs. Claus observed her sitting on the windowsill, just about to hurl the eggs, and said kindly, "I see you found the lost eggs. Now we can have fresh eggs for breakfast. How lucky for us that you are here." Mrs. Claus attributed a positive motive to the girl's actions and a bond formed between the two. This bond brought out the best in the girl, and provided the motivation she needed to shift her thinking and actions from being hurtful to being helpful. When you attribute positive motives to your child, you both feel closer. You set the stage for positive thinking and a happy outcome.

Your discovery of positive reasons for your child's words or actions encourages him to see the best in himself. Let him know that you are there to teach and guide, not humiliate or punish. If you align yourself with your child, you will build a safe atmosphere in which he will want to learn sound ways to reach his goals.

THERE'S NO TIME LIKE THE PRESENT!

Begin right now attributing positive intent to all people, starting with yourself. If you are ready to embrace the idea that mistakes are opportunities to learn, and to pass this belief on to your children, you must begin with yourself.

- Attribute a positive motive to drivers who cut you off in traffic by thinking, "You wanted to get somewhere on time and are rushing; I've felt that way, too."

- Attribute a positive motive to clerks who seem rude by thinking, "You want everyone to know you are having a hard day; I have felt that way, too."

- The next time you make a mistake, attribute a positive motive to yourself and reflect on what you will change next time. When you do this for others and for yourself, you will have harnessed the Power of Love and the words you will want to offer to your children will come naturally.

- To help you be successful in turning a conflict moment into a teaching moment, remember to start your interactions with, "You wanted _____."

The skill of attributing positive intent is rooted in the Power of Love.

EMPATHY—THE POWERFUL PARTNER
OF POSITIVE INTENT

Sometimes attributing positive intent is not enough. Sometimes children become so angry they simply cannot "hear" *anything,* including your message about a positive intent. When your child is so upset that he has lost all self-control, the skill you must employ is empathy. Empathy represents the next stop on your journey.

Positive intent and empathy offer a powerful combination. If you use these two skills together, while maintaining your own self-control, you can transform almost any situation from chaos into a teaching and learning moment.

8

Empathy:
Handling the Fussing
and the Fits

I adore the Olympics. One night, during the 1998 Winter Olympics, my assistant and I were driving back to our hometown in Florida after having conducted an out-of-town workshop. I was determined to be home by 8:00 P.M. in order to watch every minute of the Olympics. Heavy traffic scratched my plans. This disappointment did not sit well with me, and I refused to accept the fact that I was missing the Olympics. I asked my assistant to find the Olympics on the radio. When she said, "I don't think they're on the radio," I exploded. First I negated the situation, "They have to be on the radio." Then I attacked: "What kind of country is this? We can go to the moon, but we can't broadcast the world's greatest sports events on the radio?" I was raving because the world was not going my way.

This was not my first adult fit. Nor would it be my last. Over the years, I have become aware of how many fits we adults have. I estimate that adults are throwing fits more than fifty percent of the time. Adult fits range from mild (complaining, whining), to moderate (verbally attacking through criticism, name-calling, and judgments), to severe (hurting one another).

"Fussing and fits" is my general term for the emotional upset people display when the world does not go their way. A toddler scribbling on the walls cries when you take away the crayon. A four-year-old boy who wants crackers ignores the fact that you have none. His nine-year-old brother slams doors when you deny his request to sleep at his friend's house on a school night. A thirty-year-old woman wants her children to get up, get dressed, and eat breakfast. She may have a fit when one child refuses to wear long pants. A fifty-two-year-old grandfather throws a fit when the car in front of him on the freeway has its blinker on unnecessarily.

Disappointment is tough. We all need to learn how to handle frustration, and we certainly have ample opportunities to do so ourselves and to teach our children. Every time your child whines, stomps her feet, or screams, you receive such an opportunity. To teach children to cope with disappointment, you need the skill of empathy.

You must teach your child how to handle disappointment and frustration.

I cannot stress enough the importance of empathy. Empathy is not weak-kneed permissiveness, nor is it passive acceptance of misbehavior. Your empathy helps your child organize herself, process disappointment, and move on. When you empathize with your upset child, you help her restore the cooperative spirit which allows her to do as you have asked.

Parents often ask me, "How can I get my children to happily do what I want, when I want?" I surely do not have the answer. (I'm still working through the absence of the Olympics from the radio!) However, I do know some helpful approaches. First, use the Power of Acceptance: This moment is as it is. Only when you accept the moment that exists can you offer empathy to others, staying relaxed enough to see the other person's perspective. When you resist what is, you become so enmeshed in your own perspective that no one else's seems to matter. Second, let go of your expectation that your child can give up what she wants in order to follow your wishes and still be happy about it. Third, stop trying to control your child's feelings. She has a right to all of her feelings. Without them, she would be lost. Feelings serve us as our core system for discerning right from wrong. Feelings are our moral navigators. We do not need to stop having them. We need to express them more appropriately.

THE SKILL OF EMPATHY

Many people mistake being empathic with trying to "happy up" others and rescue them. Empathy means understanding what another person feels, and having insight into his or her thoughts and actions. When you empathize with your children, they realize that you care about their ideas and feelings. Your empathic response to your child's emotions helps her to feel validated and gain insight into herself. True empathy demands that you listen to your child's feelings and thoughts *without needing to change them.*

When you empathize with your child, you teach your children the following:

1. self-awareness
2. self-control
3. recognition and acceptance of emotions
4. the knowledge that emotions can be expressed to others
5. the ability to label feelings with appropriate words
6. the understanding that feelings influence behavior
7. the realization that relationships are based on mutual esteem and communication.

Your empathy builds a foundation for your child's sound emotional development. It plants the seed for a healthy family and sets the cornerstone for a happy, loving life. You can give yourself and your family no greater gift than an empathic environment.

You realize how vital empathy is when you see what becomes of people who never develop it. Heinous criminals—rapists, child molesters, and perpetrators of family violence—lack empathy. Only when empathy is absent can people willfully hurt others.

Think about yourself. When frustrations and fears surround you, are you more likely to scream at the people you love? At such moments you simply cannot see or care about anyone else's perspective. When it is your child who is feeling frustrated or fearful, no matter how pressured you feel, in order to connect with your child, you must put your worries aside and think about her viewpoint.

Hundreds of studies have shown that the way in which a parent treats a child—with harsh discipline or warm understanding—has deep, lasting consequences for that child's emotional health. Recently, too, hard data has shown that being raised by emotionally adept parents is itself a great advantage for a child (Hendrick, 1992). The way in which spouses handle feelings between themselves, in addition to their direct dealings with their child, teaches a powerful lesson to that child. One 1994 study showed that emotionally competent spouses did much better at helping their children deal with life's ups and downs. That study also showed that children of parents who are adept (instead of inept) at handling feelings have many emotional advantages (Harris, 1989). These children:

◆ Get along more easily with their parents and show more affection.
◆ Better soothe themselves when they become upset, and get upset less frequently.
◆ Are more relaxed physically, with lower levels of stress hormones.

Socially, the children of emotionally adept parents:

◆ Are more popular.
◆ Are viewed by teachers as more socially skilled.
◆ Have fewer behavior problems, such as aggressiveness.

Cognitively, they:

◆ Pay attention better and learn more effectively.
◆ Have higher achievement scores than others do in math and reading when they reach third grade.

The moral of this story is the theme of this book. We must discipline ourselves first and our children second. Some people seem to empathize naturally with others, while others find the skill difficult to acquire. Whatever your skill level, you can always improve your emotional competency.

How you respond to your child's upset teaches her how to respond to the upset of others.

HOW DO YOU RESPOND TO YOUR CHILD'S UPSET?

The way in which you respond to your child's distress teaches her how to respond to the distress of others. Two factors tend to shape the amount of empathy with which a parent responds. The first factor is the parent's own level of upset: A calm parent responds much more empathically than one who is near the edge. The second factor is the degree to which the parent equates misbehavior with disrespect. If you perceive your child's misbehavior as disrespectful, your ability to offer empathy will plummet. If, instead, you perceive your child's fussiness as a signal that she is having trouble handling a disappointment, you are in a better position to summon your ability to empathize.

Before you can empathize, you must stop equating disobedience with disrespect.

EXERCISE: Write how you would respond to the following situation. Jot down the exact words you would probably say.

SITUATION: You give your child a warning that bedtime is in ten minutes. She throws herself on the floor and screams, "I'm not going to bed! I hate you!"

YOUR LIKELY RESPONSE: _____.

Did you ignore the tantrum, give in and postpone bedtime, punish your child, or show empathy? Your response indicates your parenting style. Researchers have identified four styles. Here are brief descriptions of them. Which characterizes you?

Style #1: You ignore feelings. Some adults treat a child's distress as a bother. They fail to use emotional moments to get closer to the child, or teach her about emotions. The child's emotions are ignored.

Heather, age 9, was visiting a cousin she adored. Her dad said, "Heather, we leave in ten minutes." A little later, he said, "Five more minutes, then we go." Finally, he said, "Time to go, Heather." Heather immediately dropped to the ground, screaming, "I won't go. You can't make me." Her dad responded, "I told you ten minutes ago that we were leaving. There is no excuse for this." Heather kept thrashing on the floor until Dad picked her up and said, "Now we are going." As he carried her out the door, he said, "As you can see, Heather is out of control. See you later." He placed her in the back seat of the car as if she were a package.

Parents who employ the ignoring style simply do not acknowledge feelings. Emotions that underlie misbehavior are considered irrelevant. My guess is that Heather probably started expressing disappointment using tantrums when she was around eighteen months old. Since no one ever taught her a better way, she continued to throw tantrums at age nine. Look back at your response to the situation above. Did you ignore your child's feelings and focus entirely on the bedtime issue?

Style #2: You let the child cope alone. Some adults notice a child's feelings but expect her to handle them independently. Like parents who ignore feelings, these adults rarely step in to help the child manage emotions. They may try to soothe, distract, or bribe the children to end the period of upset or anger. Some common ways of noticing feelings with the aim of ending them are saying:

1. "Why are you sad?" or, "Why are you angry?" This teaches children to analyze feelings, not feel them. It says *think,* not feel.
2. "Pull yourself together. It's not that bad." This teaches children to "stuff" their feelings. They learn to deny their feelings, and ultimately to deny the feelings of others.
3. "Are you okay? Everything will be fine. Ssssh. Ssssh. There is no need to cry." This teaches children that their feelings upset others. They learn to take care of others' feelings at the expense of their own. This promotes "other-control," not self-control.

Here's an example.

Michael wanted to visit his friend Eric. His mother explained that this did not fit in with the family's plans to go to a barbecue at his aunt's house. Michael angrily dismissed his mother's explanation and threatened to ignore everyone at the barbecue. His mom then sent him to his room to calm down. He stayed briefly but came out and verbally attacked his mother with rude remarks. She advised him to go back and cool down before things got worse. Finally Michael collapsed, sobbing, in his room. After fifteen minutes, his mother came to him and said, "It's not the end of the world. You can see Eric another day. Why don't you take your new video game to show your cousins?"

This mother failed to help Michael feel and accept his emotions so he could work through his disappointment and move on. She sent him off to "magically" cool down twice and then bribed him to suppress his feelings by using the video game as a distraction.

Style #3: You punish feelings. Some adults criticize their children's feelings. They may forbid *any* display of anger or punish irritability. Such parents treat their child's emotions, especially negative ones, as signs of disrespect. The hallmark statement representing this style is "I'll give you something to cry about."

One afternoon, Jerod's father, Mark, told Jerod they had to run errands. Jerod hated errands and asked to stay home alone. His father replied, "No, it isn't safe. You'll come with me." Jerod screamed, "That's no fair, you idiot!" Mark grabbed Jerod by the shoulders, shook him hard, and shouted, "Don't you ever talk to me like that again!"

Mark lashed out at Jerod's rude expression of anger and threatened the boy with physical harm. Both Mark and Jerod had lost control.

Style #4: You offer empathy and help with emotions. Some parents understand that misbehavior represents an intense feeling without an appropriate outlet. These parents realize that moments when their child is upset are opportunities to teach emotional good sense.

Arthur badly wanted inline skates. His mother had offered to help him with strategies to earn the money and buy the skates, but Arthur wanted the skates immediately, and he became belligerent. One morning, Arthur was dawdling as if he wanted to miss the school bus. When his mom said, "Hurry up, Arthur," he sarcastically responded, "What do you think I am doing?" His mom felt ready to strangle him, but she breathed deeply, using the Power of Acceptance, and told herself, "This moment is as it is. Relax." Then she tried empathy. "Arthur, you seem upset," she said. Arthur resisted his mother's nurturing and responded, "What do you care? You're not the one without inline skates." Finally, she realized that this obnoxious behavior was Arthur's way of expressing his disappointment.

Mom then opened her heart to her son and replied, "It's hard to want something and not get it immediately." As Arthur started to relax, tears came to his eyes. "Mom, everybody is skating on the street but me." Mom responded, "You think that if you don't get in there soon too, you may lose your friends." Arthur tearfully said, "Yes, I won't have *any* friends." Mom answered, "It's scary to feel left out. I will not buy you the skates, but we can work out a plan so you can earn the money and get out there faster to skate with your friends. I also think that if you ask one or two of your friends to sleep over, you can stay connected until you get your skates." With sullen movements, Arthur headed out the door.

This mother helped her son process and express his emotions in a socially acceptable manner. When she reflected back the feelings behind his behavior, she opened the communication channels between herself and her child. He saw that she was not the "bad guy" but rather an ally. She listened from her heart, so she heard Arthur's unspoken fears of being left out and friendless. She responded to the fears, yet held the limit. A parent's understanding need not change the limits on behavior, but it does help a child accept them.

Go back to the exercise where you wrote your response to the child throwing a fit because she did not want to go to bed. What style did you use? What style do you typically use?

FIRST, FEEL YOUR OWN FEELINGS

To understand the emotions of another person, you must first accept and acknowledge your own. This is a challenge, because most of us have been programmed to deny our feelings. Many of our parents taught us that if our feelings were hurt or we didn't like something, we ought to ignore our emotions. They said things such as: "It's not that bad"; "Don't worry about it"; or "Don't think about it." It is impossible for us to teach children skills we have not mastered ourselves. Therefore, we must learn to *feel* our feelings and to *express* them in acceptable ways. Doing both requires skill.

Until you *feel* your feelings, you will not allow your children to experience theirs. Thinking about your feelings and feeling them are two different things. Many adults think about their emotions and confuse thoughts with feelings. If you ask a friend, "How do you feel?" and she responds, "I feel like nothing is going my way," your friend has expressed a thought, not a feeling. Your friend *explained* how she came to feel a certain way, but not what the feeling is. To get in touch with your thoughts and feel your feelings, you must know the difference between them. Practice discerning whether what you are focusing on is a thought or a feeling. The difference matters enormously.

When you think one thing and feel another, you will experience confusion. When you align your thoughts with your feelings, you will become centered. From this position, you can communicate effectively with others. Now, just for practice, how do you feel? Did you answer with an emotional word such as happy, sad, or scared? If you answered without using a feeling word, it was probably a thought.

To empathize with your children, you must first offer yourself empathy and compassion. You must accept your feelings instead of telling yourself, I shouldn't feel like this. Out loud, tell yourself, "I feel frustrated and it's okay." If you don't verbalize your feelings, you will act them out like children. Of all the languages in the world, the most difficult language in which to communicate is the language of feelings. Emotions are energy in motion and they can be difficult to label, but you should do the best you can. Feel the emotional energy in yourself, label it, and express it verbally. If you don't, you will fuss and throw fits. The choice is yours.

Roberta, a mother of three, was returning to work after staying home with her children for years. She felt scared about her job and her abilities. Usually she succeeded in hiding her terror at work, but at home it was a different story. She felt depressed, angry, and anxious. Roberta tried to stay busy to avoid her worries, but she simply could not escape a deep sense of inadequacy.

Roberta's fear manifested itself in her actions at home. She tried to silence her self-doubt by being positive and by convincing her children that they were splendid. As Roberta struggled to feel better inside, she made comments such as, "Jamie, you are wonderful," and "Mardell, you are such a good little girl." Desperate to stifle her anxiety, she attempted to control and forbid feelings her children might express. She made comments such as, "You are all right," "There's no need to be upset," and "I will not tolerate outbursts." Roberta could continue using her children to play out her own emotional issues until she achieved a level of comfort at work, or she could become conscious of her own battle with emotions. Parents cannot use children to reflect their own internal state and at the same time help their children recognize their feelings. As an adult, you can consciously choose to be egocentric or empathic. Whichever you choose is what you will teach your children.

Of all the languages in the world, the most difficult language in which to communicate is the language of feelings.

Practice feeling your feelings today, recognizing that feelings are like the weather. Some days are sunny, others are cloudy, and some bring storms. Weather simply comes and goes. Resisting a rainy day is insane. Use the Power of Acceptance—the moment is as it is—and relax. Feel your internal weather patterns come and go. You are not bad if it rains today!

The more skilled you become at reading your own feelings and those of others, the more caring you will be. Conversely, the less skilled you are at empathizing with others, the less caring you will be. In our Western culture, people rarely verbalize their emotions. You must read the feelings of others through nonverbal cues such as tone of voice and facial expression. In fact, ninety percent or more of an emotional message is nonverbal. Practice reading your child's nonverbal cues. You might say, "Look at your face. You seem excited," or, "Your body seems tense. Something on your mind?"

Notice that these comments are voiced as inquiries. Use your voice inflection to express this. You must never *tell* another person how to feel. When you make educated guesses, your child can either confirm your guess or correct you. Confirmation can come in two forms, nonverbal and verbal. Nonverbal confirmation may come in an exaggeration of the feeling described. The child's face and body will say, Yes, I do feel sad, by looking even sadder. Verbally, the child may confirm your reading by telling you what bothers her, or she will correct you, saying something like, "No, I'm just tired."

EMOTIONAL COACHING: SEE, FEEL, HEAR

To help children who have lost control or feel distraught, you must offer empathy. Empathy has two sides, one cognitive and one emotional. The cognitive side means you see from the other person's perspective. The emotional side means you understand her feelings. When your child is upset, your task is to act as a mirror to her feelings and experience. Reflect back to her your best guess as to what you believe she is experiencing. Offer her a clear description of her feelings and perceptions. Your observations will help your child to "see herself" and become aware of her situation. When your child achieves an awareness of her feelings, she has taken the first step toward managing these feelings. She is better able to become organized again.

When your child is upset, your task is to act like a mirror.

When you empathize, you symbolically say, I see you, I hear you, and I feel you. There is no room for judgments in these reflective statements.

When your child is upset, use these three types of statements to let her know you understand:

- Reflect back what you see.
- Reflect back what you feel.
- Reflect back what you hear.

EMPATHY HELPS ORGANIZE THE BRAIN

The brain always works as a whole, but for discussion's sake, it can be viewed as operating on three levels. The lower level deals mainly with survival issues; the middle level deals mainly with feelings; and the upper level focuses more on thinking and problem solving. When children become upset, they may be operating from the middle levels of their brain. This is evident by their whining ("This isn't fair"), their complaining ("This is stupid"), or their name-calling ("You're an idiot"). They are expressing their feelings inappropriately in a verbal manner. To help these children, reflect back what you think they are feeling. This helps them move into higher-organized processes. Children who display their feelings more through physical tantrums or actions (stomping their feet, throwing objects) are operating out of the lower levels of the brain. These children are expressing their feelings inappropriately. To help children gain control over an out-of-control body, it is very helpful to reflect what you see. This helps move the child from the survival level to a feeling level. So, if a child is out of control, flailing her body, describe what you see: "Your arms are going like this, your feet are stomping, your eyebrows are pulled tight." (Demonstrate it for the child.) More than likely her body will organize and her mouth will take over. ("Stop it. I hate you!") Now she has moved to verbalizing her feelings inappropriately. At this point you can reflect back what you think she is feeling: "You seem very angry." This will help the child organize her emotions enough to begin expressing the problem. "You won't let me do anything," she might venture. To help the child begin solving her problem, it is important to reflect back what you thought you heard. "You don't think I let you do what you want to do?" At this point, the child may be capable of sharing the real issue with you: "I wanted to play with Carmen and you said I had to do my homework." With the problem out in the open, you can then sum up what happened and teach the child another way of expressing herself: "You were disappointed when you heard you couldn't play with Carmen. It is hard not to be able to do what we want to do. What can I do to help you get started on your homework so you can visit Carmen sooner?"

You do not always need to use all three kinds of statements (see, feel, hear) to build empathy, but the combination is powerful. Each type of reflection becomes a bit more abstract. When you reflect what you see, your words are concrete. When you reflect what you have heard, you must listen carefully and understand the child's

meaning. When you reflect back your child's feelings, you are relying on a certain level of guesswork. If you are wrong, though, your
child will usually correct you.

**Understanding does not change the limits on behavior. It
does help a child accept them more easily.**

YOUR INTENT IS CRITICAL: ACCEPTANCE IS THE KEY

Your intent is critical to the use of empathy. If you intend to *make*
your child stop acting or feeling a certain way and you try to use
empathy to manipulate her, your tone of voice will betray your
motives. I once heard a frustrated parent say, "I know it's hard to
leave. Now, go get in the car." Her attempt at empathy was aimed
at getting her child into the car, so of course it did not help defuse
the situation.

If you intend to help your child feel—and label—her feelings,
and realize that you understand, you must speak from your heart.
Empathy is not a manipulation strategy. It comes from the Power of
Acceptance. You must first accept where your child is before you
can facilitate her willingness to change. Acceptance is love and
compassion in action, and it teaches their value.

Reflecting Back What You See

Jake stomped into the house and threw down his backpack so
hard, it knocked over the chair. Mom reached out to touch him on
the shoulder to get his attention and he jerked away. Compassionately and with total acceptance of her son, she said, "You pulled
your arm back just like this [she demonstrates the action] when I
reached to touch your shoulder." Jake looked up and made eye
contact with his mom for the first time since he entered the house.
At that point she further reflected back what she saw. "You came
in stomping your feet, your face looked strained, and you threw

your backpack so hard the chair fell. Something terrible must have happened at school." By reflecting back what she saw, Mom helped Jake become calm enough to begin talking about his upsetting experience.

When reflecting back what you see, focus on the child's body. Pay close attention to facial expression and posture. If you reflect back what you see to your child without using the Power of Acceptance, your tone will be sarcastic as you attempt to manipulate your child into "happying up." It is critical that you be conscious of your intent in reflecting. You are there to help the child regain control of himself. This is done through helping the child gain self-awareness. Jake was *physically acting out* his feelings. Saying what you see is the most helpful avenue to helping him understand how his feelings are driving his actions.

Reflecting Back What You Feel

Children are not born knowing how to handle emotions, so they often rely on unproductive strategies. Children will attempt to get you to feel the way they are feeling. It is their way of communicating their internal states. If you are feeling frustrated, there is a good chance that your child is, too. If you are at a loss to understand what she is feeling, reflect on your own feelings. To reflect back what your child might be feeling, focus on her body language. Do not rely too much on your child's words. They can be misleading. ("I'm fine.") Listen for the feelings beneath the words. Reflect them back to your child. Common reflections are "You seem angry," "You sound sad," or, "You seem really excited."

Mistakes to Avoid When Reflecting Feelings

◆ **Reflecting rather than questioning.** The purpose of questioning is to elicit information. The purpose of reflecting is to increase your child's self-awareness. If you are asking questions, you are *not* reflecting feelings. Questions ask children to think, not feel. Children then grow up like us, unable to distinguish between thinking and feeling. Avoid asking questions like:

"You're pretty sad, aren't you?"

"Why are you angry?"

◆ **Sounding all-knowing**. Your reflections need to be tentative and correctable. You want to leave room for your child's response or possible correction. Statements that sound all-knowing are *not* reflections. For example:

"You must be feeling sad."

"I know you are angry."

"You are angry."

Tentative inquiries such as "You seem angry" are more helpful.

◆ **Noticing feelings with the intent of altering them so that you feel more comfortable**. Parents sometimes say things like, "I tried reflecting. I said, 'You seem angry,' but it didn't work." These parents assume that the reflected feeling will vanish, leaving the child suddenly happy again. Empathy is not a tool to eliminate children's feelings. It is a process that helps children recognize and understand their feelings and themselves. Feelings do not need to be fixed. They are not wrong or dangerous. Feelings are a part of our humanity, helping us grow and learn. Without them, life is empty.

Reflecting Back What You Hear

To reflect back what you hear, listen closely to your child and then summarize the essence of her statements, paraphrasing in your own words what you think she has communicated. Your reflections offer tangible evidence to your child that you have listened to her with empathy and have understood her perspective. A child might say, "You can't make me take a shower. It's my body." You could reflect back the following to the child, "You want me to know that it's important to you to be responsible for taking care of your own body." The child might respond, "Yeah." You can then begin to solve the problem by offering consequences, or whatever skill you choose. In this situation, you might say, "To take care of your body, you must shower every day. When will you be taking care of your body today?"

With a nonverbal (young) child, you must summarize the expressions of her body. If her face looks angry, say, "Your face is telling me that you wanted to do that by yourself." If she kicks the door, you could say, "You foot is saying, 'Let's go.'" Then prompt the child to say, "Go," or, "Bye-bye."

ANGER: THE MOST DIFFICULT EMOTION TO REFLECT

Sadness shows up in posture (being curled over like a steamed shrimp). It may also show up as tears, pouting, and withdrawal. Happiness announces itself with smiles, joyful shouts, and hugs. Fear comes out in nail-biting, fidgeting, and wide eyes. Many adults will tolerate these expressions if they do not reach extremes. However, anger may make itself known through kicking, hitting, spitting, and swearing—behaviors that tend to scare adults. Therefore, adult empathy for anger is rare. Paradoxically, though, empathy is the best skill you can use to help your child gain control over angry emotions and behaviors. In light of the dangerous aggression many children display today, teaching ourselves to reflect anger would be extremely helpful to children and to society.

Research on infants shows that parents are more likely to mirror positive emotions. When a baby smiles, the dad smiles back. When a pouty face is presented, dad lowers his lip to mirror the child's sadness. However, parents usually respond to anger with a different emotion. Rarely will you see an angry infant receive a mirrored grumpy face in return that says, "You seem angry." This special treatment of anger becomes more skewed as the child gets older. Parents usually ignore angry girls, while they lavish angry boys with negative attention such as bribes, threats, and spanking. In order for children to become aware of their feelings, including anger, so that they can then label, express, and control their emotions, parents must start to behave differently.

Girls whose anger is ignored learn that they are not entitled to feel anger, so they subvert it. In adult life, this anger surfaces as nagging, criticism, and depression. Denied their full emotional range, girls fail to develop full self-awareness. They have trouble pinpointing what they want and expressing their desires.

Boys who receive undue attention when they are angry often grow up to be violent men. Men commit 92 percent of all violent crimes. You can see how bribery grows up into extortion, threats become stalking, and spanking leads to battering.

Work diligently on your *Seven Powers for Self-Control* and start reflecting back your children's anger. They need to learn how to manage it. Children often use inept expressions they learn from parents and others. Listen for the emotion underlying children's words in the exclamations below and note how a parent can reflect those emotions.

Children's Words	Parental Reflections
"You're stupid."	"You seem frustrated with me."
"I hate you."	"You seem angry with me."
"He's a jerk."	"You seem irritated with your brother."

PUTTING IT ALL TOGETHER: DEALING WITH TANTRUMS

A temper tantrum is an uncontrolled outburst of anger that usually arises from a child's (or an adult's) thwarted efforts to control a situation. The tantrum says, "I have tried desperately to make the world go my way. Now I'm so frazzled I can barely speak. I feel terrified, helpless, and powerless."

Both children and adults have temper tantrums. Think of your last tantrum and how awful it was to think that you might have hurt someone during it. Think of the comfort you would feel if you knew that although you had spun out of control, someone else stayed calm to assure your safety and that of your loved ones.

Parents need to understand temper tantrums and help children move through their rage without coming to feel abandoned. Rejection, abandonment, and shame create more rage, and increase the odds of more tantrums. A calm adult close at hand creates safety for the child, and teaches children that their anger and rage is powerless, thereby reducing the chance of future tantrums. If you can help your child move *through* a temper tantrum, you can then begin teaching her better ways to affect her world or cope with it.

For children between the ages of fifteen months and three years, tantrums are typical. For these small children, the battle between dependence and independence rages. They are constantly asking themselves, "Do I do it my way or my parent's way?" For toddlers, the conflict between "My way or the grown-up's way?" is intense, and takes one to two years to resolve. The question resurfaces during adolescence and sometimes during the forties. Although most parents blame themselves for temper tantrums, the outbursts reflect the child's inner struggle. Actions by parents may trigger the tantrums, but they are not the root cause. Many toddlers have daily tantrums, and flare-ups strike at least once a week for most preschoolers. Certain adult practices encourage tantrums. These include inconsistency, expectations that are too high, undue strictness, overprotectiveness, and overindulgence.

Remember, only by staying in control yourself can you help your out-of-control child. (As the flight attendants say, "Put your own oxygen mask on first. Then put the mask on your child.") Shift your focus from stopping tantrums to helping your child move through them by reflecting back what you see, feel, and hear. Pay close attention to the next example. Be alert to the mother's reflections of what she sees, feels, and hears.

Melissa, age 6, hated anything that itched. She especially disliked tags in clothing. One frantic morning Melissa and her mother, Bobbie Jo, found themselves in power struggle after power struggle. As the time for the carpool to arrive was approaching, Bobbie Jo pulled out a new tee shirt and said, "Put this on. You need to hurry." Melissa took the shirt, but the minute she saw the tag, she went into a tirade. In an attempt to move the child out of the house in time, Bobbie Jo located some scissors and headed toward Melissa to remove the tag. Upon seeing the scissors, Melissa said, "I can cut it out myself," and dashed off on a fruitless search for her own small scissors. Meanwhile the clock was ticking and the carpool was due, so Bobbie Jo grabbed the shirt and clipped the tag. Upon seeing that, Melissa totally lost it. She collapsed to the floor, screaming and thrashing about.

Bobbie Jo looked at her child and thought, I don't like you very much this morning. She resisted the temptation to feel guilty for that thought and remembered "Discipline yourself first and the child second." She took several deep breaths and told herself, "This moment is as it is. Relax and solve the problem." She started describing what she saw. "Melissa, your arms are going like this." (She demonstrates.) Melissa continued flailing her arms and hollering. Bobbie Jo ignored the hollering and focused on her body: "You face is scrunched up." Bobbie Jo made her face look as much like Melissa's as possible. Melissa looked up and made eye contact with her mother. Bobbie Jo continued to breathe and knew she was starting to reach her daughter. She said, "Your whole body is telling me you feel angry." Melissa said, pouting, "*I* wanted to cut the tag." Mom recognized her daughter's return to an almost rational state and said, "You wanted to cut it, but I cut it." Melissa crossed her arms and her body began to tense up again. Bobbie Jo responded, "You were so disappointed and frustrated that it was just too much to bear. This has been a rough morning for the both of us." Melissa began to sob and crawled into her mom's lap. Bobbie Jo rocked her gently and they stayed connected until the carpool ride arrived.

In this story, Bobbie Jo kept herself calm enough to help her child through her tantrum. When you remain calm, you will be most helpful to your child. If calmness is not possible, removing yourself from the child (or the child from you) is the next best approach. You might say, "I am too upset to help you now. I am going to my room to calm myself down." Conversely, you might say,

"You and I are both upset. You go to your room and I will go to mine to calm down." If your child tries to hit or kick you, restrain her and say, "I will not let you hurt me or anyone else. I am here to keep you safe. When I think both you and I are safe, I will let you go."

Research involving eight hundred families showed that parents managed tantrums with the following methods: complying with the child's demands (74.6 percent); demanding that the child stop and criticizing the child (53.6 percent); physical restraint (48.2 percent); isolating the child for a period of time (31.1 percent); reasoning with the child (26.8 percent); and spanking the child (20.4 percent). When parents react to temper tantrums by caving in, rejecting, abandoning, or shaming their child, they increase the likelihood of more outbursts. Yet these are among the most common methods parents employ.

Research has also shown that ill-tempered children become ill-tempered adults. Children who were still having temper tantrums at age ten were studied for the next thirty years of their lives. The explosive tendencies of these children carried through into adulthood (Caspi, Bern, and Elder, 1987).

IT TAKES PRACTICE, BUT IT'S WORTH IT

A mother I trained to use the *Seven Basic Discipline Skills* saw me recently. She hugged me and said, "Thank you! You saved my daughter's life." One of her teenage daughter's close friends had died in a car accident and the woman's daughter had grieved deeply over the loss of her friend. The mother told me that before studying with me, she would have tried to "fix" her daughter's feelings by saying things such as, "I know it's bad, but you will soon feel better. Remember the good times and stay busy." This mother was deeply grateful that she had learned to accept her daughter's grief as it progressed, and to help her daughter feel her feelings. The well-meaning parents of another friend of the deceased girl tried to minimize their daughter's grief. Tragically, she committed suicide. The mother I had coached said, "My daughter looked at me and said, 'I wish she'd had a mom like you. She'd still be alive.'" The power of empathy is phenomenal.

THERE'S NO TIME LIKE THE PRESENT

Start now to use the skill of empathy. Use it when your child is upset to help her feel understood and thus more inclined to cooperate. Empathy, like all of the *Seven Basic Discipline Skills*, is used in combination. Once you offer your child empathy, you might follow with the need to set a limit, or offer a consequence. Practice doing the following:

◆ **Feel your own feelings**. Where does anger arise in your body? What does it feel like? Where do you feel sadness, happiness, or anxiety? How do they feel?

◆ **Accept your feelings and express them** by practicing completing the following statement: "I feel _____." Fill in the blank with a feeling word.

◆ **Catch yourself saying**, "I shouldn't feel _____," and replace the statement with, "I feel _____, and it's okay."

◆ **Provide empathy to your upset child by reflecting back to her what you see, what you hear, and what you sense she is feeling**. Do not judge. Describe.

◆ **Listen to your child's feelings and thoughts without trying to change them**. Your child is capable of change if you show her a clear mirror.

◆ **Disconnect disrespect from disobedience**. To do this, take two deep breaths, use the Power of Acceptance, and tell yourself, "This moment is as it is." Then respond calmly to your out-of-control child.

9

*

Consequences:
Helping Children
Learn from Their Mistakes

When I noticed recently that my favorite jeans were getting tight, I decided to exercise more and stick to a healthy diet. I kept up my new regimen for two weeks and then, feeling proud, rewarded myself with a new pair of pants. Soon after this, business travel disrupted my healthy routine and the pants (both new and old) got tighter again.

Immediately, I began beating myself up with fault-finding self-talk. I said to myself, "Why am I so stupid? I never finish anything. I deserve to be fat and ugly." I felt guilty for backsliding and considered myself a failure. In those few weeks, I had replayed all my childhood lessons on reward and punishment. For following my plan, I rewarded myself (new pants). For failing, I punished myself (Becky-bashing self-talk). Neither the reward nor the punishment effectively motivated me to resume my healthful ways. Upon reflection, I realized that rewards and punishments had never really helped me to learn or grow.

Punishments and rewards are consequences that parents often use to try to manipulate the actions of children. Parents sometimes equate punishments and rewards with discipline. One parent with whom I worked had an aggressive child. I was showing her how to *teach* her child to communicate with words instead of fists. Finally, she said, "I can do that, but when does he get his punishment?" Many parents believe that nothing has been accomplished or learned until a child receives a punishment. Such parents often use rewards and punishments to the exclusion of all other discipline strategies.

Do any of these comments sound familiar? "Finish your homework right after school or there will be no television tonight." "What a wonderful report card. Each A is worth $2.00. Each B is worth $1.00." "You know not to hit your brother. Go to your room for ten minutes."

A reward or a punishment is based on an adult's judging a child's behavior to be "good" or "bad," and then delivering something good or bad to express that judgment. When adults rely regularly on rewards and punishments, children come to depend on the judgment of others as the basis for their own moral decisions. Rewards and punishments create "other-control." Children grow up focusing on what others demand of them and what they in turn will demand from others. Many parents are surprised to learn that consequences can take forms other than rewards and punishments. In this chapter you will learn how to shift from using punishments and rewards to using other types of consequences.

Consequences help children think about the effects of their choices and draw conclusions about the wisdom of those choices. This builds responsibility—the ability to respond appropriately to situations. Consequences can take the form of natural consequences, imposed consequences, or problem solving. Children who experience these types of consequences develop their own inner compass for moral living.

A LOOK AT THE INSANITY OF OVERRELYING ON PUNISHMENTS AND REWARDS

Tomorrow, I want *you* to meet me at Johns Hopkins Hospital. At that time, I want you to perform open-heart surgery on me. To help you, I will use punishments and rewards. If you do the surgery, but I die, then your car will be repossessed (punishment). If I survive the surgery and recover, you will receive a new car (reward).

Could the punishment or reward help you perform heart surgery? Obviously not. Whether you lose your car or win a new one does not help you perform heart surgery because you (at least most of you) are unequipped to do it. Often, we demand behavior from children for which they are equally unprepared. If you use punishment and rewards as a basis for discipline, you will fail to teach children the *skills* they need to behave well. You are holding them accountable for not using behavior skills they have not learned in the first place. As a result, they probably feel inadequate for failing to meet your expectations.

Research indicates that the brain operates differently under the threat of receiving a punishment or losing a reward. Under this threat the brain reacts with increased blood flow to the survival centers of the brain and decreased blood flow to the higher-thought centers. When the brain goes into survival mode, it becomes less capable of planning, pattern-detection, receiving information, creativity, classifying data, and problem solving. Most of us have experienced this restricted blood flow phenomenon during exam time in high school or college. We would frantically search our brains for an answer that we knew we knew, but the answer would not come. The moment we turned in the test and walked outside, free from the pressure, the answer popped into our mind. Children under threat make choices that are biologically driven. Over time, this approach creates impulsive children who resist change and lack the ability to solve problems constructively. Loving guidance requires a shift from the reliance on punishment and rewards to a reliance on consequences in order to help children learn from their mistakes.

LEARNING FROM OUR MISTAKES

How many of you have truly embraced the concept that mistakes represent learning opportunities? Think of the last mistake you perceived yourself to have made. Perhaps it was a small one, but, in your mind, it could have seemed huge. How did you handle your error? Did you tell yourself: "I have made a mistake. What can I learn from it? How can I improve?" Or, did your mind work on the theme of your worthlessness: "How could I have done this? I am horrible. This is all my fault." Perhaps your mind spun to the rottenness of others: "He should have told me. Some friend he is. I would never treat anyone like that."

Conversely, when you feel you have done something right, do you view yourself as worthy and lovable? How do you think we learned these inner dialogues, in which we bash ourselves over the head for our mistakes, or build ourselves up over things we view as accomplishments? You may think that doing this is human nature, but it is not. It is a learned pattern. We have internalized a value system in which we set ourselves up to feel good if we believe ourselves to be right, and bad if we believe ourselves to be wrong. With this system in place, we regularly get into power struggles in desperate attempts to be right, always right. Being wrong is too painful. Here's the mental pattern: Pleasing others makes you good, and disappointing others makes you bad. We pass this system on to our children.

It is not human nature to feel bad about mistakes and good about accomplishments. We learn this mind-set.

The rewards and punishments that most adults impose upon youngsters actually prevent the children from learning from their own mistakes. Parents need to help children behave like *scientists studying their own behavior*. Did the child achieve the desired outcome? If not, what other strategies could the child try next time in a similar situation? Children can learn to examine their own behavior and make changes until their true goals are reached. Such children become conscious of their own actions, and in turn, take responsibility for them. With this consciousness, they feel empowered, increase their emotional intelligence, and learn from their mistakes. Punishments and rewards rely on judgment; consequences rely on reflection.

Parents need to help children behave like scientists studying their own behavior.

INTENTION: THE KEY TO SUCCESS

The skill of using consequences with children grows from the Power of Intention. Your intention in giving consequences will determine their effectiveness. The Power of Intention reminds us to use moments of conflict as opportunities to teach, not punish.

All of us have experienced the consequences of our behavior. Everyone has overeaten or had too much to drink. The consequences may have been uncomfortable, yet most of us have repeated the behavior. At other times, though, we have really learned from an experience, telling ourselves, "I will never do that again," and kept that commitment. What determines whether we change our ways or repeat our mistakes? The answer lies in our intentions. When we impose consequences on ourselves with a punitive or permissive intent, we block our ability to reflect and learn. Instead, these kinds of intentions initiate an orgy of blame. The blame may be aimed at ourselves or at others. Blaming blocks positive change because it focuses you on finding fault instead of finding solutions.

Punitive Intent: Making Them Feel Bad

If you deliver consequences with the aim of making your child feel guilty, you will focus the child on his inadequacy. Two things are then likely: 1) your child may chastise himself and feel bad about himself, or 2) he may blame others for being mean in order to defend himself against feeling bad. Neither of these states will inspire him to reflect. Parents often think that if a child feels bad about some misdeed, he won't repeat the behavior. That is a myth. Here is an example:

Situation: The mother of a nine-year-old child had told him repeatedly to keep his bicycle out of the driveway and store it in the garage. He consistently forgot and finally the bicycle was hit by a car.

◆ **Punitive Response (meant to inspire guilt):** "You didn't listen and now look! Don't cry to me about it. You will not watch TV for a week and you can go without a bike. You are so irresponsible, you don't deserve one."

Here the parent dictated to the child first how he should feel about the smashed bike. "You should feel miserable," was the message. The mother's diatribe actually shielded the boy from experiencing his own feelings of loss, of having disappointed her, and of having failed to heed good advice. Second, she clearly said that if only he had listened to her, these "bad" things never would have occurred. To govern himself, a child needs to know what *he* feels, not what *others* think he should feel. He must also learn to trust his own feelings because they will guide him through life. A person without access to his own feelings is like a rudderless ship.

Blaming inhibits future change from occurring because it focuses you on finding fault, rather than reflecting on solutions.

Permissive Intent: Meant to Rescue the Child

Parents also keep children from learning from their mistakes by rescuing them. When adults withhold (or impose) consequences with the goal of shielding a child from the discomfort that grows naturally out of that child's choices, the child's chance to learn is blocked.

Here are two examples—one illustrates rescuing by withholding consequences; the other illustrates rescuing by imposing consequences.

Situation: The same situation as in the previous example—the bicycle has been left out and then hit by a car.

♦ **Rescuing Response (withholding consequences):** "Look at your bicycle. Oh, honey, don't cry. I tried to warn you, but it will be all right." The child cries and carries on until the mother says, "We'll just buy a new one."

Situation: It is dinnertime and the menu consists of hamburgers, peas, and rice. The whole family knows that Jacob likes only cheeseburgers, but on this night there was no cheese in the house. The evening plan is to have dinner and then go to the park for a pumpkin-lighting ceremony.

♦ **Rescuing Response (imposing consequences):** Jacob announces, "I'm not eating this. I only eat cheeseburgers." His mother responds, "I have no cheese. Just eat your hamburger. Then we can go to the pumpkin-lighting ceremony." Jacob flatly refuses. His mother is worried about him being hungry and cranky at the park, so she says, "Eat the burger or we won't go to the park." He responds, "I don't care. I'm not eating it." The power struggle continues until she finally says, "You decide—eat the hamburger and we go, or don't eat it and we stay home." Jacob's sisters, who love the ceremony, are going "off the deep end" with their fate riding on Jacob's clean plate. In the end, the family stays home.

TEACHING RIGHT FROM WRONG

When your intentions are punitive or permissive, your ultimate goal is really control. You are dictating the feelings your child should have, or shielding him from feelings he would have had. Both these positions cut your child off from his own feelings, which would have resulted naturally from his choices. The child who was made to feel miserable over the bike and the one who was shielded from feeling its loss both missed the opportunity to experience their own emotions about having been careless. Jacob never got to feel hungry at the park. In all three cases, the parents took charge of what their children would feel.

A child who is cut off from his feelings lacks the essential emotional equipment he needs to decide whether he is on course or off course. Lacking this equipment, he cannot decide to change course and depends upon others to direct his life. Your child can grow up learning right from wrong from others, or he can learn it himself through awareness of his emotions. The choice is yours.

If you deliver consequences with the intent of making your child feel guilty, you will not see a lasting change in his behavior.

TEACH EFFECTIVE CONSEQUENCES

When you are about to deliver a consequence, ask yourself, "Where am I focusing my attention?" Intention depends upon attention. If you are focused on what you want your child to feel and think (or, not feel and think), your goal is control. To teach, you must focus on what actually happened, those aspects of your child that you want to highlight, what you want him to reflect upon, and what you want him to learn. Using the bicycle example, let's go through the teaching process.

Being conscious of your intent when delivering consequences is the key to their effectiveness.

◆ **What happened?** Jacob left his bicycle in the driveway and a car destroyed it.
◆ **What aspects of your child do you want to highlight?** The message might be "You can handle this and learn from

it. You can become more conscientious and make better choices."

◆ **What do you want him to reflect upon?** His feelings of loss and his own desire to be more careful.

◆ **What do you want him to learn?** If he does not take care of his belongings, they may not be there for his enjoyment. Replacing material things requires money and effort.

◆ **What you might say:** "Jacob, you seem upset. You left your bike outside and now it is destroyed. What a horrible loss."

Let your child dispose of the old bike himself. You might have to guide his actions: "On Wednesday, take your bike to the curb where it will be picked up by the sanitation workers." If your child asks for a new bike, you could respond, "You left your bike out. If you want another one, you must earn and save money to buy it." If he fusses or throws a fit, it is okay (see chapter 8 on helping children handle frustration). Set your limit, and stick to it. You might help your child come up with a plan to earn money ("You can start earning money by doing special projects around the house").

A child whose loss is handled in this way will learn the following lessons: 1) My choices can have disappointing outcomes. 2) I can have strong feelings and they may hurt. 3) Painful feelings do not excuse me from responsibility for my actions. 4) Authority exists to set limits and help me successfully operate within them. 5) Having things I want demands energy, effort, and care. 6) To get what I want, I may have to wait. 7) When I make a mistake, I can recover and solve the problem I created.

Compare Jacob's example with this one: At the gym, I overheard a woman discussing why she was running late that morning. The previous night, around 8:00 P.M., her eight-year-old son had informed her that he had to build a log cabin for school the next day. His bedtime was 8:30 P.M. To "help" him, she and the boy stayed up past 11:00 P.M. working with Lincoln Logs. She laughed as she described the cabin's leaning walls, but she was glad it was finished on time. After describing how she had rescued her son, she launched into a long harangue about the irresponsibility of children. This mother had taught her child many lessons: 1) People will rescue you from your own choices. 2) If you let others save you, you will be better off than if you didn't. 3) Authority exists to bend the rules for you so you are sure to succeed. 4) Without help from others, you will fail. 5) Doing something by yourself will not be good enough. 6) Waiting until the last minute pays off. 7) You can't fail because others will save you.

Quiz Time—Do You Get It?

Below are five consequences that an adult might deliver to a child. Read each scenario and write **P** for punitive intent, **R** for the intent to rescue, or **T** for the intent to teach.

◆ SITUATION: While eating, Carl intentionally belches and tosses his food in the air. His brother is about to join the fun.

◆ STATEMENTS A PARENT MIGHT MAKE

1. "Carl, you are making noises and throwing food. Your actions tell me you are done with dinner. Say, 'May I be excused,' and take your plate to the counter." _____

2. "Carl, you are being rude. That is no way to behave. Keep it up and you can forget about TV tonight." _____

3. "Dinner is a time to talk and enjoy being together. Your behavior bothers me. You can finish your dinner at the counter by yourself or stay with the family." If Carl continues to belch, he is told to move to the counter to eat alone. _____

4. "What's the matter? Don't you like the food? Would you like something else?" _____

5. "Your rudeness is ruining our dinner. You know better than to act like this. Shape up or you will not go to the gymnastics meet." _____

Answers: Teaching intent is occurring in responses 1 and 3. Responses 2 and 5 represent a punitive intent. Response 4 is a rescue intent.

If you use consequences with the intent to punish or rescue regularly, your child is likely to avoid taking responsibility for his actions. He probably will engage in the following types of thinking based on blame and retaliation:

◆ **Resentment:** Your child will compare his behavior to that of others. He will focus on why he got caught, and others didn't.

Examples: "This isn't fair." "You always pick on me." "You are just being mean."

◆ **Revenge:** Your child will focus on getting back at the person who punishes or the person he blames for the problem.

Examples: "I'll show her." "I'll just fail fourth grade, then she'll be sorry." "I'm never cleaning my room now."

◆ **Rebellion:** The child focuses on not being caught.

Example: "I'll do what I want and just be more careful not to get caught next time."

◆ **Reduced self-esteem:** Your child will focus on pleasing others.

Examples: "I must really be bad and deserve to be punished." "This is for my own good." "I must try harder to be good."

◆ **Apathy:** Your child may focus on avoiding others.

Example: "I give up. I can't win, so why try? I just want to be left alone."

How often do you engage in these types of thinking patterns? Can you see the relationship between the discipline you received as a child and your current thoughts?

Recently I was on a flight to Montana, en route to a workshop. I sat in front of a family of three. Directly behind me was a boy (around the age of four) who had two action figures to play with for a four-hour flight. Eventually, to amuse himself, he began banging the tray table up and down on the back of my seat, jarring me.

Given that I'm a discipline expert, you might imagine that I could handle this one easily. My first decision was to remain silent in the hope that he would stop. During my silent period, I seethed, and blamed his mother. The more critically I judged her, the madder I got. I was just about to speak to the boy when I asked myself, "Becky, do you want to have this child pay for the discomfort he is causing, or do you want to teach him?" My answer to myself was, "He must pay!" With that, I spun around and addressed that family in a cold, hurtful way. The child did stop flapping the tray table, but that whole family was on edge. The baby started fussing. The mother became hypercritical of the boy and slapped him. He cried.

You must consciously choose to maintain self-control and focus on teaching in every conflict situation.

I chose to forgive myself for my clumsy handling of that situation and to work on the skills I would need the next time something similar occurred. I knew I did not want to repeat this behavior, so I used the unfortunate event to deepen my resolve to change my old patterns. I had initially imagined that when I became more conscious of how I was handling children, I would steadily be a loving, yet firm, disciplinarian. I discovered that this is simply not the case. You must consciously choose how to conduct yourself *in every interaction.* I had "forgotten" to use the Power of Intention, reminding me to use conflict as teaching moments rather than as opportunities for attack.

TYPES OF CONSEQUENCES

Sometimes, consequences come naturally. You walk in the rain without a raincoat and you get wet. A child touches a hot stove and gets burned. Natural consequences arise without any prearranged adult intervention. If your son does not tie his shoelaces, he may trip over them. If a child repeatedly treats his friends poorly, he may find himself friendless. These consequences are possible—sometimes proba-ble—results of personal choices, but remember that our interactions with the environment yield a wide range of possible results. A child with untied shoes may *not* fall. Adults tend to overdo their predic-tions of harm: "If you run, you *will* fall"; "If you don't eat vegetables, you *will* be unhealthy." These dire warnings send two messages:

1) Adults are all-knowing and can predict the future. You must listen and depend on them.
2) You have no control over the events of your life.

Children who internalize these beliefs grow into adults who give their power away to others, feel victimized by life, and shed respon-sibility if they can. Luckily, natural consequences offer *very powerful* learning opportunities.

Sometimes consequences occur because of imposed structures. If you don't pay your taxes, there are prescribed penalties. If a child refuses to eat dinner, he may experience hunger before the next meal. Imposed consequences arise out of pre-established codes of conduct. They come from the limits we have set, such as, "You can play outside until 5:00 P.M."; skills we have taught, such as, "When you want your brother to move, say, 'Move over, please'"; and expectations we hold, such as, "Eat with your silverware." When a child has been taught how to behave in a situation and then makes a poor choice of how to act, an imposed consequence is forthcom-ing. A child may be restricted from playing outside after school for several days, restricted from playing with his brother, or told to leave the dinner table without finishing his dinner.

To be powerful learning opportunities, children must be allowed to feel the consequences of their choices. This is probably one of the hardest tasks any parent can face, yet it is so important. Children will experience anger, disappointment, embarrassment, fright, and other painful emotions. Pain is our body's signal that something is out of balance. It says, "Pay attention and make dif-ferent choices." People who ignore their pain put themselves at risk for possible disasters. One summer while vacationing in Alaska, I decided to hike up to the Harding Icefield with some friends. Halfway up the climb, I felt pain in my knees. I ignored the pain and climbed to 14,000 feet. That poor choice damaged my knees.

Psychological pain works in the same manner. Disappointment, embarrassment, sadness, and frustration are all signals. The signal is "Pay attention and make different choices." If we ignore our feelings or project them onto others ("Look how you made me feel"), we will continue making the same poor choices and blaming others. Allowing your children to feel the feelings associated with their choices is a critical part of teaching responsibility.

STOPPING THE "BLAME GAME"

Children who are allowed to feel their feelings, instead of hearing about yours through lectures, threats, and anger, learn how to be responsible for their actions. The "blame game" ("He started it"; "I didn't do it"; "She made me do it") is minimized. The following five steps will help you teach your child to learn from the consequences of his mistakes. Together they spell the acronym GAMES:

G = Give guidance through limits, possible outcomes, and choices.

A = Allow the child to experience the consequence of his choices.

M = Model self-control.

E = Offer empathy to your child.

S = Help the child reflect on new strategies.

G (Step 1). Give guidance through limits, possible outcomes, and choices. Limits can be stated by telling children what to do (using the Power of Attention). For example, you might say to your child, "Walk around the pool. The deck is slippery." Then you could describe for your child the possible outcomes of certain behaviors: "If you choose to run, you *may* fall and skin your knees." This sends two important messages: 1) your child is in charge of what may or may not happen to him in this situation, and 2) through awareness, he can develop his own wisdom. After telling a child what to do, you may offer choices and imposed consequences. You might say, "You may play outside until five o'clock. At five o'clock you have a choice. You can come inside or continue to play. If you choose to stay out later, you will not be able to go outside for two days."

A (Step 2). Allow the child to experience the consequence of his choices. Do not attempt to save your child with excessive warnings, "Remember to walk." Do not attempt to get your child to feel bad: "If you had come in by five o'clock, you wouldn't have had this problem." "What did I say would happen?"

M (Step 3). Model self-control. Stay calm and peaceful. Use your mouth for breathing only, and stay quiet.

E (Step 4). Offer empathy to your child if he makes a poor choice. Empathy helps the child feel his feelings and take ownership of his choices. You might say, "Oh, look at those knees; they must really hurt. That fall looked really scary." Or, you might say, "How disappointing. I know how much you like to play outside after school. It is going to be hard to stay inside. You can play in your room or in the family room. It is up to you." (Choices added to empathy are very helpful.)

S (Step 5). Help the child reflect on new strategies. You might say, "Are you interested in learning ways to remember to walk around the pool or how to make sure you come in by five o'clock?"

Below are three examples of the GAMES technique in action. The letters, GAMES, highlight which step is being used.

HUNKERING DOWN TO HOMEWORK—TEACHING A CHILD HOW TO DO IT

Julie noticed that her son Mark, age 10, was being slipshod in completing his homework. She wanted to help him to do better. She walked over to Mark, waited for eye contact, and said, "When you come home from school, before you can go play, you will do your homework at the table. If you choose to sit at the table and day-dream, or if you do your homework quickly with little thought, you may not get passing grades." (**G**)

Mark continued to sit staring into space and put little effort into his work. On his next report card, he received five D's and two C's (his previous grades had been all A's and B's). (**A**) Julie knew Mark was upset and she resisted the urge to say, "I told you so," or to give him a lecture. (**M**) Instead, she said, "You seem upset about your grades." (**E**) Mark said that he was worried and proceeded to blame various people and events. She replied, "It's hard not to get the grades you wanted. I imagine it is disappointing." (**E**) Tears started to well up in Mark's eyes and he said, "I really didn't put my all into it." Julie responded by putting her arm on Mark's shoulder and asking, "What are your plans for doing homework differently in the future? Have you thought about it?" (**S**) Mark replied, "No." Here was Julie's chance: she continued by saying, "Would you like some help in making a plan?" Mark nodded assent.

STOPPING THE HITTING HABIT:
TEACHING OTHER OPTIONS

Nathan and Ashley were close in age. Their constant bickering had really worn down their mother's patience. Rebecca had been work-ing with both children on how to talk to each other, rather than hit-ting to get what they wanted. She thought she was making progress—until Monday morning. Rebecca heard Ashley screaming from the bedroom, and she entered the room to find Nathan hitting Ashley on the arm. As soon as Rebecca appeared, Nathan backed off and startled shouting, "She took my book." Rebecca took a deep breath and said, "You have a choice. You may hit your sister to get the book, or you may ask your sister for the book by saying, 'Give me my book.' If you choose to hit your sister again instead of talk-ing to her, you will play in your room alone for the rest of the day."

(G) After this, she left the room. (A) Within five seconds, Ashley began screaming again. Rebecca felt like screaming herself and telling both children that they would never live to see the age of 16, but she refrained. (M) She walked back into the room and calmly said, "Nathan, you seem really upset about that book. It must be terribly important to you. Feel free to read, do schoolwork, or just hang out in your room for the rest of the day." (E) Nathan starts shouting, "It's not fair. You always take her side and pick on me." Rebecca responded with empathy, "It does seem like that sometimes." (E) She continued, "Let me know at dinnertime if you are interested in learning other ways to get things from your sister instead of hitting." (S)

The following situation is described two different ways, based on the respective teaching styles of two parents. The first parent uses the GAMES technique based on the Power of Intention: Conflict is an opportunity to teach. The second parent uses punishment and lecturing. As you read the scenes, imagine being both of these parents. How do you think the rest of the evening went for each of them?

Coming Inside When Called—A Parent Teaches How

Jeffrey has been taught the following about playing outside in the neighborhood (G):

1) When leaving the house, you must tell a parent where you are going (to Sam's house, etc.).
2) If you change locations, you must call home, or come home and tell a parent where you are going.
3) You must come home immediately when you are called.

One spring day, Jeffrey, John, and David (ages eight, eight, and nine) went out to play. (A) Toward dinnertime, all three parents called for their children to come inside. None of the boys responded, and they could not be found. The parents then phoned each other and began a neighborhood search. Finally, one mother spotted the boys walking through a backyard.

Linda, John's mom, was the first to speak to her child. She was extremely upset, but she managed to own her own upset and began talking to her son with an "I-message": "John, when I couldn't find you, I was so afraid that something terrible had happened to you. Then I felt angry with you for not telling me where you were." **(M)** Having expressed her feelings, she continued, "John, you have a choice. You can let me know where you are at all times so I can reach you, or you can go off and play somewhere without telling me. If you choose not to tell me where you are again, you will not be allowed out of our yard for a week. [**(G)**] I love you, and when you are in the yard, I know you are safe and I can find you when I need you. Do you understand what will happen if you do this again?" The child responded, "Yes, I do." Then Linda said, "Tell me." John said, "I will play in my own yard." Linda asked, "For how long?" John replied, "One week." She ended the exchange, "Now get in the car. We are going home. You will help me prepare dinner, since I spent my cooking time searching for you."

But the next day, John was allowed to go out to play in the neighborhood. **(A)** At dinnertime, John was nowhere to be found. Just as Linda was about to get in the car to search for him again, he reappeared. At this point Linda was boiling mad and knew it was best not to say anything. She just kept quiet.

The next day, John came home from school and started to leave the house. Linda said, "I can see you were looking forward to going outside. It is going to be hard for you this week staying inside and not seeing your friends. Feel free to stay in your room and use the phone all you want between four o'clock and four-fifteen. [**(E)**] Toward the end of the week, I want you to think of a plan for how you will make it home by five o'clock. If you need help, let me know." **(S)**

Coming Inside When Called—A Parent Punishes

Sally, David's mom, spotted her son walking down the street on that first night. She lost control and spoke harshly to him: "Get over here! I've been worried sick about you and have been searching this whole neighborhood. I could paddle you right here in the street. Don't you ever do this again! You might have been kidnapped, for all I knew. You'd better start thinking of someone besides yourself. When we get home, you go straight to your room. You're grounded for a week—no friends, no video games. Understand? I don't know what gets into you."

The difference between relying on fear and relying on love is that one leaves both the child and parent feeling good, or good enough, while the other leaves each participant with a sour taste of inadequacy.

Put yourself in the place of John and David. Which child is more likely to accept responsibility for his behavior and make changes? Which child is more likely to sulk and blame his parents for being mean? Loving guidance sets up guidelines, hopes children will make poor choices, offers empathy for poor choices, and asks the child to think and choose again. Why on earth would you ever *hope* your child made a poor choice? Because it gives you the opportunity to teach him how to think and reflect at a time when the price tag for his errors is cheap. The older one gets, the more expensive and dangerous poor choices become.

PROBLEM SOLVING AS A CONSEQUENCE

Poor choices create conflicts and problems for children. Many times, the consequences of such problems require problem solving. The logical consequence of fighting is to learn how to solve problems without fighting. Many of us are so trained to think in terms of punishment, or the child's loss, that we forget to think in terms of solutions. We constantly impose consequences on children. The examples above showed how we can more effectively impose consequences by using empathy instead of lectures. More often than not, however, problem solving is the better approach to take.

When children are actively engaged in solving their own problems, peaceful homes and peaceful worlds become a reality. The following steps are helpful in assisting children to solve their own problems. The acronym to help you remember the steps is PEACE:

P = Discern who owns the *p*roblem.

E = Offer *e*mpathy to the child who has made the poor choice.

A = *A*sk the child to think, "What do you think you are going to do?"

C = Offer *c*hoices and suggestions.

E = *E*ncourage the child to come up with his own solution.

P (Step 1). Discern who owns the problem. This step is critical. All too often, parents make the children's problem their own and spend enormous amounts of energy and critical thinking skills attempting to solve it. Imagine that your friend smokes. You decide for some strange reason that this is your problem. You spend years trying to come up with solutions to your friend's smoking problem. Nothing seems successful and you end up frustrated and angry with your friend. This is basically what is happening in homes everywhere with children. Here is a list of some common problems:

1) not eating
2) not getting dressed (or undressed)
3) not going to bed
4) not doing homework or chores
5) fighting with siblings

My guess is that you thought the items listed above were *your* problem. You cannot solve children's problems, and children cannot solve your problems. To facilitate the problem-solving approach with your children, start the interaction by letting the child know he has a problem. You might say, "You seem to be having a problem." If your child is having a problem getting dressed in the morning, step one might look like this: "Oh, Mica, you seem to be having a problem this morning. You are not dressed and the car is leaving in five minutes."

E (Step 2). Offer empathy to the child who made the poor choice. Often when you inform children they have a problem, their first tendency is to blame others and deflect responsibility. This is not disrespect—it is a normal reaction to a potential threat. When we perceive ourselves to be threatened in any way, our brains shift into defense mode. We then attempt to transfer the responsibility of a poor choice to something outside of ourselves. Such comments as, "He started it," or, "If you loved me, you wouldn't make me go," are common deflection statements. Very young children who lack the verbal skills to blame others will simply scream, run, or throw fits. Either way, empathy is the skill to use. Empathy calms the brain, removes the threat, and allows a person, even a very young child, to take responsibility for his own behavior.

In the situation above, Mica ignores his mother and her comment (another typical way to deflect responsibility). Now it is time to leave the house, and he is still in his pajamas. Mom, ready to leave, says, "Oh, Mica, this could be upsetting. It is time to go and you are not dressed." Mica looks up and is surprised to see Mom with her coat and keys. Mica begins to scream, "I hate you. I am not going to school. I am not dressed. I want Daddy." Mom takes a deep breath, uses the Power of Acceptance—this moment is as it is—to calm herself, and says, "You seem very angry. It is hard to think of going to school in your pajamas." By offering empathy, Mom continues to let Mica know the problem belongs to him. Had she lost her self-control, she would have made the problem hers by screaming, lecturing, or issuing threats.

A (Step 3). Ask the child to think, "What do you think you are going to do?" It is important to ask children to solve their own problems. This can be done by asking thinking questions. Educators Jim Fay and David Funk (Fay and Funk, 1995) suggest saying, "What do you think you are going to do?" or, "I'd like to hear your ideas." You could also ask, "How could you solve your problem?" or, "What could you do now that would be helpful?"

In the situation with Mica, Mom says, "What are you going to do?"

C (Step 4). Offer choices and suggestions. Often, children, especially young ones, have not developed a repertoire of solutions to problems. When asked to identify one, they simply respond, "I don't know." To this you could say, "It's hard not to know. Are you interested in some ideas?" or, as Jim Fay (Fay and Cline, 1996) suggests, you might ask, "Would you like some ideas of what other children have tried?" These initial questions conjure up a sense of willingness within children. Willingness is critical to the change process; ask for it.

Offer children ideas, starting with some poor choices and moving up to more helpful choices. After each suggestion you offer, ask older children (seven years and up), "How do you think that would work?" This encourages them to think about how their choices will influence their lives and the lives of others. For younger children you could say, "Do you think that would be helpful or hurtful?" or offer them choices.

In the situation with Mica, Mom offers him a choice: "You could put your clothes in a bag to take to school or go to school in your pajamas. Which would be better?" Mica starts to scream, "I hate you," and begins to throw things. Mom offers empathy: "You are really upset. It is scary to think of going to school in your pajamas. Do you want to put your clothes in a bag to put on in the car, or do you want to go to school in your pajamas?"

E (Step 5). Encourage the child to come up with his own solution. End the interaction by encouraging the child. You might say, "I know you will come up with a solution to your problem. You can do this. Let me know what you decide to do and if you need my help."

Problem solving asks children to think and reflect on their choices. It demands that they accept responsibility. Sadly, too many of us associate responsibility with admitting an error, or confessing to the crime, so to speak. How often have you heard, "If you are honest and take the responsibility, it will be better for you." Responsibility does not come from accepting blame and punishment for one's actions. It comes from resisting the temptation to blame others, and then seeking solutions instead through problem solving.

MOVING BEYOND PUNISHING OURSELVES— BECOMING PEACEFUL PEOPLE

The truly sad part about the overuse of rewards and punishment is the damage that has been done to us. We have internalized our punishing parents. Even as adults, all we need to do is make one mistake and this punitive voice is activated.

Recently, I had a luncheon appointment with some leaders in education to discuss a new program. I was busily working at my computer when the phone rang. As soon as I heard the voice on the other end of the line, I knew I had missed the meeting. Immediately my inner voice began ranting: "Becky, you should know better. You have let down the children who would have benefited from the program. You are disorganized and rude." With this voice bombarding me from within, I was apologizing in torrents to the woman on the phone. After hanging up, I finally silenced the battering voices in my head by empathizing with myself. I thought, I got so absorbed that I lost track of time and missed the meeting. I let a lot of people down. In the future, I will keep my date book open on the floor beside my chair and will set an alarm clock, too. I made a mistake. I can change this behavior. All is well. Breathe deeply. I will focus on ways to change.

My decision to shift my intent from punishment to teaching allowed me to learn from my mistakes. Incidentally, I have followed through on my plan to keep appointments and I haven't repeated that mistake. I have still been late for a few meetings, but my life is easier whether I am late or prompt because I am kinder to myself. By being kinder to myself, I have reduced my stress level. My immune system is stronger now and so am I. With this strength and energy, I direct my focus to fulfilling my commitments. I find that the more I practice these techniques with myself, the more natural they feel when I use then with children.

Responsibility comes from resisting the temptation to blame others, and then seeking solutions instead.

LEARNING THROUGH FEAR OR LOVE

At every moment, you have a choice between approaching the world with a spirit of love and learning or one of fear and punishment. That choice is yours. How you teach your child to learn from his mistakes depends upon your handling of consequences. If you use traditional punishments and rewards, you opt to teach your child through fear. If you use the Power of Intention, using conflict as an opportunity to teach, you will be able to effectively use consequences as a teaching tool. Consequences can be a wonderful tool because consequences help children realize that they are the key authors of their life scripts and must, therefore, act responsibly.

THERE'S NO TIME LIKE THE PRESENT!

Start to use your life experiences as opportunities to learn today by doing the following:

◆ **Begin with yourself.** The next time you make a mistake, stop your punitive self-talk. Focus instead on these questions:
   1. What choice did I make?
   2. What happened as a result of my choice?
   3. How did my choice and its results feel to me?
   4. Did my choice achieve what I wanted?
   5. What new strategies might serve me better?
◆ **Notice how often you blame others for your actions.** The next time you catch yourself playing the "blame game," stop.

Take a deep breath and say, "I have a problem." Then offer yourself empathy instead of harassment and proceed to solve your problem.

♦ **Decide if you have relied overly much on punishments and rewards as a means of discipline.** If you have done so, be willing to change.

♦ **When conflict occurs, ask yourself,** "What is my intention in this situation? Do I intend to make my child feel bad and pay for his crime?" or, "Do I want to teach my child to reflect on his choices, change them, and develop self-control?"

♦ **The next time you deliver a consequence to your child, use empathy** and self-control instead of threats, lectures, or moralizing. Refer to the GAMES steps for assistance on page 200.

♦ **Pick one chronic problem you have been having.** Instead of imposing consequences, use the problem-solving PEACE plan on page 206.

Why Children Do What They Do: The Development of Misbehavior

Parents who hear me speak often say, "You have just described my child to a T. I could swear you have been to my house." The reason I hear this comment so often is that children develop abilities according to a rather orderly schedule. They misbehave in fairly predictable ways, too. At different times in their lives, children hit, call their friends names, appear deaf, have an attitude, lie, and break their curfew. Misbehavior, although annoying, is part of the normal developmental process children undergo. Again, your responses to these unavoidable but necessary behaviors teach your children how to view themselves and the world, and how to maintain relationships.

Children misbehave in fairly predictable ways.

This chapter outlines behaviors that typify the various stages of child development and can lead to certain types of conflicts. These behaviors revolve around the level of opposition which your child presents to adult demands; how well she interacts with siblings and other children; her response to frustration; and her ability to handle the activities of daily life on her own (dressing, eating, bathing, homework, bedtime, and so on). In essence, this chapter traces the development of misbehavior.

WHY KNOWLEDGE IS POWER

Descriptions of what to expect from children at various ages help some parents feel more secure. "I feel like I can relax somewhat," said the mother of a ten-year-old boy, who had learned that many children that age still need supervision to complete daily routines. She had convinced herself that "He should know better by now," and would badger her son about remembering to do his homework, take a bath, or clean his room. Her tirades achieved nothing except compeling him to feel bad, and they trapped mother and son in frequent power struggles as they both defended against feeling inadequate.

Some parents who read books on children's development choose to feel scared. "Oh no, my child's not like that; perhaps something is wrong with her," said the mother of a six-year-old girl who had read that children her daughter's age are stubborn. Her child was generally compliant. The problem with general information about development is that it never shows you the whole picture. All children are both alike and different. Some information you receive will hit home and some will not apply—that's normal. Use what you can.

Once at a parent group, I met a young mother who was distraught about her three-year-old daughter. As I explained some discipline skills, she kept saying, "I already do that, and it doesn't work." She wanted a magic strategy that would change the natural progression of her daughter's development, and bring an end to her oppositional behavior. Eventually, the mother realized that her daughter's actions triggered her own sense of inadequacy and frustration, and that was their biggest problem. Her agitation kept her from helping her daughter learn and mature. Author Harville Hendrix says, "Conflict is an indicator of growth trying to happen." Your response to conflict can yield constructive, growth-enhancing effects or destructive, deadening effects that trap you and your child in endless power struggles.

Parents must accept that conflicts will always arise and that they serve a purpose. With this Power of Acceptance, you then can use your energy wisely. Instead of frantically trying to prevent conflicts, you can rally your forces to effectively respond to them.

BEHIND BEHAVIOR LIES DEVELOPMENT

What many parents see as cute moments reflect more than the sweet innocence of children. "Cute" behaviors also reflect how children see and understand the world. As adorable as these behaviors may be in some instances, they represent certain issues of development that can cause conflict in other contexts.

A little boy marches around singing his version of the television jingle, "The best part of waking up is soldiers in your cup." Children use their own life experiences to make meaning for new experiences. A child knows more about soldiers than coffee so, when he hears the jingle, he constructs his own meaning. Adults, too, add personal meaning to their perceptions, but adults have so many more experiences upon which to draw that the meaning they add is likely to be quite similar to the one other adults impose.

Children are also very literal. I once worked with a parent whose son Bryan flatly refused to go to school and threw fits about it every morning. This story eventually emerged. On the first day of school the teacher did not have enough tables and chairs in the classroom. While moving the children about, she told Bryan, "You sit here for the present." Bryan waited for that gift for over a week. She never brought him his present and he became totally disillusioned with her and school.

Parents in the grocery store often tell their children, "Don't touch that!" Minutes later you hear, "Don't touch that!" again. And soon thereafter you will hear, "What did I tell you?" and other comments of utter frustration. From the child's point of view, "that" was just the one can of soup they originally had their eye on. There are a million different "thats" on the shelves. To the parents, "that" meant anything on display. Young children take your words literally. You must be conscious of what you have said *and* what they have heard. If you understand your children, guiding them will be much easier.

A mother was driving a group of little children to a movie when a car abruptly pulled in front of them, forcing her to swerve to avoid a collision. In fright, she yelled, "Asshole!" A child in the back seat asked, "Where? Where? My mommy saw one yesterday." The point: Our brains seek patterns. Classifications are very helpful—they help us make sense of our world. For instance, we divide the animal kingdom into categories (mammals, reptiles, insects, etc.) and then we subdivide each of those groups into smaller categories.

Young children scrutinize every verbal and nonverbal action, looking for every possible pattern in order to create categories. The young girl in the car was trying to figure out a category for "assholes." Children do not learn to classify completely until around the age of nine or ten. Prior to that age, they are in the process of setting up a filing system, yet adults often want them to use the system before it is completed. We tell young children to "be nice" to visitors when what we need to do is explain to them how to be nice—"Greet our friends at the door"; "Show them your room"; "Ask what they would like to play."

When you speak to children in terms they cannot understand, you create anxiety in them. Their inability to respond appropriately fosters a feeling of "being not good enough." Such feelings of unworthiness create a less than/better than schema of relationships, preventing the ability to feel connected with one another. When children feel disconnected, they choose to be defensive instead of cooperative. In this way, misbehavior is fostered. Adults must understand child development in order to offer children loving guidance rather than opportunities to disconnect and defend.

ORGANIZATION AND CHAOS:
THE PROCESS OF DEVELOPMENT

You can compare the development of a child to the growth of a business you might start. All businesses need certain basic systems—a computer system, an accounting system, and a phone system. As your business grows, you will need to upgrade these systems until one day when you must replace them. Then you might post a sign saying: "Please bear with us as we upgrade our systems to better serve you." During the transition period, disorganization will prevail as you train everyone in the company to use the new systems. Employees will resist, learning will be hard work, customer service will drop, and profits may too. Once the new systems are finally in place and running smoothly, however, your business will operate more efficiently and serve your customers better. In time, the cycle will need to be repeated if growth continues.

A similar process happens with children as they grow. Stages of chaos precede stages of organization. Your child may at one stage make strides (upgrades) in certain abilities and then need a "new system." During its "installation," chaos may prevail and your child's behavior may fall apart. Skills that she seemed to have mastered will be suddenly unavailable. You will have to stifle the voice in your head that says, "I know she knows better." Her disorganized state will be followed by a period of relatively calm, organized behavior during which she will demonstrate new or more advanced skills.

Children's cycles of organization-chaos-reorganization occur about every six months, starting at the age of 15 months (when the first bout of chaos strikes). Two-year-old children are fairly delightful compared to eighteen-month-olds. However, two-and-a-half-year-old children truly challenge their parents. Three-year-old children seem charming and bright, and then comes the dreaded three-and-a-half-year mark of total opposition.

Reflect on your own life and you will see these same cycles. Haven't there been times when you felt in charge of what you were doing, where you were going, and what you wanted, interspersed with periods when you didn't "have a clue"? All of us have times when our confidence and sense of being in control of life comes in and out of focus.

While we know that stages of disorganization must occur before the child can move on to stages of higher organization, no one can say just when these stages will occur with any individual child. Nor can you foresee the extent to which your child will "break up" during the disorganized stages or how smoothly the times of reorganization will go. Some children seem to always live a bit on the side of chaos. Even during their calm stages, they challenge themselves and the people around them. Other children seem to enjoy life easily and are usually cooperative. During their "chaotic" periods, they simply seem out of sorts. These variations reflect aspects of a child's inborn temperament. One mother recalled that when her third child was born and the nurse placed him on her stomach, he raised his head and arms, looked at her, and screamed. As a child, too, he was always loud and demanding. Now that he is a young adult, his character traits have manifested themselves as determination and an ability to lead.

Generally, times of disorganization reveal that a great deal is happening internally. This is true with a business in transition—or with a child. People are grappling with new concepts and new information. They are trying to learn fast and use new tools to their advantage. A child in the midst of a developmental shift may seem resistant, and even mean sometimes. Her internal struggles reduce her ability to cooperate. The greater the struggle, the less the cooperation. You've probably observed the same phenomenon within yourself. The more problems you have, the more likely you are to be short-tempered and grumpy.

"IRRITATION POINTS"

I call certain kinds of behavior that reflect normal processes of development "irritation points." You might also call them parental "hot buttons." Parents are not born with these buttons; they actually install them themselves by clinging to certain beliefs. When parents equate misbehavior with disrespect, they definitely set themselves up to be irritated by typical developmental issues. If you believe "My child should know better by now," you have created neon buttons screaming to be pushed. How do you know if your buttons are being pushed? You totally forget the *Seven Powers for Self-Control*. Here are the warning signs:

◆ You act like a nut. You scream, shout, threaten, bargain, plead, beg, spank, bribe, or cry.

◆ You focus on what is wrong and what your child is *not* doing, losing the Power of Attention.

◆ You attribute a negative intent to your child: "She is doing this to get back at me." When you attribute this kind of negative intent to your child, your focus shifts from your child and her developmental journey to yourself and how your child is supposedly trying to upset you. You forget the Power of Love.

◆ You blame the child for your upset and try to make her feel bad through guilt, fear, or the use of force. You refuse to own your own upset and use the Power of Perception.

◆ You forget the Power of Acceptance (this moment is as it is), and think any one of the following thoughts:
"This child should know better than this.
"I shouldn't have to give constant reminders. She ought to be able to get up and get dressed by her age."
"I shouldn't have to tell her again. She should do what I say when I say it."

◆ You become alarmed and wonder, What happened? What have I done wrong to make my child act like this (forgetting the Power of Free Will)? How can a delightful child one month become a monster the next? If she's this bad now, what will her teens be like? By projecting fear into the future, you attempt to feel "special" through suffering, losing the Power of Unity that holds everyone together.

As human beings develop, their behavior goes from being organized, to being chaotic, and then to being organized again at a higher level. This process is cyclical, not linear.

I will discuss four stages of children's development: infancy, toddlerhood, the preschool period, and then the school-age years, providing some background about each stage. I will also describe the irritation points that typify each stage. This will help you see the contexts in which children develop misbehavior and why it actually contributes to the growth process.

Infancy: The First Year of Life

The first upsetting behavior that parents confront is crying. To insure its own survival, an infant is born programmed to signal for care. A parent's job is to pick up the signal and respond. When parents respond reliably to their baby's cries, they lay the first underpinnings for the child's own sense of responsibility. Sadly, parents often misinterpret crying. Some parents attribute a negative motive: "She's just crying because she knows I'm a pushover," or, "He fusses when I'm on the phone because he wants all of my attention." Everyone is happier when a parent attributes a positive intent: "She's trying to tell me something." The parent feels better about his child and himself, and performs the caretaking the baby requires.

Tiny babies are simply incapable of scheming. In the first three months, they have no capacity for conscious intentional behavior. Infants can only react unconsciously to internal feelings (such as pain or hunger) and to external sensations (things they see, hear, taste, or smell). Between the ages of three and ten months, babies start to communicate intentionally. As a parent, you can foster this developmental process by learning to decipher your baby's signals.

When you read and respond to your baby's signals, she learns that her actions and the feelings she broadcasts result in reactions from the world. This experience sets a pattern that is the foundation for learning about cause and effect. Later in life, this pattern will help your child connect rules with consequences, or make the connection between hitting and hurting.

Your infant's major developmental tasks are to send signals, to accept nurturing, to bond with an adult, to learn that the world will respond to her, and to develop a sense of trust. In short, she will fuss, cry, cuddle, make sounds, imitate, and look at—and respond to—faces, especially eyes.

Infants' Irritation Points

◆ **Failed communication.** A baby sends out signals to a parent through cries, laughter, and fussing. If the baby's first signals are not heard, or are misread, she will usually pump up the intensity. Fussing and crying can be irritation points for parents who are tired, overwhelmed, or unable to figure out the baby's signals and soothe her.

◆ **Face exploration.** Between eight and ten months of age, infants begin to intensely explore their parents' faces. In the process, they may pull hair, pinch, stick their fingers in your nose, and grab your earrings or beard. To teach your baby, you can say, "Ouch!" (make it clear that the action hurt), and, "I don't like it when you pinch me." Then, by attributing positive intent to your child, you can teach her a new way of behaving. You might say, "You wanted to touch Mommy. Touch me like this [take the child's hand and show her how]." If the baby continues to be hurtful, put the child down so she cannot hurt you.

◆ **Biting or pinching.** Around twelve months of age, your baby may bite or pinch you. She is exploring the experience of biting and seeing how you react. Let the child know the bite hurt and put her down. When you pick her up again, let her know you will accept a hug but not a bite. If she continues to bite, firmly separate her from you and assertively say, "Look at my face [look of pain].

Biting hurts. You may give gentle touches." Take the child's hand and show her exactly what you mean. Use your Power of Attention and the skill of assertiveness.

Toddlers: The Second Year of Life

Toddlers are a force to be reckoned with. During the second year of life, most children say no before they say yes, throw things before they care to pick them up, and run away from you before they respond to, "Come here, precious." Leaving infancy behind, toddlers make a huge cognitive leap in their ability to remember things and make crude mental manipulations. Toddlers have several developmental tasks to perform. They advance the development of cause-and-effect thinking through explorations of "What happens if . . ." activities. Accordingly, they love light switches, cabinet doors, buttons on the TV remote control, and all other objects they can manipulate. Their boundless curiosity and irrepressible urge to explore test the patience of every parent.

Moreover, toddlers must investigate, test reality, push against boundaries set by other people, and learn ways to express anger and other feelings. They begin to follow simple commands, but as they are also starting to separate from their parents and develop a sense of autonomy, they say no a lot. In short, toddlers fiddle with everything, often grow frustrated, and throw temper tantrums.

Adults tend to get angry at toddlers who are angry. This is counterproductive and usually produces a power struggle. Every angry moment for a toddler is a teaching opportunity for an adult. As a parent you can label the anger ("You seem really mad") and then redirect it with positive choices ("You can play with the blocks or the dolls. Which one do you pick?").

Toddlers' Irritation Points

◆ **Anger and frustration.** Toddlers are moving from the total dependency of infancy to a state of some independence. This journey is riddled with frustrating situations and anger. Toddlers may get angry when they are:

Restrained from independent movement, play, or exploration.

Restrained from declaring everything as "Mine."

Frustrated by their own physical or cognitive limits while attempting something new.

Hearing repeated "No" and "Stop that" commands.

Bidding for attention but being ignored or misunderstood.

◆ **Temper tantrums.** If you can stay calm during a toddler temper tantrum, you have half the problem solved—*yours.*

◆ **Negative oppositional behavior.** At around fifteen months, toddlers enter an age of decidedly firm negativism. They must have their own way, whatever the cost. A toddler's frustration at not getting her own way often prompts a tantrum. Tantrums respond to empathy. Remember to reflect what you see ("Your arms are going out like this"); reflect what you feel ("You seem really angry"); and reflect what you hear ("Your body is telling me you wish you could play longer").

◆ **Impulsive behaviors.** Toddlers must be protected from their own impulses. They will dash into the street and pull things off shelves, regardless of your warnings. Vigilant supervision, child-proofing, and redirection are vital security measures. For a child, visual triggers to action (seeing a desired object) usually override the child's auditory system (hearing your no). This situation prevails until around the age of four.

◆ **Possessiveness.** "Mine," "My daddy," "I need," "Me do it," are all favorite exclamations of toddlers. Things may seem to matter more than people do as the child continues to explore the meanings of "me" and "mine" versus "not me" and "not mine." When your child says "mine," you can help her understand this word by saying, "You are carrying the garbage can. It belongs to the family. We all carry it at different times." If your child grabs your coat and says, "Mine," you can respond, "You are holding Daddy's coat. Yours is by the door." Your child may continue to say "Mine," but you will have provided usable information that your child will eventually integrate into her concept of "mine" and "not mine."

◆ **Aggressive behaviors.** Toddlers often display a need to control any and all toys they see. This tendency conflicts with your attempts to promote cooperation and sharing. Some aggressive acts on the part of toddlers seem to be unprovoked. One toddler may push another down for no obvious reason. The child who pushed will then look back to the adult to see what will happen next, almost as if to ask, "Was that okay?" When the parent declares that such behavior is unacceptable, the toddler may next try hitting another child with a stick, asking, in effect, "Might this be okay?" Remember, in these situations you teach both parties new skills. Go to the victim first and say, "Did you like it when he hit you? Tell him, 'Stop! No!'" Then teach the aggressor by using the Power of Love and the skill of positive intent. Say, "You wanted her to play with you, so you pushed her. You may not push. Pushing hurts. When you want to play, give her a toy. Do it now. Give her the truck. That's it! You are doing it!"

◆ **Nothing seems right.** If Mommy is reading the child a story, the child declares, "Daddy read." After the child asks for *Goodnight Moon,* she throws it onto the floor and demands a *Spot* book. If the child notices her brother reading a magazine, she will attempt to seize it. Whenever she gets what she wants, she doesn't want it anymore. Remember, when your child is upset, use the skill of empathy first. I would then follow up with a choice by saying, "You have a choice: Mommy can read the book or you can read it yourself."

◆ **Endless rituals and love of repetition.** "Do it again." All the conflicts the toddler creates in the outside world reflect her inner conflict, which vacillates between dependence and independence. To feel somewhat in control of a world that feels out of control, the toddler relies upon routines and rituals. With these, she attempts to impose order on her world. The rituals of toddlers can become all-consuming. One little boy said goodnight every night to twenty-one stuffed animals. Plan time for rituals with toddlers.

The time spent performing rituals will spare you untold time lost in power struggles.

What does all this mean for parents of toddlers? It means that no matter what skills you acquire and how well you master them, if you can help your toddler choose to be cooperative fifty percent of the time, you are blessed.

Preschoolers: Ages Three to Five

A key developmental task faced by all preschoolers is to acquire power and an identity. Preschoolers continue to develop their sense of separateness from others. They learn about their world, themselves, their body, and their gender. In relation to cause and effect, they begin to learn that their behavior has consequences. They define their own place in a group and practice socially appropriate behavior. They learn to distinguish fantasy from reality, and figure out where they have power and where they do not.

How do you think your child learns so many complex concepts? You got it! Repeated trial and error. Preschoolers repeatedly act in ways that have an effect on others and then observe the consequences. They must perform these behavioral experiments many times in order to process the resulting information and internalize the knowledge.

In their quest for learning about power and control, preschoolers try all kinds of tactics. Teachers hear, "My mommy said I could," or, "My daddy always lets me do what I want." Conversely, parents hear, "My teacher never makes me take a nap." These are not intentional lies. They represent embellished wishful thinking. As preschoolers grapple with issues related to power (what it is, how it is used, who has it), many of them resort to a "higher power" such as, "My mommy says." Listen as Cassandra and Maggie try to figure out how to influence one another.

Cassandra, who is big and domineering, and Maggie, who is usually shy and sensitive, play together daily. Today, though, Maggie is not in the mood to take orders for long.

"You be the baby," said Cassandra to Maggie. "I will be the mommy getting you ready for school. Lie down in bed. I'll tell you when to get up." Maggie stretched out and pretended to be asleep. Cassandra soon said authoritatively, "Wake up, baby. It's time for you to go to school. Come sit in this chair for breakfast." Maggie got up, went to the table, and shouted, "Bring my food now! I want my food!" This annoyed Cassandra, who said, "You can't talk— you're a baby." Maggie then objected, "I don't want to be a baby. I want to be big." "You have to be the baby," insisted Cassandra. "If you do, I will be your friend."

Maggie ignored her and played with a rubber band. "My daddy said you have to be the baby, so get back in your chair," Cassandra said, hands planted on her hips. Maggie looked intimidated, but said, "I'm telling." Cassandra responded, "You're not my friend anymore and you can't come to my birthday." Maggie, by now crying, said, "So what, I have a new Barbie." Cassandra hit Maggie, and then went to tell her mother, "Maggie's not playing nice." Maggie followed her and said, "She hit me."

This is a typical episode for four- and five-year-old children. The girls were trying to exert their power and influence each other. Unlike toddlers, however, they were not immediately hitting, grabbing, or throwing tantrums, because they truly wanted to play together. Nevertheless, the skills they possess for influencing each other are still crude. Adults must teach them.

Preschoolers' Irritation Points

◆ **The simplest event or routine may trigger total rebellion.** The child seems determined to control the adult and will go to amazing lengths to have her own way. This extreme willfulness is especially noticeable with three-and-a-half-year-old children. The intensity will ease as the child grows older. Breathe deeply. Use the Power of Perception to own your own upset. Remember, no one can make you angry without your permission. Then calmly respond to your child.

◆ **Your child may be shy one minute and impossibly bossy**

the next. This can be extremely confusing for you. Testing her power, your child may attempt to dominate you with orders such as, "Don't laugh," or, "Stop talking." Frightened by her own power, she may revert to infantile behaviors such as thumb sucking or genital rubbing.

◆ **Whining.** When your child whines it means she longs for the security of infancy, before her struggle between dependence and independence took hold. If your child whines, play the following game with her at bedtime. It is called "When You Were a Baby" (Bailey, 1997), and in it, you tell your child stories about her infancy. Show her the games she loved, and talk the way you talked to her then. This will meet the underlying need your child is expressing by whining and help her handle this stressful time of development. The game is not designed to stop the whining. It helps you respond to the message the whining conveys. If whining irritates you, it will persist. That which you resist, will persist.

That which you resist, will persist.

◆ **They may begin to swear and use elimination swear words** ("doo-doo head," "poo-poo brain," etc.). This usually starts around the age of four.

◆ **They exaggerate and brag.** "I have twenty zillion toys."

◆ **They tend to be aggressive with friends and siblings.** They are also likely to make faces and stick their tongue out, even at you. Your response to these actions is the teaching moment. If these behaviors upset you, the child learns to exert power by getting a rise from others. You can choose to remain calm and instruct, "I don't like it when you make faces. You wanted me to notice you. When you want me to see you, say, 'Look, Daddy.'" This teaches your child that power is acquired through communication.

◆ **They hate for mom to talk on the phone.** They misbehave to communicate this. Favorite strategies include fighting and screaming, acting crazy and chasing each other, engaging in activities that are clearly forbidden (such as jumping on Mom's bed), and interrupting you ("Can I watch *Nickelodeon?*" or, "Will you turn it on?"). Your child hates to see all your attention devoted to another person. Your conversation also intrigues her. She hears you exclaiming, "Okay, great!" and wonders what is happening. She wants to be involved. If you truly don't want to be interrupted, talk on the phone after your child has gone to bed if at all possible.

◆ **They do not do what they are told to do.** Young children can only focus on one experience at a time, and they do so with their entire being. Imagine seeing a magnificent sunset. You are so captivated, you almost become the experience; you melt into it. Most of the time, we adults are able to juggle many different points of focus at once; we hold to-do lists in our heads. Preschoolers cannot do this. Colors, sounds, and movements grab their attention and they melt into the moment. Your preschool child needs your help in attending to matters that you deem important. You must state your instructions over and over again, yet remain calm. (To do this, use the Power of Attention [what you focus on, you get more of], and the Power of Free Will [you are the only person you can *make* change].) Then, give an assertive command by walking over to where your child is located. Get as close as necessary until she makes eye contact with you. Then say, "There you are," in a soothing voice. Follow up with: "It's time for lunch. You can play more after lunch." Finally, offer two positive choices. "You have a choice. You can help cut your sandwich in half sitting in your chair, or standing next to the table. Which would you like, sitting or standing?"

◆ **When they know that an action is wrong, they may do it anyway.** Young children imitate your words before they can integrate your teachings. Although they might say the right buzzwords, they are not necessarily ready to use the concepts the buzzwords imply to govern themselves. They will look straight at you, say "It's not nice to push," and then proceed to knock the baby flat. Children under the age of seven do not have inner speech and do not talk to themselves inside their heads. Only when they reach the age of eight or nine can a child use concepts conveyed by language to override their own impulses.

Adults use inner speech to plan, organize, and foresee conse-quences of possible actions. In other words, we adults can think before we act. Young children act first and then bargain, "I'll be good next time." Inner speech also allows adults to quickly process information. As you probably have noticed, most of what you say to children goes in one ear and out the other. They simply cannot process our words as quickly as we can say them. To determine whether or not your child has developed inner speech, do the fol-lowing: 1) Ask her, "Do you hear yourself talk to yourself in your head?" If she looks at you strangely as if to say, "No, do you?" it is not there yet. 2) Ask your child to lip-synch a song without making any sounds. In order to do this she must be able to hear the words in her head and then move her lips to form those words.

◆ **They are gloriously funny and love the ridiculous . . . but they ask lots of questions.** I was in an airport bathroom. In the next stall was a mother and child. I heard, "Mom, why does the light flush the toilet?" "Why is the suitcase inside with us?" "What's this little box?" "Why is the roll of toilet paper so big?" The mother answered two of the endless questions. Suddenly the girl's doll shot into my stall. I pushed it back to them as the woman apologized for the incident. I said to the woman, "It's tough being four." She asked, "How do you know my daughter's age when you haven't even seen her?" I responded, "Four-year-olds ask about four hundred questions every day. She just asked you at least ten in two minutes." "Four hundred," she sighed. "I'm exhausted."

The School-Age Years: Six to Eleven Years

Between the ages of six and eleven, your child becomes capable of classifying objects and events. She will also use language to express those classifications. This allows her to become more aware of her-self in relationship to others. Meaning: School-age children com-pare and compete. Children focus intensely on their peers and form relationships based on perceived similarity. Boys play mostly with boys and girls generally stick with girls. Likewise, boys emulate their fathers and girls emulate their mothers. Children cement their gender roles. They strive to match cultural norms as boys learn to suppress fears and girls learn to dampen aggressiveness. School-age children begin to realize that they have more in common with other children than adults, and the value they place on friendship rises accordingly.

School-age children gradually become more logical. The journey starts slowly. One first-grade child told his pastor that at Easter, Jesus comes out to look for his shadow. Children of seven and eight often complain, "It's not fair." With stronger language and cognitive skills, they are more apt to argue, analyze rules, and view situations as unjust. Comparing, they ask, "Why can Sarah stay up till ten when I have to go to bed at nine?" They reason and protest until frustrated. Out-of-control parents end the debate with "Because I said so."

As children become better at evaluating their own performance (around age seven), they become more eager to master new skills. They can also become highly self-critical. Repeated failures can create severe self-esteem problems and children may start to avoid risks. While a four-year-old will do anything and keep trying, school-age children often shy away from possible failures. They say things like, "I don't care about sports; they're stupid," to cover up a potential area of failure.

School-age children are more aware of themselves and of others. They study other people and amass information about them. They are receptive to modeling and fixate on athletes or musicians they admire and imitate. They may do wonderful impersonations of relatives.

A school-age child has a huge list of developmental tasks to accomplish. The biggest one is learning the skills that she perceives she will need in adulthood. For some children, these skills are reading, writing, and math. For others, they are learning how to manipulate, con others, steal, or fight. A school-age child must learn from her own mistakes and decide for herself that "I am capable." She must learn to listen in order to collect information and think logically.

She must learn about rules and the consequences of breaking them. She must test her own ideas and values, and see that she can disagree with others and still be loved. School-age children grow in their ability to cooperate during the same years in which they contrast their abilities with those of others. They grapple with the concept of responsibility and strengthen their internal control mechanisms.

Each one of these many tasks requires trial and error. Reread the paragraph above and let it register in your brain. For the truth is that in order to learn to listen, children must learn the consequences of not listening. In order to learn from mistakes, they must make them. In order to develop cooperation, they must sometimes be resistant. These skills slowly become more and more refined between the ages of six and twelve. Some children reach adulthood still working on these tasks. I number myself among these children!

School-age Children's Irritation Points

◆ **Resisting your directions.** Six-year-old children may consistently choose to be uncooperative. They may throw fits like younger children or they may start being "fresh." You may hear remarks such as, "Why should I?" or, "I don't have to." At seven, children's energy is usually focused inward. They may be moody and withdrawn and spend time sulking. When told to do things, children of seven often resist, with comments like, "Why do I have to?" or, "It's not fair." Yet if you firmly remind your child that she needs to do something, she will complete the task. Advances on the road to compliance usually come during the eighth year of life. Your child will obey and then walk off, mumbling face-saving gripes you can't quite decipher. Nine- and-ten-year-old children tend to worry, complain, and make excuses. These excuses, some of them fairly plausible, are often physical. ("I can't practice the piano because my head hurts.") Our job through all this is self-control. Breathe deeply. Use the Power of Acceptance (this moment is at it is). Use the Power of Attention and repeatedly remind the child what to do.

◆ **Bickering with siblings or friends.** At age six, children begin exploring the depth and breadth of friendships. These younger school-age children tend to criticize their friends. "You're cheating," and "I'm not your friend anymore," they announce. They resort regularly to name-calling and fighting. At seven, children tend to retreat to their room and withdraw from the struggle, instead of "duking it out" like their younger counterparts. Seven-year-old children are concerned with themselves and how others treat them. They need extra encouragement from their parents. When siblings are close together in age, as their needs for parental attention increase, so too do acts of sibling rivalry and bickering. When squabbling between children intensifies, read this as a signal to devote extra time to each child individually. By the age of eight, children are able to conduct good two-way relationships. This brings real "best friends" on the scene. With this development comes intensity in demands and fights. At home, much less tattling occurs because, at this age, children want relationships to go well. By age nine and older, friends become more important than siblings.

Nine is a quieter, more thoughtful age than eight is. By age ten or so, children adore their friends and their mother as well. You might think that peace would prevail with siblings, too, but this is not usually the case. Generally, the more "in love" a child is with her parents, the more she competes with her siblings. In blended families, all these issues intensify until the stepchildren establish firm, healthy relationships with each other. That process can take at least two to three years.

◆ **Needing endless reminders.** As children grow older, parents often assume they should know how to manage themselves. Indeed they do "know," but their energy is usually focused on other areas, ones that are not priorities for parents. Have you ever been so busy you forgot to eat or brush your teeth? Have you ever been so consumed by your work that you had trouble focusing on your children? Reread the list of developmental tasks faced by school-age children and you will see how much they have to do. Learning to read, write, and establish friendships takes so much energy that brushing your teeth can seem inconsequential. A seven-year-old child simply gets lost in her own world and forgets life's daily routines. If you don't tell her to wash her face, she probably won't. If you don't remind her to say "Excuse me" or "Thank you," those words probably will not be said. A seven-year-old child is usually compliant in obeying your reminders. Mercifully gone are the flat refusals and fits of earlier years.

Eight-year-old children are generally good self-starters, but they need some freedom in accomplishing tasks. They tire easily because they work, play, and eat fast. They need your encouragement, reminders, and help to finish what they have started and to clean up their own messes. By age nine, these skills strengthen, although children still tend to accomplish their tasks at their own pace (which may not strike you as appropriate). When your child turns ten and you think, Surely by now she must be old enough to accomplish these basic tasks independently, you will find she still needs to be reminded about bedtime and a bath. By age ten, though, you may only need to say one word ("Bath") in order to get your child to comply (albeit with an attitude).

◆ **Feeling unjustly treated.** "The teacher always picks on me." "You pay more attention to him than you do to me." These are common complaints voiced by school-age children. It's useless for you to try to convince your child that the complaints are unjustified. Your child is comparing herself to others, trying to establish herself as a group member, and making sense out of differences as well as she can. The best kind of help you can offer is empathy. This can only be done by using the Power of Acceptance. If your child says, "You like her better than me," listen carefully to your child's underlying message and reflect back to her what you see, what you think she is feeling, and what you think she really needs. You might respond, "Your whole body is slouched down. You seem discouraged. It sounds like you and I need some time together."

◆ **Being overly sensitive.** School-age children hold themselves to high standards. They are beginning to truly internalize all they have been taught, and they struggle to live up to the expectations they now place on themselves. Self-critical, they are also quite sensitive to outside criticism. For the first time, they fully recognize their own failures and mistakes. Accordingly, they often make self-effacing comments, engage in odd behaviors to reduce tension, and withdraw from certain situations. Your child may say, "I never do anything right." Instead of rushing to correct her, use your best listening skills and offer a response such as "Things didn't turn out the way you had hoped?" Your child may deal with tension by drumming her fingers, picking her cuticles, biting her nails, or with other nervous habits. In this case, redirect your child toward more socially acceptable anxiety-reducing behaviors. Get her outside, running, and playing. Some children may try to avoid mistakes by adopting an "I don't care" attitude about nearly everything. When children get to the point of saying "I don't care," they are really saying, "I don't feel cared for." Use your Power of Unity to encourage and connect with your child. Children who are being too hard on themselves will need a great deal of your attention and praise. Take time to notice them and join them in pressure-free activities. Go to the movies or ride bikes together. Choose books that are somewhat difficult for your child to read herself, so you can continue reading to her as you did when she was young. You'll both enjoy these times.

◆ **Saying "What?"** Before you have even finished giving your child a directive, she blurts out, "What?" You want to scream, but there is a reason why your child does this. Older school-age children are starting to develop inner speech, so they now have conversations going on both inside and outside their heads. When their inner speech is relatively "young," it is hard for them to listen to both conversations at once. Calmly repeat your statements, and remember to disconnect disobedience from disrespect.

◆ **Bending the truth.** Your child may look you in the eye and deny having done something you know that she did. Brittany wrote her name in a felt-tip pen on the van's armrest. Her mom said, "Brittany, you wrote your name on the armrest." Her response was,

"No, I didn't. Jimmy did." "Jimmy is two—he can't even write yet," her mother answered. Brittany said calmly, "I taught him." Unlike preschool children, who explore the difference between fact and fantasy through play, older children who are in the midst of developing their reasoning abilities need to test the difference between fact and fiction in real life. They do it by making up delightful stories. To maneuver through these developmental challenges, use the skills in this book. Brittany's mom started the interaction by focusing on behavior she did not want. This led to an argument. Using loving guidance, Brittany's mom could have said, "Brittany, look at your name in the car. You have a choice. You can clean it with a washcloth or a sponge. Which will you use?" As Brittany chooses and begins the clean-up process, her mom must encourage her by saying, "You did it! You cleaned up the armrest and your seat!" She could then use the Power of Unity to connect with Brittany and watch her write her name on a piece of paper in the house.

YOUR RESPONSE TO IRRITATION POINTS IS THE KEY

The key fact you must remember is that many irritation points serve a healthy purpose. As annoying as these behaviors are, they are also crucial to your child's development. Distinguishing between what is a problem and what is normal involves understanding children's developmental stages. Consider temper tantrums. Temper tantrums are typical if the fits are being thrown by a toddler, but they can signal real problems that must be addressed if they're being thrown by a seven-year-old child. As a parent, you must gauge whether or not the behavior is typical for your child's age group.

One parent told me that her seven-year-old son's dawdling and distractibility worried her: "I say it's bedtime but he doesn't seem to hear. Eventually he heads to the bedroom, but he gets distracted by a magazine and starts riffling through it. I feel like such a nag. Every day it's the same thing—dawdling about bedtime, tooth brushing, prayers. . . . His father thinks his hearing needs to be checked." As you know from reading this chapter, the behaviors that concerned these parents are simply typical of a boy who is seven.

Another mother told me about her eight-year-old daughter's refusal to comply with any of her commands. Their house is the scene of endless power struggles as the girl challenges her mother to "*Make* me go to bed," and, "*Make* me do my homework." Young children communicate by trying to make you feel as they feel. An older child who is still doing this is screaming for help. Something more than development is at work. If you feel hopeless around your child, your child probably feels hopeless. Give up the fear-based discipline measures you have been using and use the loving options taught in this book. If you still cannot reach your child, seek professional help.

There are no magic tricks to overrule development. Use the Power of Acceptance—this moment is as it is. You only aggravate yourself if you cling to the belief that through better handling of discipline your child will always comply. Conversely, increasing your knowledge of child development does not mean you should ignore misbehavior or forego disciplining your child. You must respond to misbehavior in order to teach your child more socially acceptable ways to express herself.

Misbehavior is communication.

Toddlers throw fits. Preschoolers scream, "I hate you." School-age children "talk back," mumble, and stomp off. Through the ways you respond to each troubling behavior, you teach your child acceptable ways to express anger. Eventually, you will hear your child say, "I don't like it when you take my things. Ask first." This day will not have arrived by serendipity. You will have taught your child to speak in this manner. Your teaching is called discipline.

11

Loving Guidance in Action: Solving the Top Discipline Problems

Many of my friends have older children ranging in age from 15 to 25. As part of my research for this chapter, I called several of them to ask what they remembered about discipline problems. Although my friends vaguely recalled problems with sharing or tattling, they really didn't remember any details. Interestingly, though, my friends could recall their own childhoods and give detailed descriptions of events that had occurred with their own parents when they themselves were as young as four. When I called the children of my friends, they, in turn, remembered every detail of long-past discipline encounters. Their parents' statements and behavior had made lasting impressions. As a parent, your words and actions are extremely powerful, which is the reason that this book is about becoming conscious of what you say and do to yourself as well as to your children.

This chapter presents real-life scenarios that demonstrate the use of the *Seven Powers for Self-Control* and the *Seven Basic Discipline Skills*. In each situation, adults use the skills of loving guidance. The parents also demonstrate an understanding of why children misbehave, as discussed in chapter 10. I illustrate the *Seven Powers for Self-Control* by "broadcasting" the parents' inner speech (what they say to and do for themselves). I illustrate the *Seven Basic Discipline Skills* by describing how the parents handle their children. My goal in sharing these scenarios is to give you concrete models of what you can say and do in specific discipline situations with your children. Athletes visualize success. So will we. Together, we will create new parenting images. So read, relax, and open your mind to these new possibilities. This chapter prepares you for chapter 12, which presents a seven-week program to help you change your habitual responses to conflict. Changing habits is difficult but doable. When you stumble, pick up this book and reread this chapter. Refresh yourself, remind yourself, renew yourself. Then share that internal state with your children.

These scenarios cannot describe the exact approaches you might take, but each one presents a responsible approach which demonstrates the skills I teach. As you read the vignette, remember:

◆ **Your job is to help your child to be more likely to choose to comply with your wishes.** Your job also involves keeping your primary focus on safety. Safety is a relative term. Sometimes your best option is to remove your child or yourself from the scene rather than screaming. You could say, "I am concerned about you and this situation. I am going to calm myself down before we discuss the problem." Sometimes you are calm enough to create a teaching and learning moment; sometimes you are not.

◆ **Your child's job is to test the limits, based on his current developmental level.** Children learn from their testing, from your responses, and from their own natural development. As they learn, they form and test new hypotheses. The testing never ends. Change occurs constantly and conflict plays an integral part in it.

THE "DISCIPLINE TWO-STEP"

Discipline reminds me of the country-and-western two-step. This dance involves two different rhythms—first slow-slow, and then quick-quick. Discipline also involves two steps: slow-slow and quick-quick.

The slow-slow part involves the building of healthy relationships. Parents must build healthy relationships with themselves, each other, and their children. Your loving relationship with your children, built over time, serves as a deeply motivating force for good behavior. When your children feel loved, valued, and capable in your presence, they are far more likely to choose cooperation over opposition.

Think about this in your own life. When your relationship with your mate is going well and you feel close to each other, a willing spirit prevails. Imagine yourself and your partner sitting on the sofa. If your partner got up and you asked, "Would you get me a soda from the refrigerator?" the response would probably be "Sure, honey." If your relationship were strained, however, communication and closeness would suffer. You might hear a different response to the same request—something like, "Get it yourself." Bitterness kills the cooperative spirit in adults and children. If your child persists in being more resistant than cooperative despite your patient, loving guidance, then your relationship needs repair.

Sarah was raising her son almost single-handedly. Her husband, Bob, brought home a paycheck and occasionally played with Michael, but did nothing else on the domestic front. Sarah worked as a beautician and took full responsibility for their child, house, chores, and meals.

Fearing that Bob might leave them, Sarah even tried to keep Michael "out of Daddy's way" while he rested. Sarah was overwhelmed and her life was a continual rush. She often surrendered to Michael's demands just to save time. Michael, in turn, became more and more resistant and difficult—far beyond the norm for his stage of development. "Go clean your room," Sarah would command, and he would shout back, "No, I won't!" Sarah would then snap, "Well, then you won't watch TV today." Michael, showing no emotion, would reply, "What do I care?"

Sarah and Michael are "out of relationship." Sarah's stressful existence has left no room for her to connect joyfully with Michael.

He feels neglected and conveys his sadness with his apathy and opposition. In effect, he is saying, "I don't care about my life because you don't seem to care about me." If your child seems totally resistant or apathetic, he is begging you to make time to connect with him. Do enjoyable things together regularly and rediscover your joy in one another. Children who need attention often capture it through misbehavior. Don't let their misdeeds distract you from the important underlying message. Take charge not by punishing, but by planning time to be close with your child. The slow-slow minutes and hours you spend together now—reading, playing, talking—build the motivation for a lifetime of good behavior.

Togetherness, though, will not teach children how to behave. That comes in the quick-quick part of discipline.

The quick-quick part of discipline involves your conduct in the heat of conflict. What can you say or do to help your child choose to clean his room? How can you help your child reflect upon his choices? What can you do to solve immediate problems? The skills you use in the quick-quick part of discipline can build up or tear down your relationship with your child. The following scenarios demonstrate the quick-quick strategies you have learned in this book—but never forget the importance of the slow-slow. A loving relationship is the foundation for your success.

PARENT TRIGGERS, CHILD TRIGGERS

As I mentioned in chapter 3, there are two kinds of triggers for discipline encounters. One kind involves you wanting your child to do something he is not doing. The other kind of trigger involves your child wanting something to happen that is not happening. In essence, one kind of trigger involves you trying to do your job; the other involves your child trying to do his job. The following scenes are divided accordingly.

Parents Doing Their Job

"Stay in the yard and play"

"Bailey, stay in the yard and play with Michelle. In the yard, you are safe from cars." Bailey's mother, Doreen, has assertively stated a limit, but the girls are excited and are not listening. To make sure the limit is clear, Bailey's mom says, "On three, I want you girls to run around the edge of the yard. Trace the whole yard as if it were a rectangle. One, two, three, go!" The girls take off squealing. Upon their return to Doreen, she says, "You did it. You ran around the whole yard. Bailey, your hands were pumping like this [demonstrates arm positions] and Michelle, your legs came up in the back like this [demonstrates leg position]. So now you know the limits. Play inside the line that you traced." As she goes inside, she calls out, "Have fun!"

When Doreen checks on the girls ten minutes later, they are in the neighbor's yard, gathering pinecones. She goes over to them and says, "I see you got excited about your project and forgot about staying in the yard." Both girls look up, their faces fall, and their little voices reply in unison, "We forgot." After giving it some thought, Doreen concludes that she has adequately taught the girls about the yard limits, and not just on that day, but also on other days. She decides that consequences might help: "Girls, I have shown you the safe boundaries. You had a choice to remember them or to forget. It is important that you pay attention to help keep yourselves safe. If you forget and leave the yard again, both of you will come inside, and then Michelle will go home. Do you understand what will happen if you leave the yard?" They both nod. "Tell me," Doreen says. Both girls repeat the consequences they have heard.

"Get in your car seat"

Martha felt harried. She was ten minutes behind schedule and her three-year-old child, Gary, had been singing a chorus of noes all morning. Lately, the car seat had been an issue and Martha was apprehensive. She thought, I don't have time for this, not this morning. Martha was in knots, but she finally decided to take hold of herself. "Breathe," she commanded herself. "You must relax. Remember, discipline yourself first and your children second. You're already late, but don't panic. The more you hurry Gary, the more trouble he gives you. Focus on what you want, Martha. You can do it. Keep breathing. All is well. This moment is as it is."

Out loud, Martha calmly said, "It is time to go. Get in your car seat." Gary ignored her. Martha continued, "You have a choice. Do you want me to lift you up so you can open the door, or do you want me to open it for you?" Gary ran toward the car yelling, "Me do it." When Martha reached the car, she started to pick him up to open the door. He pushed her arm away and collapsed to the ground with his lip protruding and arms folded. Martha thought, Oh no, here we go again, but stopped short and said to herself, "I know what to do—reflect what you see." She said, "Gary, your arms are crossed and your lip is quivering [demonstrates his position]. Your body is telling me, 'I wanted to do it myself.'" Gary made eye contact and seemed to relax. Martha told herself, "Don't give up now. Stay calm." She said, "When you were a baby, I carried you in my arms like this [shows him]. I used to put you in your car seat [opens the door to show him]. Now you can do it by yourself. Climb in and hook it up. I will watch you." Gary slowly got up, his body still slightly tense. Martha said to herself, "Have faith; stay calm." Gary climbed in, pulled the belt over his head and buckled up. Martha exclaimed, "You did it! You climbed in and put your seat belt on yourself." Martha jumped into the car and drove off, late but fairly calm, as Gary started singing.

"Clean your room"

Nelson was a meticulous child, and organization was his strong suit. His brother Carlson was exactly the opposite. Mayhem was comfortable to him and his unwillingness to clean his room was a chronic problem.

Since chronic problems require problem-solving, not consequences, a family meeting was held to define the problem and create an action plan. The question the boys' parents posed to Carlson and to the entire family was "How can we help you [Carlson] be successful in keeping your room clean?" The first comments were not productive (Carlson suggested hiring a maid). However, in order to encourage Carlson to really tackle the problem, his parents acknowledged these comments without getting upset. The final plan turned out to be that there would be a designated time every week during which the whole family would clean their respective rooms. Periodically, each person would go to another's room to offer encouragement. The boys practiced giving encouraging statements such as "You did it! You are almost done. Keep at it." After the cleanup, pictures would be taken of each room for display and the family would enjoy some time together. Each person could request help. The boys practiced this by saying, "I'm having trouble with this. Would you help me?" Their parents reminded them to say "Thank you" for encouragement or help. The family decided to try this plan for two weeks and see how it worked.

When Mom checked on Carlson during that week's room-cleaning session, she helped him stay focused by noticing his accomplishments: "Carlson, you put all the baseball cards in their box." She would also help him to continue by offering choices if he seemed overwhelmed: "You could put the dirty clothes away, or sort out the pile on this chair. Which will you do?" When he made a decision, she would encourage him: "You decided to start with the chair. You can handle it."

"Finish your homework"

To help Chelsea succeed with her homework, her dad arranged a time and place for her to do it. Chelsea shopped for the supplies she needed and arranged her desk neatly. One Thursday night, Dad said gently, "Chelsea, remember to study your spelling words." Chelsea made a face and started mumbling. Her dad ignored the mumbling and continued to encourage Chelsea to do her task: "Would you like me to call them out to you in person or put them on the tape recorder?" Since the idea of making a tape was novel, Chelsea selected that option. As she pushed the button on the tape recorder to hear the first word, she heard a surprise from Dad instead. "Twinkle, twinkle little star, what a wonderful child you are." Chelsea hollered, "You're corny, Dad," and then studied her spelling list.

"Stop hitting your brother—be nice"

Chad was pounding on his younger brother Danny when their mother, Nancy, walked by. "Stop!" she shouted as she pulled them apart. Danny began crying and said, "Chad punched me. I hate him."

Nancy reflected this back to him: "Chad was hitting you and you're mad because he wouldn't stop?" Chad jumped in with, "The little twit was in my room. When I told him to leave, he stuck his tongue out at me." Nancy, losing patience, took a deep breath. She reminded herself that if she listened now and taught the boys how to resolve conflicts rather than simply punishing them, one day her efforts would be repaid. She vigilantly kept her mind focused on the positive intent of the boys. She knew this was the key to teaching. She created a mantra in her head, telling herself, "Positive intent, positive intent." "You wanted Danny out of your room so you asked him to leave, but he wouldn't." (Nancy summarized Chad's positive intent.) "Yeah," said Chad. "So then you started punching him? You may not hit your brother," Nancy said. "When you ask him to leave and he does not listen, come and get me. I will help you solve the problem without hitting."

Danny said, "I wanted to play with Chad and see his airplane." Nancy, exasperated, wondered how many times they had been over this. "Relax," she said to herself, "You can do this. Focus on the positive intent." With renewed spirit, Nancy said, "You wanted to play with Chad and see the airplane, so you came into his room and stood there?" Danny said softly, "Yes." Nancy continued teaching. "Danny, when you want to see the plane, you must say, 'Chad, may I look at your plane?' Say that now." Reluctantly, Danny said, "Chad, may I look at your plane?" Danny responded, "No, you twit."

At this, Nancy's patience evaporated. She heard her inner voice saying, "I've got more to do than mess with these two. I have taken enough time to teach them. I can't spare any more." Before she could regain her self-control, she shouted, "I have tried to teach you boys how to treat each other decently, but I give up. You can both forget about that stupid toy." With this, she grabbed the airplane and stomped out of the room towards the kitchen.

Within a few minutes, she felt guilty. She knew that guilt can lead to overly permissive parenting unless an adult restores his or her sense of equilibrium. She thought of the Power of Free Will, reminding herself that the only person you can make change is yourself, and then she was able to draw on the Power of Attention and focus on what she wanted to have happen. She went back to find the boys. "Boys, I do care about you and about how you behave," she said. "My job is to love you and teach you how to love each other. Chad, name-calling is hurtful. So was my loss of control. I'm sorry for what I said. At dinnertime, we will make a plan about going into each other's rooms. Both of you, think about how we can solve this problem together."

"It's bedtime"

Jeffrey, age two, was watching television when his mother, Eileen, announced, "When that show is over, it will be time for a bath before bed." When the show ended, Eileen headed toward the TV to turn it off. "No bed!" screamed Jeffrey. Eileen immediately felt her body tense and heard her inner thoughts saying, "Not again. I can't take this every night." She decided to breathe deeply and relax. Eileen talked herself through her own upset in order to help Jeffrey handle his. She reminded herself, "He is only two, and he is testing me. That's his job. My job is to stay calm, hold the limits, and offer compassion if possible. I can do this. When he digs in, I will lighten up."

She focused her attention on his arms and face, and said compassionately, "Your hands made fists [demonstrates], and your face got tight [another demonstration]. Your body said, 'I feel angry. I want more TV.'" Jeffrey relaxed a little. She quickly offered him a choice, saying excitedly, "Jeffrey, you have a choice!" His face relaxed a little more. "You can play with dolphins or frogs in the tub. Which would you like? Last night, the dolphins swam and swam." Eileen took her hand and pretended it was a swimming dolphin. Jeffrey immediately announced, "Dolphins."

Eileen celebrated his ability to decide by saying, "You chose the dolphins. You can swim with them in the tub tonight." Jeffrey ran to get the dolphins and happily climbed into the bath. After a while, Eileen told him, "In five more minutes, it will be time for pajamas and toothbrushing." Jeffrey immediately said, "No, more play. More dolphins." Eileen felt her heart sink and her body tense up once again, and she said to herself, "It doesn't have to be this hard. I don't have to put up with this. I was patient but this is endless. I'm tired."

She almost lost it, but pivoted by using the Power of Attention to regain her course. She told herself, "What you focus on, you get more of. If I am upset, I am focusing on what I don't want. I sure am upset. Do I want more of this demanding behavior? No! Okay, what do I want? I want him out of the tub and into the towel. I'll take it step by step." Eileen took two more deep breaths, saying to herself, "This moment is as it is. Relax." She decided to be playful this time and have some fun. "Oh, no, did you hear that?" she asked Jeffrey. He looked interested, and she continued, "It is the dolphin distress call, Wheo-o-eo. The poor dolphin is sick! Quick, get him out of the water and into the rescue towel immediately!" Eileen started examining the dolphin and talking to it softly. Jeffrey stood up to hear. Eileen said, "I need your help. Come dry off; we may have an emergency." He quickly dried off and sat in Eileen's lap as they examined the dolphin. She asked him, "What do you think is wrong?" He started to tell a story about what he thought might be wrong. She listened, responded, and put on his pajamas. Jeffrey was still worried about the dolphin, and Eileen felt ready to pass the parenting ball to her husband. She said, "I'm not sure what made your dolphin feel sick, but your father will know. Hop in bed. I'll send Dad in and he will tell you the whole story." As Eileen passed her husband in the hall, she said tiredly, "I got him into bed. Now it's your turn. Tell him a story about how his dolphin got sick." Dad looked totally bewildered, but Eileen had just enough energy left to say, "Good luck." Jeffrey's dad sat on his son's bed and asked, "You have a sick dolphin?" Jeffrey threw the dolphin on the floor and said, "No sick dolphin—juice." Dad hollered out to Eileen, "What do I do now?" She responded, "The best you can, dear."

Dad felt totally out of his element. He thought that his child *should* just do what he was told. Jeffrey knew that it was bedtime. When Dad heard the word "should" resonate in his brain, he immediately started breathing deeply, calming himself by saying, "This moment is as it is; relax." As he relaxed, so did Jeffrey. Dad took the opportunity to say goodnight to Jeffrey's head, shoulders, fingers, legs, and feet. This ritual brought them together and the fight over the juice disappeared as quickly as it had manifested itself.

"I'm stopping this car right now"

Linda was taking a three-hour car trip with her son, John (age ten), and his friend Michael (age nine). The boys talked and joked until boredom set in. Then they grew loud and started shoving each other. Linda hoped they would calm down, but they did not. As the volume climbed, she became edgy. Without thinking, she yelled, "Don't make me pull this car over!" As soon as the words flew out of her mouth, she wanted them back. She said to herself, "I don't want to give my power away to these boys. They can't *make* me pull the car over. I am in charge. I will decide if I am going to pull over or not. Linda, take control back of this situation." She then said to the boys, "I am driving at seventy miles an hour, and you are distracting me with your ruckus. I cannot drive safely when you are so disruptive, so I'm pulling the car over."

She pulled to the shoulder and got out of the car. Then she went around and opened the back door so she could talk with the boys eye-to-eye. She said, "This is a long trip and we have an hour left. What could you do that would be enjoyable and safe?" The first three suggestions from the boys were funny to them, but not to her. Linda was in no mood for silliness, but she said calmly, "Come on, work with me on thinking of things to do." They decided to draw pictures and play a modified form of Pictionary. Linda got back in the car and drove off. As the boys began to organize themselves and the game, she encouraged them: "You boys found everything you needed for the game and you wrote down the rules on a napkin. That took a lot of creativity and thought."

Children Doing Their Job

"I had it first"

Little Emily was wandering through the house when she passed her big brother Landon. He was drawing at the kitchen table and she decided to draw, too. Focused totally on her wish to draw, Emily grabbed a marker from Landon. Shocked, he looked up, hit her, and shouted, "I had it!" Emily, stunned by the blow, screamed, "I need it!" All the screaming drew their father to the scene.

In situations like this, Dad has many options. He can view the children as "bad" and put all the markers away until the children can learn to share. He can view the children as "mean" and put them both in time out until they can "be nice." He can view them as "helpless" and solve their problem himself by saying, "Landon, you use the marker for five minutes and then Emily will have a turn." He can consider one child "good" (Landon) and the other "bad" (Emily) and say something like this: "Who had it first? Emily, you know better than to grab things. Why don't you think before you act?" Alternatively, Dad could view this conflict as a teaching opportunity. This father chose to teach.

"Stop! What happened?" he asked. Both children began shouting at once. Dad said calmly, "Landon, you tell me first." As Landon spoke, their father stood beside Emily with his arm around her, verbally and nonverbally assuring her that she would get a chance to tell her side as well.

Landon said, "I was drawing and Emily grabbed my marker.

Now my picture is ruined." Emily jumped in and said, "But he hit me." Dad asked, "Landon, did you like it when she grabbed the marker?" "No," replied Landon. Dad knew that if he was going to successfully use the conflict moment as an opportunity to teach, he needed to focus on the positive intent of each child.

"You wanted to stop your sister so you hit her? Hitting hurts; you may not hit," said Dad. "When you want her to stop, say, 'Stop! This is my marker. Get your own!'" "But I needed one," Emily whined. Dad explained, "You wanted a marker right away so you grabbed one from Landon. You may not grab things from people. You need to ask, 'Landon, where are the markers?' Say that now, Emily." Emily asked the question and Landon told her where to get a marker. Dad walked off and noticed he was attributing positive intent to himself. As he listened to his inner speech, he heard, "You wanted the kids to solve the problem, so you stayed calm and taught them. Good for you." With this, he just grinned.

"I'm telling"

At a table in the backyard, Tracy and McKensie were playing house. As they quietly set the table for dinner, Albert, Tracy's slightly older brother, stormed through announcing that he was a Power Ranger. McKensie dropped his role as Dad and joined Albert in the game of Power Rangers. Albert declared Tracy the "bad guy," and both he and McKensie began to chase her. Tracy, repudiating her new assigned role, proclaimed herself a "princess." She raised her head high and marched back into the house. Disregarding her royal role, Albert and McKensie kept chasing her.

Finally, Tracy dropped her princess stance and said, "I'm telling." She began screaming for her mom. Then McKensie stuck out his tongue at Tracy and called her a baby. Mom soon arrived. She approached Tracy, took a deep breath to relax her body and said to herself, "Stay calm. You can handle this. Focus on teaching."

Her mother then spoke to Tracy: "You seem upset. What happened?" Tracy said, "They were chasing me." Mom responded, "Tracy, tell them both now, 'I don't like it when you chase me.

Stop.' " Before Tracy could do so, McKensie hollered, "We were just playing." Mom again told Tracy, "Tell them, 'Stop. I don't like it when you chase me.' " Tracy stated this firmly.

The Mom then followed up on what McKensie had conveyed to her by saying, "McKensie, you wanted to play with Tracy, so you chased her?" He nodded. Mom continued, "You didn't notice she wasn't enjoying the chase, because you thought it was fun?" He dropped his head. Mom knew that he felt bad that he had not considered Tracy's point of view. She told him, "McKensie, when you want someone to play with you, you must ask them. You must say, 'Do you want to play?' If they say yes, you can play. If they say no, you must find something else to do." Firmly and compassionately, Mom then said, "Ask Tracy now. Say, 'Do you want to play with me?' " McKensie asked the question and Tracy responded, "No; you called me a baby." McKensie said, "I'm sorry." Tracy said, "Okay, then I will play with you, but I'm the princess, not a Power Ranger." Albert quietly observed the entire exchange and said nothing but learned a great deal.

"Look at me!" "Watch me!" "Watch me!"

Reggie and his older sister Casey usually got along fairly well. Today was Casey's seventh birthday and she was having a party at home. Reggie was going to invite one friend, too, so he would have a special visitor with whom to play.

Just before the party began, Reggie began demanding attention. He shouted, "Watch me climb. Watch me dance. Look at me—my pants are backward." Casey complained to their dad, "He's a jerk. He's going to ruin everything."

Dad decided to take some time to bring the children together. He said, "In our family, we love and help each other. Sometimes when Casey has a special day, it seems hard to know what to do, Reggie. You think there may not be enough love for you. But it's not true. You are both loved." He grabbed them and picked them up and twirled them around. They giggled happily. He had successfully used the Power of Unity. Then he set the children down and said, "Today is Casey's birthday, so we all must do our part to make it a happy one. Reggie, your job will be to open the door and say, 'Hi, come on in.' If the guest brings a present, say, 'Please put the present on the counter.' Then take a break to play with your friend. After your break, we will need you to take pictures. Let's practice your part. Casey, go outside and ring the doorbell so Reggie can rehearse." As Reggie practiced, Dad noticed him and encouraged him, saying things such as, "You did it. You opened the door and said, 'Hi. Come on in.' Practice again. This time say, 'Please put that present on the counter,' and point to it." Dad hugged both the children and said, "We make a great team."

"I didn't do it"

Ellen went grocery shopping with Matthew, her eight-year-old son. When they got home, he helped bring in the packages and then went up to his room. He was very quiet. After putting away the food, Ellen decided to check on Matthew. She found him sitting on his bed holding a Milky Way. Wondering where he had gotten it, she asked him, and he answered, "I just have it." Ellen then realized that he had probably picked it up while they were shopping. She asked, "Did you get it at the store?" Again, he responded, "I just have it."

Ellen realized that her son had stolen the candy bar. At first, she thought, How am I going to get him to admit it? Breathing deeply, she realized that forcing him to be honest was not the point. Mentally, she shifted gears and reframed the question. She asked herself, "How do I help him to be more likely to choose to tell me the truth? I must create a safe space so he can admit to his mistake." With these thoughts in mind, she spoke. "Matthew, I think when we were shopping you saw the candy bar. You knew I wouldn't buy it but you wanted it so badly that you couldn't stop yourself from taking it." Matthew lowered his eyes and said, "I really wanted it."

Ellen replied, "You wanted it, so you stole it. How do you feel now about what you did?" "Bad," said Matthew. "The candy bar is not yours," said Ellen. "It must be returned. Get your coat and the candy bar and get in the car. We'll go back to the store." They drove back in total silence.

At the store, Ellen instructed Matthew, "Find the manager by asking a clerk, 'May I speak to the manager?' Then tell him what you did and anything else you would like to say." Tears welled up in Matthew's eyes but he located the manager and explained what had happened. Then he returned the candy bar.

On the way home, Ellen started to lecture him about stealing, but stopped herself. She thought, I want him to figure out about right and wrong without my telling him, and I want to help Matthew reflect on his experience. She decided to say to him, "You chose to steal the candy bar. Then you acted responsibly by returning the candy to the manager. How do you feel now about what you did?" Matthew answered, "I'm glad I took it back. I feel better now." Ellen said, "You made a mistake and you learned from it. You can tell if something is right or wrong by how it makes you feel. It feels rotten to steal and it feels good to correct your mistake."

"I hate you"

In a sporting-goods store, five-year-old Jeremy was shooting basketballs while his Dad shopped. Jeremy was totally absorbed in his game when his Dad said, "Let's go. I'm done." Jeremy slouched down, kicked some items off a shelf, and said, "I'm not going. I hate you."

His father felt his heart beat faster and felt like shouting, but instead he took several deep breaths and told himself silently, "Don't see this as disrespect, Greg. Remember, he is young. Put yourself in his shoes. He was happily shooting hoops when I suddenly said, 'Let's go.' I need to start this departure over again." Out loud, Greg said, "Son, you seem angry. You were having fun and I just said 'Stop,' without giving you any warning." His son ignored him, pretending not to hear. Greg got closer to his son, waited for eye contact, and said, "Shoot the ball five more times. Then it is time to go. I want to watch you shoot."

Jeremy was reluctant to relinquish his anger. His dad took the ball, tossed it to him, and said, "Think fast!" As Jeremy began to shoot baskets, Greg noticed and encouraged him. He said, "You shot using both your arms and your legs for extra power. Looks good, son." Greg also counted aloud the number of shots. After the fifth shot, he caught the ball in the air to help his child successfully stop. Jeremy started whining, "Just one more, Dad." Greg commented, "Five means five. It is hard to stop when you are having fun, but it is time to go. You can walk out holding my hand, or you can ride in the cart. Which will you choose?"

Jeremy said nothing. He scowled and crossed his arms. Dad read the nonverbal language of resistance and said, "I can see by your action that you have chosen for me to hold your hand." He took Jeremy's hand and began to walk. Jeremy pulled back, refusing to move. Greg had had enough. He dragged Jeremy for a few feet. Greg attempted to breathe deeply and relax, but he was not willing to calm himself down totally. He said to himself, "Just get out of the store as safely as possible." He decided his best option was to pick Jeremy up, carry him out, and keep quiet. He said only, "I'm going to carry you so I will not hurt your arm since you are pulling against me."

"Why can't I? Everyone else does."

"Why can't I swim in the lake? Ricky does," Leah said angrily. Another Saturday morning and it's the same issue, thought her mother, Donna, who wanted to scream, "You're not Ricky!" Instead, she quietly said, "You can't swim in the lake for one big reason. I love you and plan to keep you safe. There are alligators and bacteria in the lake. I don't want you to get hurt or sick." Still insistent, Leah replied, "Ricky swims in the lake and stays safe. He doesn't get eaten or sick."

Donna, though feeling desperate, willed herself to remain calm and solve this problem. She decided to draw on the Power of Perception to own her own upset, and the Power of Free Will, realizing that the only person she could make change was herself. She said, "I will not let you swim in the lake. I know you don't like it, but I won't change my mind. You can be angry at me and we can keep fighting, or we can work together to find some solutions. Tell me what is so special about swimming in the lake."

Leah sat silently for what seemed to be an eternity, but Donna waited patiently for her answer. Finally Leah said, "Everyone does it but me."

Listening carefully, with empathy, Donna said, "So you feel left out." Leah nodded and said, "Carmen gets to swim with Ricky." Donna then said, "If you could swim in the lake, you would feel closer to Ricky. So the real problem is that you want to play a lot with Ricky and get to be even better friends." Leah said nothing but her mother intuitively felt that her grasp of the situation was accurate. Donna continued, "You may not swim in the lake, but you can invite Ricky to come with us to the beach or the town pool." Leah decided the beach would be more fun. (Later that year, Leah cultivated bacteria from the lake for a science project.)

"Sydney isn't eating her peas"

At dinner, Madeline blurted out, "Sydney isn't eating her peas." Their father, Daniel, looked at Madeline and asked, "Are you telling me to be helpful or hurtful?" Madeline thought a moment and replied, "Helpful."

This surprised Daniel. He stopped himself from making a sarcastic remark and reminded himself to be conscious of his intent. Eventually he resisted attributing a sarcastic negative intent and said, "How is telling me about Sydney helpful?" Madeline responded, "She needs good bones." Daniel smiled (although he felt like laughing) as he responded, "So you want Sydney to eat her vegetables so she will be healthy?" Madeline smiled, too. Daniel said, "Madeline, you need to tell Sydney, 'I care about you. I want you to be healthy. I think eating peas will help you.'" Madeline stared at her dad as if he had gone mad. He winked at the girls and said to Sydney, "I think your sister likes you." Attributing positive intent to Sydney and utilizing the Power of Unity strengthened the entire family.

"I DON'T HAVE TIME . . . " "WHAT IF . . . " "IT LOOKS GOOD ON PAPER, BUT . . . "

I hope that by now you have tried some of the skills in this book and have enjoyed moments of success. Such moments will occur more frequently as your skill level, confidence, and self-discipline increase. While reading the scenarios in this chapter, you may have felt your doubts and worries about loving guidance rearing up. If so, relax. Listen closely to your inner speech and learn your own language of resistance. Attribute a positive motive to yourself. Empathize with your difficulties. By treating yourself kindly, you can turn your own resistance into cooperation with the program.

For one last time, I want to remind you that the way in which you treat yourself is the way in which you will treat your children and the way in which they will treat others. The last chapter of this book is a seven-week training program to help you incorporate these principles into your daily life. Do it—for yourself, for your children, for your community, and for us all. Each time you watch the news and think, What can I do?, pick up this book and practice loving guidance. When you hear of senseless youth violence, of children killing teachers, parents, and each other, pick up this book and keep practicing. Your choice to rely on love instead of fear can and does make a difference. It all comes from your willingness to learn, grow, forgive, and change.

12

❦

The Loving
Guidance Program:
Change Your Life
in Seven Weeks

Any one of the many programs available for weight loss, relaxation, and positive thinking would probably work if you followed through with it. For me, following through has always been the kicker. I have found many excuses for not changing. ("I'm too tired." "Other things demand my energy.") Finally, I admitted to myself that when I don't do something, it's because I really don't want to. Frequently what I want to do is muddle through, griping, or even throw the occasional fit. Muddling through as usual simply seems easier than disciplining myself to change.

This chapter summarizes and makes concrete the information you have already read, in the form of a concise, seven-week program. Each week focuses you on one of the *Seven Powers for Self-Control* and the discipline skill that evolves from that power, centering on attitudes that will help train and focus your mind, and lead to strategies to use with your children. For many parents this book demands a philosophical shift, one which most people find makes sense. Still, integrating the principles of loving guidance into your life demands practice and commitment. I myself worked on these attitudes and skills vigilantly for five years before many of them felt natural. Over the past 15 years, thousands of adults and children have grown closer and happier through adherence to these sensible practices. When self-control is your guiding principle, mastering loving guidance is worth the work. You will feel so much better about yourself and your family and will experience much more peace and joy together. I guarantee it.

What if this were an instructional book for golf? Could you read it, put it aside, and then go play golf like Tiger Woods? No. You would need to practice, make mistakes, forgive yourself, and try again. It's unrealistic to expect yourself to read this book and automatically become a more positive parent. If you hold such impossibly high expectations for yourself, you will hold your children to the same unattainable standards, and then both of you will feel deficient and simply not "good enough."

To help you stay calm and focused so that you will succeed with the seven-week program, here are some tips:

◆ **Begin by recognizing how resistant your mind is to change.** Often you will find yourself not practicing or forgetting these techniques. Instead of saying, "I forgot," or, "I've been too busy," ask yourself, "Why don't I want to remember? What am I afraid of?" Listen quietly to the answer, without judgment. You are not bad. You're simply afraid of something. What is it?

◆ **You will resist practicing this program at some points.** When you become aware of resistance, tell yourself, "Resistance is my friend." Resistance acts as the brakes in your life. Without resistance, change might come too fast. Sometimes we do need to slow things down; doing so can be wise. Notice that when your children are changing the fastest because of their natural development, they are the most resistant to you (see chapter 10). They must use their brakes, just as you must.

◆ **Forgive yourself when you feel you have failed.** Give up the need to make yourself feel bad in order to change. Feeling rotten about yourself actually ingrains old habits and hinders change as you obsess about your shortcomings. Use the Powers for Self-Control to regain your self-esteem and your self-discipline.

◆ **Be patient with yourself.** You may need to do the exercises in week one for two months, then take off three months before starting on week two. This book is yours—use it at your own pace, extracting what is helpful and letting go of the rest.

◆ **Have fun, laugh at yourself, and enjoy the process.** Try not to let yourself get sucked into seriousness. You cannot have a happy ending to an unhappy journey.

◆ **Celebrate your successes.** Remember that although you cannot stop conflict, you can respond to it with integrity. When you do, you have succeeded. Consciously use your Power of Attention to focus on each tiny success you achieve.

◆ **When all else fails, take time to be thankful for something.** There is always something to be grateful for. Gratitude will refuel your soul and bring you renewed energy to begin your efforts again. It taps into the Power of Unity, the mother of the *Seven Powers for Self-Control.*

WEEK ONE

ATTITUDE SHIFT: Harnessing the Power of Perception
REASON: To own your own upset.
DISCIPLINE SKILL: Composure
VALUE: Integrity

◆ **Notice how your thoughts create your feelings.** When you feel angry, overwhelmed, or anxious, check to see what you are thinking. Where is your mind directed?

◆ **Listen to how often you blame others.** Carefully note any "make me" language. Notice how often you say, "Don't make me _____" or, "You made me _____." Replace "Don't make me _____" with "I'm going to _____."

◆ **When you are upset, say, "I feel angry, and it's okay."** Accept all your feelings. They are signals. Anger is a signal that you need a change. Take a deep breath and say, "I am willing to see this differently."

◆ **Remind yourself, "Whomever is in charge of my feelings is in charge of me."** Take back your power by owning your own upset. To own your own upset, say to yourself, "Each day, each hour, every moment, I choose the sounds I want to hear, the sights I want to see, and the actions I want to focus on."

◆ **When you are upset, *you* have a problem.** Your upset is a signal to you. You need to use one of the *Seven Powers for Self-Control* before you do anything else.

Composure: Living the values you want your child to develop

◆ **Breathe deeply and decide that you are going to stick with these exercises.** Maintaining composure is an option you always have available to you. Even when you lose your composure, in the next moment it can be yours again. You may feel ready to explode, but you can breathe deeply, choose to stay calm, and see the situation differently. If you explode anyway, you can still return to a state of calm—all is not lost. Self-control is a moment-by-moment decision. When you are upset, say to yourself, "I am willing to see this situation differently." Then, use one of the *Seven Powers for Self-Control* on yourself before you use one of the *Seven Basic Discipline Skills* with your child. Remember, discipline yourself first, and your children second. The use of these exercises will allow you to live the values you want your children to develop. It allows you and your child to live with **integrity**.

WEEK TWO

ATTITUDE SHIFT: Harnessing the Power of Attention
REASON: What you focus on, you get more of
DISCIPLINE SKILL: Assertiveness
VALUE: Respect

◆ **Tell yourself at least five times daily, "What I focus on, I get more of."** Do this when you wake up, at meals, and at bedtime.

◆ **Pay attention to your focus.** Are you focusing on what you want, or on what you don't want?

◆ **When you are upset, *Pivot*.** Tell yourself, "Okay, I'm upset. If I'm upset, I'm focusing on what I don't want. Do I want more of this in my life?" If the answer is no, take a deep breath. Focus on what you want your child to do more successfully. Then calmly tell your child what to do and why.

◆ **Tell your child what you *will* do.** "I will be happy to talk to you when you are calm," or "I am going to stop the car and make sure all children are safe, with seat belts on."

Assertiveness: Saying no and being heard

◆ **Listen to yourself talk to your children.** Are you passive, aggressive, or assertive? Change passive and aggressive statements into assertive commands. Use a calm, sure tone of voice.

◆ **Complete the following chart.** Check to see how much you have already changed by comparing it to your previous score recorded on page 85.

Week Ending	Passive Communications	Aggressive Communications	Assertive Communications
_____	_____ %	_____ %	_____ %

◆ **Give assertive commands to your children** when you want obedience. Use the following steps.

1) Gain your child's attention. Move close to your child until she looks at you. Say, "There you are," and smile.
2) Tell her what to do in understandable terms.
3) Gesture like a traffic cop to provide additional information.
4) If your child chooses to obey you, praise her in specific terms. Start with the words, "You did it," then describe what she did that led her to success. Avoid general praise such as, "Great job!"

◆ **If your child ignores you, say, "I will show you what I want you to do."** Then guide your child to success. If she still resists, offer her two positive choices. Alternatively, try using empathy, or ask, "What would help you ____ right now?"

◆ **When you feel frustrated with your child, express your thoughts or feelings directly** by saying, "I don't like it when you ____," or "When you ____, I feel ____." Then assertively tell her what you want her to do.

◆ **Teach your child to handle intrusions by other children in the following manner.** Go to the victim and say:

1) "Did you like it?"
2) Listen to the no you receive to decide if the victim's energy and confidence level are high or low. If her confidence and energy are low, accompany her to speak to the other child.
3) Say to the child, "Go tell ____, 'I don't like it when you ____.'"

◆ **Teach your children how to get what they want and respect the rights of others** by saying to the aggressor:

1) "You wanted ____." (Attribute positive intent.)
2) "You may not ____. ____ hurts [or, is not safe]."
3) "When you want ____, say [or do] ____."
4) "Do it now! Practice."

WEEK THREE

ATTITUDE SHIFT: Harnessing the Power of Free Will
REASON: The only person you can *make* change is yourself
DISCIPLINE SKILL: Choices
VALUE: Commitment

◆ **Catch yourself** when you say, "How can I get my child to ____?" Change the question to "How can I help my child to be more likely to choose ____?"

◆ **Change your "shoulds" to "coulds."** Then make a choice and live with it.

◆ **Allow others to have their own thoughts and feelings.** Pay attention to what you feel when people disagree with you. (Most of us feel threatened.)

◆ **Resist the need to make others happy or convince them that you have all the answers.** Remind yourself three times a day, "The only person I can *make* change is myself." Then choose to be pleasant and share that with others.

Choices: Building self-esteem and willpower

◆ **Discern how much influence a child has in a given situation.** Can she choose to stay up or must she go to bed? Can she choose what to wear or must she wear certain attire?

◆ **Check to see when you offer your child too many choices and when you offer too few.**

◆ **Do not give children choices in areas where you are afraid to make a decision.** You are the boss.

◆ **Give children two positive choices as a way of setting limits.** Use the following formula to get started.

1) "You may _____, or _____."
2) "What is your choice?"
3) "You chose _____!"

◆ **For older children, you may want to use the phrases,** "Feel free to _____ or _____," or, "Which of these options would be better for you? _____ or _____."

◆ **Figure out when to give an assertive command and when to offer two positive choices.** For most children, assertive commands are best when they are feeling overwhelmed or anxious. Choices are more helpful when children want to feel empowered. They work wonderfully with empathy. As children make choices and experience the success that comes from their decisions, they learn the value of commitment.

WEEK FOUR

ATTITUDE SHIFT: Harnessing the Power of Unity
REASON: To focus on connecting instead of trying to be special
DISCIPLINE SKILL: Encouragement
DISCIPLINE VALUE: Interdependence

◆ **Take five minutes (or more) daily to "just be" with each of your children.** Put aside any agenda, and simply enjoy their company.

◆ **Ask yourself in all situations,** "Do I want to be special or do I want to connect?" or, "Do I want to be right or happy?"

◆ **Celebrate your successes in changing your behavior.** Decide two things you want to accomplish in a day *(only two)*. After you accomplish them, honor yourself by saying, "I did it." Then describe what you did.

◆ **Practice changing your self-defeating statements into encouraging ones.** Tell yourself at least three times a day, "I can handle this. I am good enough."

◆ **Notice how often you choose to judge people or situations using a better than or less than frame of reference.** Stop judging, start noticing.

Encouragement: Honoring your children so they can honor you

◆ **Every time your children choose to obey you, celebrate their choice with encouragement.** To offer encouragement, do the following:

1) Start your sentence with your child's name or one of the following phrases: "Look at you," or, "You did it!"
2) Describe exactly what you see (or noticed).
3) Add a tag, if desired. Use one of the following: "That was helpful"; "Good job"; "Good for you."

◆ **Encourage your child every time you see her using the following behaviors:** kindness, caring, turn-taking, sharing, cooperation, honesty, staying on task, and any other behavior you value. Do this by describing, not judging. For example: "You held the door open for your mother. That was helpful," or, "You worked on your project for about two hours. That took determination."

◆ **Chronic behavior problems indicate a significant relationship has been injured.** For chronic problems, spend additional time with your child to strengthen the relationship—cooperation will follow. As children learn that they contribute to the well-being of others and that they can count on each other to be helpful and caring, interdependence is fostered. They learn it is better to give than to get.

WEEK FIVE

ATTITUDE SHIFT: Harnessing the Power of Love
REASON: To see the best in one another
DISCIPLINE SKILL: Positive Intent
DISCIPLINE VALUE: Cooperation

◆ **Wish people well.** Do this silently from your heart when you are standing in lines, driving, or passing people as you walk. Give this gift to everyone you see. Notice how you feel when you do this.

◆ **Begin each day being grateful for at least three things.** Before you go to bed, tell all your family members how thankful you are for their presence in your life. Notice what this does for your energy level.

◆ **Affirm to yourself five times a day, "What I offer to others, I give to myself."** Do this upon waking, at meals, and at bedtime.

◆ **Be conscious of how often you offer judgments or criticism to others.**

Attribute Positive Intent: Turning resistance into cooperation

◆ **When your child makes a mistake, or misbehaves, highlight her best self by attributing a positive intent to her.** Then focus on teaching her another way. To get started, you can use the following steps:

1) "You wanted _____." State a positive motive.
2) " . . . , so you _____." Describe to the child the actions she took (teasing, hitting).
3) "You may not _____. _____ hurts [or is not safe]."
4) "When you want _____, say _____. Say it now for practice."
5) "You did it." Offer some form of encouragement.

◆ **You know you love your child, but does she know?** Write up a long list of ways that you can show your love for your child. Put it on the refrigerator and add to it. Do two things from that list daily. Be generous with physical affection with young children and those who are moving through their school years. Boys need hugs and kisses as much as girls do.

◆ **When you slip up, consciously cut off the punitive self-talk and attribute a positive motive to yourself:** "You were frightened for Sarah's safety, so you yelled at her when she ran ahead of you to cross the street."

◆ **Attribute positive intent to clerks, politicians, food servers, and others.** Do this out loud to model the power of love for your children. Do it especially when these people make "mistakes." This demonstrates your cooperative spirit.

WEEK SIX

ATTITUDE SHIFT: Harnessing the Power of Acceptance
REASON: This moment is as it is
DISCIPLINE SKILL: Empathy
DISCIPLINE VALUE: Compassion

◆ **Practice being peaceful in the moment by noticing things and describing what you see, without judgments.** Notice the weather, plants outdoors, shadows, smells, and sounds.

◆ Add a ritual to your child's bedtime routine that involves saying goodnight to her body parts. For example, "I'm going to say goodnight to your ears [touch the ears], your chin, your elbows. . . ."

◆ If you find yourself getting upset when things are not going the way you think they should, take a deep breath. Remind yourself that, "This moment is as it is, and I can relax."

Empathy: Handling the fussing and the fits

◆ Practice feeling your own feelings. Observe how anger, irritation, anxiety, and contentment manifest themselves in your body.

◆ Practice accepting and directly expressing your feelings. Use this statement: "I feel _____." Complete the sentence with a feeling word.

◆ Catch yourself saying, "I shouldn't feel _____," and replace the statement with, "I feel _____ and it's okay."

◆ Provide empathy to your upset child by reflecting back to the child:

What you see;

What you hear;

What you sense your child is feeling.

◆ Listen to your child's feelings and thoughts without trying to change them. If you provide a clear mirror, your child will be capable of change.

◆ Separate disrespect from disobedience. Take two deep breaths and remind yourself, "This moment is as it is." Then respond calmly to your out-of-control child. This teaches compassion.

◆ Provide empathy to your child during a tantrum. Instead of trying to stop the tantrum once it has started, help your child work through it.

WEEK SEVEN

ATTITUDE SHIFT: Harnessing the Power of Intention
REASON: Conflict offers an opportunity to teach
DISCIPLINE SKILL: Consequences
DISCIPLINE VALUE: Responsibility

◆ Whenever conflict arises, breathe deeply and remind yourself, "Conflict is an opportunity to teach and learn."

◆ Focus on responding to conflict rather than trying to eliminate it.

◆ When conflict occurs ask yourself, "What is my intent in this situation? Do I intend to make my child feel bad and pay for his crime?" or, "Do I want to teach my child to reflect on his choices, change them, and develop self-control?"

Consequences: Helping children learn from their mistakes

◆ Start with yourself. Be a scientist of your own behavior. The next time you make a mistake, stop your punitive self-talk. Focus instead on these questions:

What choice did I make?

What happened as a result of my choice?

How did my choice and the results of it feel to me?

Did my choice achieve what I wanted?

What new strategies might serve me better?

◆ Allow yourself to feel the consequences of your choices. If you eat too much, forego the antacids. If you drink too much, forego the aspirin. This may help you in making future choices.

◆ Notice how often you blame others for your actions. The next time you catch yourself playing the "blame game," stop. Take a deep breath and say, "I have a problem." From this position offer yourself empathy instead of harassment and proceed to solve your problem.

◆ Decide if you have overrelied on punishments and rewards as a means of discipline. If you have done so, *be* willing to change.

◆ **For the next consequence you deliver to your children, use empathy and self-control instead of threats, lectures, and moralizing.** Use the GAMES technique. (For more assistance, see page 200.)

G = *G*ive guidance through limits, possible outcomes, and choices

A = *A*llow the child to experience the consequence

M = *M*odel self-control

E = Offer *e*mpathy

S = Help the child reflect on new *s*trategies

◆ **Pick one chronic problem you have been having.** Instead of imposing consequences, use the problem-solving PEACE plan. For additional information, see page 206.

P = Discern who owns the *p*roblem

E = Offer *e*mpathy to the child who has made the poor choice

A = *A*sk the child to think, "What do you think you are going to do?"

C = Offer *c*hoices and suggestions

E = *E*ncourage the child to come up with her own solutions

Congratulations! Take a moment to honor your accomplishments. Then, when you're ready, start over again, and again. . . . The next time through will be even more fun! Discipline is not a technique to use on children. It is a way of life to model for children. Life is a journey and I thank you for sharing part of yours with me. I am deeply grateful.

Epilogue

Happiness comes from learning to give, rather than seeking to get. Remember to . . .

◆ Give children the communication skills they need to solve problems rather than getting them to act or be "nice."

◆ Give children encouragement by attributing positive motives to all their acts rather than forcing them to feel bad in order to behave better.

◆ Give children lifelong skills they will need to contribute to society rather than getting them to behave in ways that impress others.

◆ Give children a model of happy, loving, responsible living rather than getting them to "act like they should."

Find something intangible that you feel you lack in life (hope, enthusiasm, courage). Give it to others and you will possess it yourself. Giving and receiving are one. The first step to resolving a problem is to give away your solution.

Have a good journey!
Love, Becky

The "What-Ifs" Page

This page is provided for you to write down your "What-If" questions. As these questions surface, write them down, as well as the page number from the book where this "What-If" was triggered. After reading the book, check back here to see if they were answered. See if the anxiety about change dissipated. If not, send me a message from my web site at *www.beckybailey.com* with your questions and, if possible, I will respond.

1. What if _____ ? Pg.#_____

2. What if _____ ? Pg.#_____

3. What if _____ ? Pg.#_____

4. What if _____ ? Pg.#_____

5. What if _____ ? Pg.#_____

6. What if _____ ? Pg.#_____

7. What if _____ ? Pg.#_____

8. What if _____ ? Pg.#_____

9. What if _____ ? Pg.#_____

References

Chapter 1: From Willful to Willing

Bailey, B. *I Love You Rituals: Activities to Build Bonds and Strengthen Relationships with Children*. Oviedo, FL: Loving Guidance, Inc., 1997.

Coloroso, B. *Kids Are Worth It! Giving Your Child the Gift of Inner Discipline*. New York: William Morrow and Company, 1994.

Hendrix. H., and H. Hunt, *Giving the Love that Heals: A Guide for Parents*. New York: Pocket Books, 1997.

Kotulak, R. *Inside the Brain: Revelational Discoveries of How the Mind Works*. Kansas City: Andrews McMeel Publishing, 1997.

Nelson, J., L. Loot, and S. Glenn. *Positive Discipline A to Z: 1001 Solutions to Everyday Parenting Problems*. Rocklin, CA: Prima Publishing, 1993.

Chapter 2: The Seven Powers for Self-Control

A Course in Miracles. Tiburon, CA: Foundation for Inner Peace, 1985.

Dyer, W. *Your Sacred Self: Making the Decision to be Free*. New York: HarperCollins Publishers, 1996.

Myss, C. *Anatomy of the Spirit—The Seven Stages of Power and Healing*. New York: Harmony Books, 1996.

Schuller, R. *Power Thoughts: Achieve Your True Potential through Power Thinking*. New York: HarperCollins Publishers, 1993.

Williamson, M. *A Return to Love—Reflections on the Principles of a Course in Miracles*. New York: HarperCollins Publishers, 1996.

Chapter 3: The Seven Basic Discipline Skills

Bailey, B. A. *There's Gotta Be a Better Way: Discipline That Works!* Oviedo, FL: Loving Guidance, Inc., 1997.

Watchtower Bible and Tract Society of New York. "War Reaps a Young Harvest." *Awake* (October 1997), pp. 12–18.

Chapter 4: Assertiveness

Canter, L., and M. Canter. *Assertive Discipline: A Take-Charge Approach for Today's Educator.* Los Angeles: Lee Canter & Associates, 1976.

Gordon, T. *Teacher Effectiveness Training.* New York: Peter H. Wyden Publisher, 1974.

Lundberg, G. B., and J. Saunders. *I Don't Have to Make Everything All Better.* Las Vegas: Riverpark Publishing Company, 1995.

McKay, M., M. Davis, and P. Fanning. *Messages: The Communication Book.* Oakland, CA: New Harbinger Publications, Inc., 1983.

Wolfgang, C. H., and M. E. Wolfgang. *The Three Faces of Discipline for Early Childhood: Empowering Teachers and Students.* Boston: Allyn & Bacon, 1995.

Chapter 5: Choices

Branden, N. *The Six Pillars of Self-Esteem.* New York: Bantam Books, 1994.

Millman, D. *The Life You Were Born to Live: A Guide to Finding Your Life Purpose.* Tiburon, CA: H. J. Kramer, Inc., 1993.

Chapter 6: Encouragement

Dinkmeyer, D., and G. D. McKay. *STEP: The Parent's Handbook.* Circle Pines, MN: American Guidance Service, 1989.

Hochschild, A. R. *The Time Bind: When Work Becomes Home and Home Becomes Work.* New York: Henry Holt and Company, 1997.

Jensen, E. *Amazing Brain Facts.* Del Mar, CA: Turning Point, 1997.

Kohn, A. *No Contest: The Case against Competition.* New York: Houghton Mifflin Company, 1992.

―――. *Punished by Rewards: The Trouble with Gold Stars, Incentive Plans, A's, Praise, and Other Bribes.* Boston: Houghton Mifflin Company, 1993.

Kostelnik, M. J., L. C. Stein, A. P. Whiren, and A. K. Soderman. *Guiding Children's Social Development.* 2d ed. Albany, NY: Delmar Publishers, 1993.

Kvols, K. J. *Redirecting Children's Behavior: Discipline that Builds Self-Esteem.* Gainesville, FL: INCAF, 1993.

Chapter 7: Positive Intent

Bohm, D. *Wholeness and the Implicate Order.* London: Routledge & Kegan Paul, 1981.

Brennan, B. A. *Hands of Light: A Guide to Healing through the Human Energy Field.* New York: Bantam Books, 1987.

Landreth, G. L. *Play Therapy: The Art of the Relationship.* Muncie, IN: Accelerated Development, 1991.

Chapter 8: Empathy

Brazelton, T. B. *Touchpoints: Your Child's Emotional and Behavioral Development.* New York: Addison-Wesley Publishing Company, 1992.

Caspi, A., D. Bem, and G. H. Elder. "Moving Against the World: Life-Course Patterns of Explosive Children." *Developmental Psychology* 23(2), 308–313.

Goleman, D. *Emotional Intelligence.* New York: Bantam Books, 1995.

Harris, P. L. *Children and Emotion: The Development of Psychological Understanding.* New York: Basil Blackwell, 1989.

Hendrick, J. *The Whole Child.* Columbus, OH: Charles Merrill, 1992.

LeDoux, J. *The Emotional Brain: The Mysterious Underpinnings of Emotional Life.* New York: Simon & Schuster, 1996.

O'Conner, K. *The Play Therapy Primer: An Integration of Theories and Techniques.* New York: John Wiley and Sons, 1991.

Truman, K. T. *Feelings Buried Alive Never Die* . . . Las Vegas: Olympus Distributing, 1991.

Chapter 9: Consequences

Bennett, M. *The Development of Social Cognition: The Child as Psychologist.* New York: The Guilford Press, 1993.

Fay, J., and F. Cline. *The Life Saver Kit.* Golden, CO: The Love and Logic Institute, Inc., 1996. Audio series.

Fay, J., and D. Funk. *Teaching with Love & Logic: Taking Control in the Classroom.* Golden, CO: The Love and Logic Press Inc., 1995.

Glenn, H. S., and J. Nelsen. *Raising Self-Reliant Children in a Self-Indulgent World: Seven Building Blocks for Developing Capable Young People.* Rocklin, CA: Prima Publishing & Communications, 1988.

Hart, L. *Human Brain and Human Learning.* White Plains, NY: Longman Publishing, 1983.

Jensen, E. *Brain-based Learning.* Del Mar, CA: Turning Point Publishing, 1996.

———. *Completing the Puzzle: The Brain-Compatible Approach to Learning.* Del Mar, CA: The Brain Store, Inc., 1997.

Kohn, A. *Punished by Rewards: The Trouble with Gold Stars, Incentives, Plans, A's, Praise, and Other Bribes.* Boston: Houghton Mifflin Company, 1993.

Lozanov, G. "On Some Problems of the Anatomy, Physiology and Biochemistry of Cerebral Activities in the Global-Artistic Approach in Modern Suggesto-pedagogic Training." *The Journal of the Society for Accelerative Learning and Teaching* 16 (2), 101–16.

Piaget, J. *The Psychology of Intelligence.* Patterson, NJ: Little-Adams, 1963.

Turiel, E. *The Development of Social Knowledge, Morality and Convention.* Cambridge: Cambridge University Press, 1983.

Chapter 10: Why Children Do What They Do

Ames, L. B., and C. C. Haber. *Your Eight-Year-Old: Lively and Outgoing.* New York: Dell Publishing, 1989.

Ames, L. B., F. L. Ilg, and C. Haber. *Your One-Year-Old: Fun-Loving and Fussy.* New York: Dell Publishing, 1982.

Berger, K. S. *The Developing Person through the Life Span.* 2d ed. New York: Worth Publishers, Inc., 1988.

Brazelton, T. B. *Touchpoints: Your Child's Emotional and Behavioral Development.* New York: Addison-Wesley Publishing Company, 1992.

Clarke, J. L., and C. Dawson. *Growing Up Again: Parenting Ourselves, Parenting Our Children.* New York: HarperCollins Publishers, 1989.

Hannaford, C. *Smart Moves: Why Learning Is Not All in Your Head.* Arlington, VA: Great Ocean Publishers, 1995.

Hendrix, H. *Getting the Love You Want: A Guide for Couples.* New York: Henry Holt & Co., 1998.

Miller, A. *For Your Own Good. Hidden Cruelty in Child Rearing and the Roots of Violence.* New York: Farrar, Straus, and Giroux, 1990.

Williamson, P. *Good Kids, Bad Behavior: Helping Children Learn Self-Discipline.* New York: Simon & Schuster, 1990.

Index